FROM OUR HOME CORRESPONDENT

Letters from Hessle in the Second World War

by
Philip Chignell

Highgate Publications (Beverley) Ltd
1989

Published by Highgate Publications (Beverley) Ltd.
24 Wylies Road, Beverley, HU17 7AP
Telephone (0482) 866826

Printed and Typeset in 10 on 11pt Plantin by
B.A. Press, 2-4 Newbegin, Lairgate, Beverley, HU17 8EG
Telephone (0482) 882232

ISBN 0-948929/21/9

British Library Cataloguing in Publication Data

Chignell, Philip, 1872 – 1947
    From our home correspondent: letters from Hessle in the Second World War.
    1. Humberside. Effects of World War 2
    I. Title
    940.53'4283

ISBN 0-948929/21/9

Acknowledgements

Grateful thanks are expressed to: Humberside Libraries and Arts for kind permission to reproduce the picture of All Saints Church, Hessle (front cover), from the illustrations collection in the Beverley Reference Library, and to the *Hull Daily Mail* for permission to reproduce the photograph of bomb damage to Hull Savings Bank branch, Holderness Road (front cover), from *A North East Coast Town* by Tom Geraghty.

Front: All Saints Church, Hessle (Humberside Libraries and Arts); Katie and Philip Chignell; Bomb damage to Hull Savings Bank branch, Holderness Road (By courtesy of the Hull Daily Mail*).*

Philip Chignell, F.R.C.O., 1872-1947

Throughout the Second World War Philip Chignell, the organist at All Saints Church, Hessle, near Hull, a retired employee of Hull Savings Bank, sat down regularly at his Corona typewriter and composed a letter full of family news for his four sisters. Each sister received a copy and Philip, a most methodical man, filed his copies in numbered sequence under the symbol 'BS' — for 'Brothers and Sisters'. Between 1 September 1939 and 18 December 1946, interrupted only by serious illness as he grew older, he wrote 128 'BS' letters, a total of something like 120,000 words, the equivalent of two full-length books.

When his granddaughter, Marion Lace, came across this monumental collection of correspondence she realised it was of more than family interest. The letters give a riveting picture of life on the Home Front and convey what people who remember the war will recognise as the authentic atmosphere of that period with its unique blend of tragedy relieved by odd moments of humour, a time when the trivia of everyday life acquired peculiar significance and people showed an obstinate, unsentimental determination to carry on normally in a world gone mad.

Philip's three sons were called-up, all served abroad, and for most of the war he struggled to conceal his concern about his son, Henry, first reported missing and later found to be a prisoner-of-war. Hessle Church choir was badly depleted and services had to be timed to comply with blackout regulations; but somehow he coped, in spite of an uneasy relationship with the vicar and a sometimes jaundiced view of his own part in the proceedings. He never understood the mysteries of clothing coupons but, like others, he quickly learnt to ignore the air-raid siren and adopt a fatalistic attitude to the possibility of imminent death. He observed the blitz on Hull, and he was overwhelmed with sorrow as he made his way through the rubble of the ravaged city.

For an apparently unremarkable member of the community, Philip Chignell had had an unusual life. Born in Bedfordshire in 1872, one of a family of seven, he was a chorister at St. George's Chapel, Windsor, 1881-8, and his occasional reminiscences about the Royal events of which he had a front-seat view are a fascinating bonus of his letters and a unique source of new information for future historians of Victoria and her family. He sang at the Queen's Golden Jubilee in 1887, and at the wedding of her youngest daughter, Princess Beatrice, he saw the tears trickling down her face at the funeral of her youngest son, Prince Leopold, and he was shocked to hear the Duke of Cambridge swear at the soldier pall-bearers. He wrote, too, about the famous musicians he had known: Elgar, Walford Davies and Arthur Sullivan.

After leaving Windsor he became an organ scholar at Norwich Cathedral, then organist at St. Peter's Church, Kirkley, Lowestoft. In 1901 he moved to Hessle and remained as organist there until 1944; when he retired, the bellringers rang a peal as a thanksgiving for his many years of service. A highlight of his life was the world tour he undertook in 1911 with the Sheffield Choir. It was on this tour that he met Katie Netherwood, who was to become his wife. The family home was 19 The Weir, Hessle, and Philip and Katie Chignell had three sons and a daughter.

Philip Chignell loved sport, played bowls almost to the end of his life, was outstanding at chess, found great fulfilment in music, had a happy marriage and took pride in his family. Yet an underlying theme of his letters is a sense of disappointment at his failure to achieve the success which should have been within his grasp. In one letter he regrets that he had been too lazy to write a book. Ironically, he was at that very moment writing the book which will be his lasting memorial. He died on 3 January 1947 and was spared the exceptionally severe winter he would have hated.

The main characters mentioned in the letters are:

Katie, his wife, who had also trained as a musician and had been a member of the Huddersfield Choral Society. She died in 1961.

John, Henry and **Stephen,** his sons. All won scholarships to Hymers College.

John, the eldest son, who was in the Territorials when war began, joined the Royal Artillery and served in Gibralter, North Africa and Italy. After training at Sheffield City Training College he taught in Beverley and Hessle. He still lives in Hessle and is a life member of the Hull Choral Union and still a member of the Hessle Church choir.

Henry spent most of the war in a German prison camp where he began to study for the degree in German he completed afterwards at Hull University, later becoming headmaster of a school in Birmingham. The father of two sons and two daughters, he died in 1986. His wife lives in North Ferriby.

Stephen worked at Spillers until he joined the army, serving in Tunisia and Italy and usually being involved with transport. He returned to Spillers after the war, moved to Head Office in London (where he joined the BBC Choral Society) and remained with the company for the rest of his career. Married and the father of two sons and a daughter, he and his wife now live in Ledbury where they are both keen musicians.

'Trigo' was the nickname of his daughter, **Ruth** (Stephen was known as

'Donaghue' and she was so called after a winning racehorse of the twenties). After leaving the Boulevard School she became a secretary with the Commercial Union Assurance Company and in 1947 married Peter, the son of Tom Geraghty, assistant editor and 'John Humber' of the *Hull Daily Mail*, and moved to London. Peter worked as a civil pilot with B.E.A. The Geraghty's had one son and four daughters, two of whom, Christine and Marion, returned to Hull to study at the University. Ruth maintains her musical interest as a member of the Ealing Symphony Orchestra.

The four sisters who received Philip's letters were:

Madge Crimp whose husband was organist at Leominster Priory Church.

Isabel ('Jezebel' in the letters) Jamieson who lived in Australia but was visiting her son in England when the war began.

Ruth, the closest sister, a retired headmistress living in Findon, Sussex.

Kittie Chaston who lived on Vancouver Island.

Others referred to are:

Arthur, his brother, the Rev. A. K. Chignell, Master of Hull Charterhouse. An author, translator, and a professional proof-reader, he wrote a column for the *Hull Daily Mail* under the pseudonym, 'Perambulator'.

Aunt Maude and the **Netherwoods** were relations of Philip's wife, Katie, née Netherwood.

Editorial Note

The quantity of Philip Chignell's letters has made it necessary to edit them for publication. A break in the serial numbers indicates the complete omission of a letter, but usually omissions have been made only within letters to avoid repetition or unnecessary detail. Alterations to the text have been almost entirely confined to correcting punctuation and obvious errors, or clarifying the intended meaning. Editorial additions are indicated by square brackets [ ].

FAMILY TREE

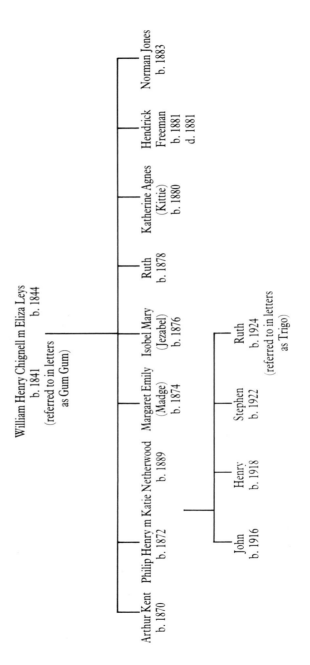

William Henry Chignell m Eliza Leys
b. 1841   b. 1844
(referred to in letters
as Gum Gum)

Arthur Kent
b. 1870

Philip Henry m Katie Netherwood
b. 1872   b. 1889

Margaret Emily
(Madge)
b. 1874

Isobel Mary
(Jezabel)
b. 1876

Ruth
b. 1878

Katherine Agnes
(Kittie)
b. 1880

Hendrick
Freeman
b. 1881
d. 1881

Norman Jones
b. 1883

John
b. 1916

Henry
b. 1918

Stephen
b. 1922

Ruth
b. 1924
(referred to in letters
as Trigo)

1939

B.S.1 5th September 1939

War, war is now the cry.

We are passing through historic days. I am not going to attempt any record of what I think about the present political or international situation but I am just going to tell you how it has affected us at Hessle. My first remark is that it has broken up our little family circle. All our four children have lived at home with us ever since they were born. There are six of us, as you know, and we have lived together happily until this time when Herr Hitler seems to have set Europe on fire with his terrible ambition. Of course, we knew that something in the way of another war was brewing. It has not come upon us as a surprise. The business seems to have had a definite beginning when Trigo came home on Wednesday with definite instructions about the school evacuation that had been arranged some time ago. We had decided that Trigo should be evacuated with the other boys and girls at the Boulevard School. I was against this idea at the first but I did not feel I could refuse to let her go when she wanted to go and Katie thought she should go, so we had signed a paper saying that we wished her to be evacuated. Well, on Wednesday (Aug. 30) Trigo came home with definite instructions. On Thursday she went off to school with everything as arranged, temporary luggage, sufficient food to last her for a day, etc. She came home at dinner time, although we had not expected her, and she then and there definitely refused to be evacuated. She just declined to go. We did not attempt any argument but we insisted that she should return to the Boulevard School and tell them that she would not be evacuated.

At about 6.45 I went off to the bowling club and I left John having his tea in the usual manner. I came home to listen to the Promenade Concert. John had gone. A dispatch rider had called for him and he had packed up and gone off at once. He left a filled-up form to be posted to Smith and Nephew to say why he should be away from his work the next morning. We have not seen John since that day but we now know that he is near Spurn Head with a gun battery.

Friday, September 1st came along. I was in my study upstairs when Katie came and told me the wireless news: Germany was attacking Poland. I knew at once that this news meant war. I went off on my bicycle to the Humber, to a place I love, half way between Hessle and Ferriby. This is a place of absolute seclusion and yet so open and free that one can see for miles and miles. It is called Redcliff Sands. One can get off the riverside path and push through a mass of rushes and wild flowers (sea asters are in full bloom just now) and you can get to where there is a regular cliff, hardened mud, but a cliff all the same. It was a glorious morning and a south-west wind bringing the waves over the river bank just as though I had been at the sea side. I had an old sack to sit on, and here I stayed for an hour or so just thinking it all out. I knew it meant war between England and Germany. Yet I love Germany. I have been in that country many times. One of the very best friends I ever had in all my life (Carl Hillerns) was a German. Beethoven, Brahms, Rheinberger, Merkel, Haydn, Mozart. Well, I just cannot forget what they have done to make my life a pleasant one. And then, while I was thinking of these things, sitting on the sunny bank of the mighty river I love so well, there was the sudden report of a gun. Where it came from I cannot tell. It may have been the blast of some quarry over in Lincolnshire. Whatever it was, it made my heart stop still for a moment and I had to stand up and take a breathful of the lovely fresh south-west breeze that was blowing. Silly ass, I might say to myself. How could it be anything but a noise you might hear on the Humber bank any day of the week?

Katie Chignell
(née Netherwood)

Philip Chignell

Probably taken soon after marriage, 1912.

On Friday afternoon I went into Hull to exchange library books. I noticed armies of school children being evacuated. The station in Hull was closed to everybody except the children and their teachers. Police and railway men were guarding every entrance and I made no effort to go into the station to see what was going on. Having changed my three books at the library I went on to the Charterhouse where I found the Master alone in the house. Do you remember how father used to clothe himself at Croft House? Any old garment he could find. The worthy Master of the Hull Charterhouse reminded me of father in Croft House days. Obviously visitors were not wanted, not even a brother. I stayed only a couple of minutes and then I cycled home the five or six miles.

At tea a dispatch rider called. This time it was for Henry. He packed up and was off in half an hour. Katie packed up food for him and he went, saying good-bye to us. We did not know when we should see him again or where he was going to.

The Vicar telephoned me — on no account was I to have a light in the church or vestry after 8.0 p.m. There was the usual choir practice at 8 coming on and I had given out a general notice that at 9.0 a presentation of a wedding present given by the choir would be made to Molly Digweed, one of our choir altos, who was to be married on the following day to John Haselhurst. We had to have the presentation in a very dim light and we had to abandon the choir practice altogether. One or two members of the choir who are in the habit of coming late to the practice found themselves too late, everything had closed down.

The Haselhurst-Digweed wedding was duly celebrated, or performed, on Saturday at 2.0. I had an awful job just getting a few boys and men together. The boys were all doing scouts' jobs, filling sandbags, etc. I had to promise them faithfully that they would be free by 2.30 and even then I only got about ten boys out of 25. However, the wedding went off all right. Later on the happy couple were unable to get away for their arranged honeymoon — no trains. They had to go to their new home and do the best they could there, friends helping them and loaning them things they most needed.

I forgot to say that Henry returned home late last night. The authorities did not know how to sleep the 1,300 young men who had answered the call and most of them were sent home. Katie fixed up all our darkened window blinds in the most wonderful manner. She had the 1914 experience and knew what was wanted. I saw crowds of people besieging the shops where dark paper could be bought but Katie had foreseen this and had provided for it. I was 'narked' that I could not get the Promenade Concert on the wireless on Saturday night. I wanted to hear it very much. Afterwards I heard that there was no concert, the Proms have been given up altogether.

We had to have evensong at an early hour because of the lighting restrictions and hardly anyone came to it. I have never seen such a small Sunday evening congregation. During the afternoon I was at the bowls club once more. A Sunday afternoon match had been arranged with a Hull club but nobody turned up, only four of our own members, including myself, and we just sat and talked and watched the traffic on the Boothferry Road, people 'skittling' out of Hull. As you know there had been a definite declaration of war at 11.0 a.m. and the fear of immediate aerial attack on Hull frightened people. I must be honest enough to say that if I had a car and nothing particular to keep me in Hull I should have been off on this big westerly trek.

After having said good-bye to Henry for the third time on this Sunday morning, we had him back at home on Sunday night. He is still with us for sleeping and meals as I write (Tuesday) but he never knows when he may be sent away or where he may be sent. We have now given up saying goodbye. If he goes he goes and that is the end of the matter.

The dreaded air raid warning came to us at 3.20 a.m. Monday morning. We have been taught to expect an actual raid about seven minutes after a warning buzzer has sounded. We cannot miss the buzzer because it is at our local town hall, only a few steps away. So it did not take us very long to get into the agreed upon funk hole, the place where we hang hats and coats under the stairs. We all got our gas masks fixed and there we waited for about half an hour. Nothing happened and we relaxed a little, took off our masks and moved about into the other rooms. At 4.30 we ventured to look out of the front door and a passing policeman told us — All clear! We went back to bed and I had just got nicely to sleep again when the blessed buzzer sounded the relief and I was wide awake once more. Once, when we were all sitting together in the funk hole and in the dark, I accidentally touched Katie's foot. She was trembling badly, as though frozen cold. I felt really bad about that. I thought she was so brave and so much stronger in nerves than I am. She has been splendid in keeping us all going, looking after the soldier boys, getting them off and so on, looking after all the arrangements due to a rigorous light restriction. The fact of the matter is that nobody, let alone a woman, should have to hide from air bombs. It is a cursed thing that such bombs should ever have been invented and here are we having to suffer because man is so darned clever and can invent such horrible things. Poor old Katie. Trembling like that. But you just come to Hull when there is an air raid on and see what your knees do and what your heart does. You may not know you have a heart until you have been through an air raid.

B.S.2 11th September 1939

Nothing much has happened in this district since my last letter. We are in a state of tension. Anti-aircraft guns are all round us and there is a large balloon barrage over Hull. Everybody carries a gas mask. All the houses are darkened at sunset. All places of amusement are shut down and life has become a sad business. We are in constant fear of an air raid but, so far, we have not had one.

You speak about the radio. All our fine concert programmes have gone overboard. This afternoon there was a violin and piano sonata turn, just for half an hour, 3.30 to 4.0, and I made a special point of listening to that. In the end it did me no good, I was just annoyed about it. Towards the end of the Grieg sonata, just as I was enjoying some good music, they switched off to announce some war news which, I bet a dollar, was untrue. I don't believe anything the wireless tells us. I know, through a bowls friend of mine, how terribly the press is censored and I have no doubt broadcasting is the same, more so perhaps. On the top of that they give nothing but stuff made for the simple minded, organ music with plenty of tremulant. Unfortunately other people in this house like this sort of stuff and there is the cry 'Why shouldn't we have what we like?'

Beyond playing the organ at Hessle church on Sundays I don't seem to have anything left to live for, and to tell the truth, I am rather tired of that with the everlasting hymn singing and obstreperous choir boys. Best love, Phil.

B.S.3 18th September 1939

Today is Henry's 21st birthday. He was born on September 18th 1918, just a few days before Armistice Day. On Thursday last, very early in the morning, he left this house in full accoutrement, off to do his share, whatever it may be, in this present war that has just broken out. We have not heard from him since. We only know that he has gone somewhere in the neighbourhood of Worksop. So we have not been able to send him even our best birthday wishes. He resolutely declined any coming of age present, saying that he would wait for it until his return home. Henry, queer chap that he is, left a trail behind him, dirty boots, old and very much dilapidated slippers, old clothes, coats, cricket shirts, dirty old trousers, books concerning all sorts of sports especially cricket but including tennis, billiards and even golf, packets of snap shots; an old camera, a nice brown suit, discarded for the present, was carefully folded and put over the armchair in my little attic study as though to say, 'Please look after this until I get back.' Now he is gone and we shall see him no more for the present.

18th September 1939 (later)

We had three letters from Henry this morning. He seems quite cheerful and happy in the military work he is now doing, sentry-go at 2 a.m. is just the sort of job that will appeal to him. Of course I feel a bit sad about it all, very sad indeed if I speak the truth. I passed the now deserted Hessle Cricket Club and I thought of Henry and how he has this season become quite famous locally as a slow bowler. He has got to be well-known all over the place just like I got to be known all over Suffolk and Norfolk as a football player. That was how I came to be famous. I never became famous at music.

John came home from Kilnsea on Wednesday on 24 hours' leave. He returned on Thursday morning, marching off just after Henry had gone. So Thursday was a day of departures. John was full of life and fun and could not stop talking, telling us all that was going on in the battery camp at Kilnsea, near Spurn. He and Henry are as different as two brothers could possibly be. We have never forgotten that Henry once spent a month in Finland and had nothing to talk about when he got home. John once flew from Inverness to the Orkney Islands and I feel as though I went that flight myself — I have heard so much about it.

We all have our trial in these days. I think the biggest bores are those people who think they are in a very unhappy condition and pour out all their troubles to anyone they may meet. I think we are all in the same boat just now. All the well-to-do people have cleared out and gone inland somewhere or other. Katie and I would do the same if it were not for the church and the home for Stephen. We have talked it over and quite decided. My church choir has fallen all to pieces. Yesterday I had two old and very fluffy bases, neither of them any good at all, Stephen and Len Emerson, tenors, both quite good. Choirboys have gone perfectly dotty lately, I have never had such a poor lot. The girls help a bit but it is a very poor show compared to our usual turn-out. We have put Trigo to a commercial college in Hull. Her school is closed, children all evacuated. Best love, Phil.

B.S.4 25th September 1939

This morning Stephen has to cycle out to Ferriby three miles away to our west, instead of cycling towards Hull and half way through it to get to his work. Spillers have taken a large house at Ferriby and transferred many of their staff, including Stephen, to work there. It means that every day Stephen has a very pleasant and country ride instead of a rather dull and sordid one. He can go from here to Ferriby along the main road, past Hesslewood with a grand view of the Humber on his left nearly all the way. When he gets to Ferriby he will have to climb half way up a rather steep hill. When he comes home he can, if he likes, continue up the hill to the pretty village with a pretty name, Swanland, and from there he can almost coast all the way home, never once touching the main road by which he travelled in the morning. He has two delightfully pleasant routes to take and he can get home for dinner quite easily provided the weather is suitable. He is to be allowed six shillings a week to make up for the lost dinners at Spillers in Hull, for the firm supplied the staff there with a dinner every day, that is five days a week. So they seem to have thrown in one shilling for fun. Another thing that has given him pleasure is when a youth of 16 or 17 is given work at Spillers he is under an obligation to attend certain night schools in Hull

Spillers' staff at Woodgates, North Ferriby, 1941.
Stephen Chignell — second left, back row. Peter Geraghty — front.

Woodgates House: Spillers' wartime office.

two nights per week. Henry and Stephen have had to conform to that rule and it has been rather hard on them. They get home for tea about 6.15 and on the two nights they have had to get back into Hull again pretty quickly for the two hours' night class. It would be nearly 10.0 before they got home again. They always refused to have their tea in Hull and go leisurely to the night class and they always complained that the night classes taught them nothing. They both passed the London matric exam when they were at Hymers College and they said these night classes were not up to the matric standard. There are no night classes now so Stephen is absolved from that irksome duty. As I say it is an ill wind . . . Nowadays I do not have to hide such things as trouser clips, safety razor blades, bicycle pump, shaving soap and all sorts of other things. A little while ago my very nice rain proof cape for use when cycling disappeared. I had given 25 shillings for it and it was a real beauty. There are now four people living in this house instead of six and that makes a great deal of difference. During the last two or three years our house has been the gathering place for the youth and beauty of Hessle. John and Henry are very popular, they have boy friends and girl friends galore. I have no objection to any single one of their very many friends, they are dear young people and two of the girls at any rate are perfectly charming. I could easily be in love with either one of them myself. The top room in our house is rigged up as a table tennis club. I have known a dozen boys and girls up there at night time. Sometimes if they get the chance, they have taken possession of our wireless set and I have come home to find six or eight young people lounging about in the drawing room listening to some variety show and filling the house with roars of laughter. I have had to join the company or move off elsewhere. Mind you, I am not grumbling. Any man who indulges in a small family has to make the best of this sort of thing and I pride myself I have accepted the inevitable with good grace. Now these young people are not all mad on variety and such nonsense. A good concert will bring some of them to the loud speaker and they have learned to follow the full score of a Beethoven symphony. The New World Symphony and César Franck's Symphony in D Minor always attracts Trigo, John and his beloved.

Katie's brother-in-law possesses a wife and two children and a motor car. This little lot have got into the habit of coming over from Huddersfield to Hessle on a Sunday. They will arrive somewhere about 2.30-3.0, spend the afternoon here, stay to tea and slip off after I have gone to church at 6.0. Once when I was away from home Trigo wrote to me on a Sunday evening and she said the TRIPE of Israel have been here, so that for ever afterwards we have referred to our Huddersfield relations as the Tripe. Now we are all very friendly and nice with our relations but, honestly speaking, I prefer a quiet time just before I go to my Sunday evening duties and I also like to have Katie and all the others in my choir at the Sunday evening services. Ten or twelve at the table does not mean a gentle and quiet cup of tea just before you go to work again. Now it is all quite in order, nothing to complain about. This petrol rationing business stops this Tripe and Onions story. So, as I say and as the story goes, 'It's an ill wind that blows no good.'

B.S.5 2nd October 1939

The black-out has had one very good result. If you go out an hour or more after sunset and if the weather is good you can see the stars most beautifully. There are no gas lights and the nights are just lovely. I often go for a walk round before I go to bed and I love a few minutes' communication with the majestic glory of the universe. One night last week Katie came out with me and we had half an hour's trot round. It was inclined to rain but there was a moon, almost at the full, spinning low down in the south-west. We saw a good lunar rainbow, a phenomenon very rarely seen in this country. Only once before in my life have I seen the lunar rainbow and I recorded the time, date and place — 11.10 p.m. at Hessle, 1st August 1905. I was 34 years old then and I have had to live almost as long again before I can say that I have again seen a lunar rainbow.

Did you ever meet the Huffam family, friends of mine at Hessle? I had not been here very long before I had a visit from Francis Huffam, a man about my own age, slightly younger as a matter of fact. I was invited to visit Huffam's family and I quickly became very friendly with all of them. Mrs. Huffam (widow), three daughters, Nellie, Cissie and Olive and the one son, Francis. We were on the most friendly terms for years. I was always invited to their house for Christmas dinner and that alone is a sign of good friendship. It was the regular and recognised thing for me to go to tea there on a Sunday afternoon and two or more nights a week I would go in for a game of cards. Yes. They were very dear friends of mine. Mrs Huffam is now dead and so is Olive, the youngest daughter. Francis Huffam just lived in a quiet way over at Kirk Ella and he had an old business in Hull. Burstall and Huffam, timber. Nothing very extraordinary. When he was married, two or three years after Katie and I fixed things up, he came to me and asked if I could lend him a top hat. He was going to be married and he had not got a topper. Funny, wasn't it? I lent him my topper, so that particular topper has been twice married. I was glad to save him a couple of guineas. A day or two ago the newspapers gave particulars of his will. Francis Huffam had left over £77,000, nearly £78,000. That is a lot of money, isn't it? . . . I have to pay an extra ha'penny for my glass of beer.

Here in Hessle we are still on the alert waiting for the long expected air raid. There is a large hall set out as an emergency hospital, everything ready for a large number of casualties with a staff there day and night. I am told the staff get £3 a week and have to put in twelve hours attendance out of every 24. They earn their money pretty easily and spend their time playing bridge etc. I would not mind a salary of £3 a week for playing bridge. Then there are very many air raid posts all over the place and someone in charge of each post, day and night. Any amount of lorries and motor cars all ready for the sudden air raid that has not taken place. I think people are getting rather tired of playing this waiting game.

Church services are booming, we get excellent attendances and very good offertories — over £20 yesterday. The people seem to like the short and hearty evensong at 6.0, all over in an hour and get home to the wireless business by 7.15.

Henry is still in Worksop. He seems to be having a good time, captain of the army football team, managing a rather large chess club, head of a bakery department and also a member of a very good church choir close at hand. He is better off than John. John is still in a camp near Spurn. Not allowed out of the camp and no friends admitted. He cannot find anywhere to spend his weekly allowance but has to send it home and ask us to post him a tin of tobacco or a book of stamps etc. etc. Ah, well. What is it all leading to? That is all for today. I forget what is the next thing I have to do. Nothing particular until choir practice on Wednesday night. Oh yes. I have promised to go out to play bridge this evening along with Katie. Phil.

B.S.6 23rd October 1939

One of my many memories of father is the time when I heard him swear in public. I could hardly believe my ears. The dear old boy was playing in an impromptu cricket match got up in the camp one evening. He was batting and was just about the last man in and the scores were very nearly level, just a run or two needed for victory. The umpire said papa was 'run out', and my worthy parent returned to the tent holding his bat aloft and publicly swore at the umpire. That was a dreadful moment for me. I was thoroughly ashamed of my dear father. Everybody else roared with laughter, which I thought was very unseemly and unkind of them.

I also see father on Finsbury Park station at about 8.30 a.m., one of hundreds of business men all wearing the inevitable top hat. It seems funny in these days to think of all those men and all those toppers.

We have had two air raid warnings this week but they led to nothing, I am glad to say. On Sunday a large motor car drew up at our door at 8.0 a.m. and five big and hungry soldiers stormed our house and demanded entry. These five men had motored 60 or 70 miles from Worksop and they left without even a cup of tea, so you can imagine the state of their little tummies. The company included Henry, of course. A local baker had lent them the large car and they came along for a run round the Hull district where they all came from. Jolly nice men too, all in khaki. Except for Henry they were all strangers to me. They swarmed into our kitchen where there was a really good fire and stood there as though to say, 'What next?' We are not big breakfast people and it was quite impossible to cater for the whole army. So we got a large teapot going and just warmed them all up and then they cleared off, leaving Henry to spend a few hours at home. I suppose each of them had somewhere to go.

We had another air raid alarm this same Sunday morning, just as we were getting ready for matins. That service was abandoned and I came home and had a bottle of beer, which suited me better than singing a *Te Deum*. Nothing followed the warning and evensong was held as usual. I was very glad to have Henry's valuable services in the choir. He sang as an anthem a little song called *England* by Owen Mase, which I arranged for the occasion, giving the choir something to sing as a refrain.

After evensong we were swarmed out by Henry's friends. Visitors, male and female, they came down on us like sparrows after crumbs at our kitchen door. A table tennis tournament was held upstairs in our large attic and Katie and I were left in peace during the evening. Once, Henry came downstairs and foraged for refreshments for his guests. It seemed rather a large order — supper for eight or nine, but there you are.

We were all up soon after five on Monday morning to get Henry a good breakfast before he went off at 6.0. His four soldier pals and their large baker's car called for him precisely at 6, and he was gone. As usual I had to go round and clear up, for Henry has the knack of leaving things about. We have had four alarms so far but none to trouble us. It appears that we shall not suffer from night raids as we did in the last war but time will tell. It was the Zepp night raids that made me feel so queer and nervous in the last war. So far I have been unaffected by raid warnings in this war. Phil.

B.S.7 7th November 1939

Nothing doing in Hull in the air raid business. I hear that more than half the evacuated children have come back to their homes and the problem now is to know what to do with them because all the Hull schools are closed. I was in Hull yesterday afternoon and evening and I noticed that the barrage balloons were not up. That may have been because there was a lot of wind about. As a rule one can see about twenty of these balloons riding the sky in every direction. I was at the Hull chess club until nearly 10.30 and then I cycled home (5 miles). You would think it a miserable business to be cycling along these dark streets. As a matter of fact it is just the opposite. It is very pleasant on such a night as last night. Twice, as I rode home, when I came to a fairly open position I got off the bicycle and had a good look round at the stars. Always interesting. The alternative way home is to catch a bus at 10.30. 25 minutes with a crowd of people, most of the men and some of the women smoking cigarettes, the windows all blacked out so that you only know where you are by hearing the calls of the conductor. You can take which way you like. I know which way I prefer. All along the road home I kept on passing A.R.P. shelters. At every one of them there were two or more men on duty. I am told that in this district alone the cost has run up to over £3,000. I don't know that anyone grumbles.

I have had several choirboys from Hull churches come to Hessle. Their parents having moved, the boys want to come into Hessle choir. I don't care for this idea for various reasons but I have sympathy with a boy in this position. He just wants a choir transfer and it seems only just to give him one. Dennis came to me one night, he wanted to join Hessle choir from a Hull choir. He was rather a big boy and I did not think he would last long, so I let him come in. Last Wednesday he had just about got his footing in the choir — got to know the other boys and their little ways, ways humorous, silly, playful and so on. Dennis thought it was about time to show what he could do in the entertainment line. His first idea was to draw a small catapult and swish a paper pellet across to another boy. That caused amusement and a warning from me. Later on he hit the next boy to him a sharp blow on the head with an *English Hymnal*. (Thank heaven it was not an *Ancient and Modern* book) The sentence in this case was, 'Get out! Hop it!' Master Dennis refused to hop it and remained in his seat. Old men of 67 do not tackle lusty boys of 14 or so, at least not with any happy feelings. However, I went for him and for the first time that I can remember I ran one of my choirboys out of the vestry. Not a pleasant job. I resumed practice and after a few minutes I looked out to see if the young hooligan had gone away or whether he was waiting for the other boys. It avoids awkward questions at home about the shortness of the practice. Master Dennis had switched on the corridor lights which were shining out to the world, only the vestry and part of the church having been blacked out. I was in terror about the A.R.P. warden and a £2 fine for the churchwardens but nothing happened. I don't know who invented choirboys. Just now, with all this air raid scare on and gas masks flying about the boys seem to be ever so much more troublesome than of yore. However, I suppose I should be thankful to have any boys at all. In Hull churches most of the boys have been evacuated. Some churches have given up their choirs altogether and I know of one church that has closed down entirely, the parson and his wife have fled, their children evacuated and nearly all the houses in the parish have been demolished.

John is now at Shoeburyness where he is having a week's gunnery tuition. Fancy a boy like John spending his time learning gunnery. He spent Saturday night here. He motored on his cycle from Kilnsea to Hessle in pouring rain and arrived home like a drowned rat. However, he is cheerful enough. I think he thoroughly enjoyed every moment he was here and I don't know how many of his pals, girls as well as boys, came to see him. I don't remember how many boxes of cigarettes he got, given to him I mean, and some of his admirers are knitting him various garments. He has grown a little Hitler moustache and he has filled out ever so much. It is quite obvious this sort of life is doing him good. The future does not seem to concern him, not in the very least. He went off to London early on Sunday morning. We expect him back again at the weekend. What the next move is to be is uncertain. John thinks he will have to return to Kilnsea. Henry is still at Worksop. We have not heard from him lately.

I don't think there is much more to write about. Business is up. I had a wedding on Saturday last and a funeral yesterday. They are all the same to me as long as they pay up. Trade has been very slack since the war commenced and September used to be such a good month. Best love, Phil.

B.S.8. 5th December 1939

A strange and unusual thing has befallen this house, a thing that has never happened before within memory. Our three boys are all away from home. Stephen is in North Wales spending his well-deserved summer holiday (?) with his Aunt Maude at Deganwy. I think Stephen had given up all hope of this deferred holiday, he was just off for a fortnight when the war broke out in the first week of September and his firm cancelled all holidays. Last week he was told that, if he liked, he could have the fortnight now. He soon fixed things up and he went off on Monday morning (Nov. 27) and since his departure our family has come down to three, Katie, Trigo and me. Nice for some things, sad and unhappy for other things. It is sad to look into that back bedroom where all three of them pass their nights during the ping-pong season when our largest and best bedroom is given up to the ping-pong club and therefore the three of them have to sleep in one room. A bit of a squash but their own desire. The room now looks very miserable and sad. All sorts of things, garments, books, papers, old photographs etc. lying about to remind us of one or other of the trio. I wonder if the old life will ever come back to us. I rather doubt it. Somehow or other I feel that we shall never again have the three of them all living at home as was the case before the war broke out. Trigo seems a different being altogether now that her three brothers are not at home to tease her and to bandy words with her. I notice that our housekeeping costs us just about £2 a week less that it did last year. In other words John and Henry were costing us about £1 a week each.

It seems to me that I am going to break a record on Saturday, December 23rd. I am booked to play at three weddings that day and another inquiry has been made about the fees for the organ for yet another wedding on the same day. Well. Three guineas and possibly four will come in very handy just at Christmas time, although I don't quite relish spending all my Saturday afternoon at the church playing the wedding march etc. over and over again. Last year I made thirty guineas in this way. So far the number is 18 for this year.

We have had no more air raid alarms lately, total number so far is five. In the previous war we laughed at the idea of any air attack until one fine night a Zeppelin attacked Hull and then we got to know what a raid meant, and ever after that I was really bad whenever a raid warning was sounded.

People in Hull seem to think that we shall have no raids this time. Well. They thought like that in 1914 and we old people know what happened in the three following years. However, for the present things seem quiet enough.

The war has taught us how to hold very delightful evening services at the church. Very little light and that darkly shaded so that the clerestory windows get none of it. All come into the centre of the nave and come as close up as possible. The choir sit along with the congregation and we have only one lesson and a short sermon and everything timed to end in exactly an hour, just like a B.B.C. turn. Everybody likes this arrangement and the offertories keep well up to the mark. Goodbye, Phil

B.S.9 19th December 1939

We have had our Christmas dinner already. Last Thursday the whole family were at home and so we celebrated the event and we had a jovial Christmas dinner. Henry came home for a week's Christmas leave before going abroad, so they say. John came home for a spell of 48 hours. So we had a very lively time. It is not only our four that makes things hum. They all have friends, Henry especially, who honour us with their company from time to time. Katie is very good on such occasions as this although, if she gets the chance, she says DRAT to me. The word I use in such cases is BLAST. It means just the same thing. I don't know how many visitors we had on that Sunday night, I should say about eight. They all got up into the top attic where the table tennis business goes on and we heard very little of them.

Last night at the Hull chess club I played three games against a Polish doctor who has somehow or other found his way to Hull. He could hardly speak a word of English but he had with him a young man I took to be his son who was able to act as interpreter. This Polish doctor was a man about my own age, he looked as though he had not had a decent meal for months and when he moved a chessman I saw that his hands were trembling. He just could not smile. I tried to speak to him in French but he knew no French. The son took up what I said in French and after the old man had spoken he gave me back a reply in English. I am still looking at that pale and sad face and wondering what is the story . . . Don't forget, if you want to write to Henry, to address the letter Sergt. H. Chignell, very important. Henry has had all the luck. John, at the out-of-the-world corner at Spurn has had none. He never will get any of it down there. It seems that John is there for the duration, as they say, but Henry is expecting to be moved off at any time. Today Henry writes for us to send along his cricket things. Well, there is no cricket going on in France just now. Goodbye, Phil.

1940

B.S.10 *2nd January 1940*

On Saturday, December 23rd, I came out from Hull to Hessle by the 6.0 p.m. bus. It was crowded with women and packages and all very excited and talkative. I felt jolly well bored in that company but there, all women are dotty at Christmas time. At Pickering Park the bus pulled up at the usual stopping place and various women gathered their parcels together to get out. There was a shrill cry from one of them, 'Oh, I've lost my rabbit.' There was a wild hunt under all the seats of the bus for the lost Christmas dinner but it was not to be found and the conclusion unanimously agreed upon was that the rabbit was dropped on to the road when the woman got onto the bus. History does not relate what happened on Christmas Day or who got a gift Christmas dinner.

Another story, not quite so funny, refers to that same Saturday afternoon. I have played at five weddings (and two funerals) during the Christmas holidays. The usual proceeding is for the bride or bridegroom to inform the vicar that they want some music and thereupon the vicar telephones me and I book the date and hour. Well. After one of these Saturday afternoon weddings, the mother of the bride said to the vicar, 'It was so kind of Mr. Chignell to come and play, it did make the wedding so nice.' Nobody had asked for the music and the vicar had made a mistake in booking me.

On Sunday, December 24th, Henry came over from Worksop by road to say a last goodbye before going abroad. He stayed the night and went off at 7.0 a.m. on Christmas Day. Katie was up that morning at 6.0 in order to give our Sergeant a good meal to set him off. He left home as the church clock was striking the hour. That will be the last we shall hear of him for some time and I expect it will be a year or two before we see him again. We understand he went to Cherbourg on Wednesday or Thursday and after that we know nothing but we think he has gone overland to Marseilles on the way to Palestine. With John still in the Spurn district and with Trigo spending Christmas with her Aunty Maude, we have had a very quiet time. Stephen alone has been at home.

My church choir seems to have gone all to pot. So many away at Christmas time, all the young men called up. On Sunday night we sang

Parry's *I Sing the Birth* without one single bass worth having. One old stager, whose voice left him altogether six or seven years ago, another, who has never sung a note in tune in all his life, and Stephen who gallantly switched over from his tenor department in order to balance things a bit. Two altos out of six, eight boys out of 24, and not selected boys either, and still we had the cheek to sing the anthem. Best love, Phil.

B.S.11 16th January 1940

How do you like this weather? I loathe it. I am only half alive. Just alive and that is all, One or two days during the past week the frost has been very keen indeed. I think on Saturday last there were at least ten degrees of frost right through the day. Now today, Tuesday, the snow has come and at the present moment there is a north blizzard blowing; the snow is so thick that I can hardly see across the road. John is home on a few hours' leave, he is now due back at Kilnsea (25 miles away) at 10 p.m. I don't know how he is going to get there in time. He was relying on his motor cycle but I think he would be foolish to try to drive the beggar through such snow as this. The cold and the frost leave me absolutely miserable. We have a lot of bother with our water in frosty weather. In past years we had several bitter experiences of water pipe bursts after frost. This house is very badly built in this respect. When the pipes were laid down the builder did not seem to worry about frosty weather and we always have much anxiety. So far I have kept the water running, except that just at present I have got a beastly air pocket in the hot water system that I do not seem able to shift. Consequently, just at the time when hot water is most needed i.e. in frosty weather, we cannot get it. Plumbers are only to be had just now by booking them for a certain hour (in the meantime, if you have a burst, you have to cut off your entire supply of water). Water only costs 19/- a year, supplied by Hull Corporation. A very cheap commodity , but just at this frosty time it is a confounded nuisance.

On Saturday, (Jan 13th) I was asked to play at a funeral. I was told it was a young airman who had lost his life, but beyond that I knew nothing. When I went to church late on Friday night I found the coffin placed in the little recess close to the organ. On Saturday the funeral was attended by a company of about 25-30 young airmen from Leconfield Aerodrome. I was so cold at the organ I could hardly move my fingers. Outside the weather was bitterly cold, a dry and firm frost which seemed to bite one's ears and nose. I was told afterwards that this young man lost his life in an accident. An aeroplane flying somewhere over Wales lost its way in fog and crashed into the side of a mountain. All five men lost their lives. And then to see these young men come to the funeral. All about 20 years of age and no older. I often wonder if my life is just a dream. One day I shall wake up and find I have been through a nightmare and that really and happily there are no such things as aeroplanes or bombing planes, no submarines. John has just come to my study to say that he has telephoned to his battery at Kilnsea and obtained permission to return by bus leaving Hull at 6.30. I am thankful he has not got to cycle through all that snow. We had a line from Henry a few days ago. It was just to say that he was well and that he was having a most interesting time. We don't know where he is just now but we fancy he has gone to Palestine. The letter gave us no clue whatever. Phil.

B.S.12 29th January 1940

This month of January will pass down to history as about the coldest month ever experienced in this country. The cold is still going on and there is no sign as yet of any thaw. Just at present if you look out from my front window you will see a huge pile of snow in our front garden, five or six feet deep. As the snow has fallen, day by day, I have cleared it from the path leading up to the front door and thrown it on to the garden. The paths, which have been cleared now and then of the snow as it fell, have about three or four inches of solid ice on them. On each side of the road is a big heap of snow, feet deep, where the path has been cleared.

On Friday last we had a blizzard after sunset. It was our choir practice night. I struggled down to church and found six or seven brave youngsters waiting for me to open up. They were not wasting their time, just having a snowball fight in the churchyard. Three men and two girls turned up; Stephen was one of the men and Trigo one of the girls. And, do you know, we had a really jolly little practice, everyone enjoyed it; even I enjoyed it. Afterwards the churchyard snowball fight was resumed, which Stephen and Trigo joined in. Nobody, not even the naughtiest choir boy, thought of attacking me, for which exemption I was thankful. All the same I kept my weather eye open in case. The great point to observe, if you are an elderly choirmaster and have to pass through a snowball battle of choirboys, is just appear to be interested in it and do not on any account appear to be in a hurry. You are in great danger and might easily be involved.

I have never seen so much ice in the River Humber before. One day last week it was firmly fixed, not moving, half a mile across the river. Huge boulders of ice on the river bank where the tide had left them. Another time all the ice was in motion, big ice floes mixed up with ice boulders. Some of the floes must have been a hundred yards long. And then on Saturday (27th), when I went to have another look at this unusual sight, the river was completely open, no ice at all, except some boulders on the bank and a few small floes drifting with the tide. I suppose some strong tide, to do with the recent full moon, had cleared the lot out to sea. Anyway it had all gone, although the severity of the weather had not diminished in the least.

Henry is now at a place called Sarafand, in Palestine. We have had two letters from him since he arrived at Haifa. He talks about lovely hot weather, jaffa oranges at ten a penny, a visit to Jerusalem with a provision lorry, where he saw a film. Poor old John is at home for one day. He has nearly frozen to death down at Spurn, which is a very exposed place. Just luck. He is very much bucked because he has had his pay increased by 6d. a day because of his expert knowledge in range finding. Even so his pay is only 2/6 a day. Henry's is nearly four times as much. Phil.

B.S.13 13th February 1940

Last Friday (Feb 9) a thaw set in at midday and the snow melted and that made things all the more unpleasant. It then froze up again on Friday night. For the first time the R.D.C. sent out a small gang of men to work on the frozen roads of Hessle., I saw these men working(?), mostly standing about smoking cigarettes. They just broke up the ice with axes etc. and left it as they broke it. I wonder what the motorist had to say about it. The broken ice became as glass upon the hard road.

Then came Sunday. We saw the sun for the first time for weeks but the frost remained hard bound as ever. With the snow and the frost and the ice and the blackout and no moon, black as sin an hour after sunset, an absent vicar leaving a deacon curate to carry on — we had a doleful Sunday. Bell ringers all ill or away or too tired to come and pull the ropes. I am proud to think that the choir did not fail. Although small, it was quite good. The music was the only thing that counted in Hessle Church that Sunday.

Yesterday was a dreadfully cold day. Katie, Trigo and I celebrated a certain birthday by going to the Regal Cinema in Hull and afterwards to a cafe for tea. I was cold at the cinema, cold at the cafe, cold at the library, where I was from 6 to 7, cold again at the Chess Club from 7 to 9.45 and starved to death in the bus on the way home from 10 to 10.25.

Trigo went to the Hull Choral Society last night for the first time. Brahms' Requiem. She is going to join. I just hesitate to repeat the flattering words the conductor (Mr. Strafford) said to Katie when she introduced Trigo. It seems that she had been admitted with no test. Admitted just on a reputation. That is like how I got into the Sheffield Choir in 1911. We are bringing up Trigo in the right way. She can now play four or five Beethoven violin sonatas, four of Mozart's and three of Schubert's quite well enough to make me enjoy playing with her.

A year or two ago a new main road was opened which relieved Hessle of through traffic from Hull to the West Riding and the south. The new road leads direct from Hull to the old Booth Ferry, over the Ouse where a fine new swing bridge carries the road over the river, and into Goole. The new road leaves Hessle half a mile or so to the south and we have been released from continuous noisy traffic. No sooner do the motorists begin to use the new and very straight road than accidents begin to happen. The driver and his mate of a local tradesman's van were knocked over and killed by a speedy motorist who was summoned for manslaughter. The chief witness was one of my choirmen who, a month or two later, was himself killed at the very same spot when riding a motor cycle at night. One Good Friday Stephen ventured on the new road on his bicycle. He was brought home by a Goole doctor, rather badly knocked about, his bicycle (borrowed from John) smashed up beyond hope of repair. A few days' rest and he was all right again but he was one of the lucky ones. I could give you more gruesome stories about this wonderful new road. Sometimes it is the motorist himself that takes the punishment. Mr Company Director, in a hurry to get to his meeting in the West Riding, failed to see a coming motor bus. That meant another funeral for me. Phil.

B.S.14 27th February 1940

On Thursday last, Feb 22nd, the hard frost that has persecuted us ever since the beginning of 1940 suddenly came to an end. A most refreshing thaw set in and soon our paths and road were running with melted snow and ice. Once it began, the thaw continued and by the end of the week we were practically clear of the snow that has haunted us for so long a time.

John is home for a week's leave. He is thoroughly enjoying himself. In a letter he wrote to us a few days before his leave commenced he used the words 'O Boy, O Boy' and that just about expresses the state of his mind today. He is thoroughly enjoying his holiday. His return home for a few days wakes us up all right. After church, (and didn't John enjoy himself in the choir, morning and evening), John's pals came round to spend the evening with him. So there we are, more company for Sunday supper. Katie seems to thrive on this sort of thing but I get a bit bored with it. You know with this younger generation it means the wireless running all the time. Strikes me as being very funny. All my four children like to have the wireless going all the time, whatever else may be going on in this house. Meals, visitors, reading, homework, never mind what it is or what the wireless programme may be, the knob has to be turned on and you may listen to it or not as you like.

We have not heard from Henry recently. He seems to be seeing a lot of things in Palestine that I have often longed to see, especially places like Jerusalem and Jericho. I wonder what the end of it all will be. Just at the present it is quite clear that both John and Henry are learning some useful lessons. The only thing that seems to vex John is Henry's recent photograph in uniform, with the sergeant's stripes very carefully in the picture. John turns this photograph to the wall. It vexes him. I could write to H.M. on that point. John is just as good and certainly more reliable than t'other chap, only H.M. does not know it and he gives t'other chap the stripes and nearly four times as much pay. But the world always was upside down and unfair. Eh! Phil.

B.S.15 12th March 1940

March 9th and March 11th are red letter days in this house. Stephen was 18 years old yesterday. One of Stephen's boy friends must have walked past this house to the local Post Office and there paid ninepence in order to send his chum a Golden Greeting Telegram. I thought that was a waste of money but The Committee agreed that is was a very charming act. You may ask about this Committee. Well, in the absence of the military members of my family, my house is well under the control of a committee — Stephen, Trigo, with a little help from the old lady. I am supposed to be on this committee but I am always outvoted and suppressed.

I shall talk of choirs. Mine is a pretty rotten task just now of trying to keep the church choir going. Take the alto department. A few week's ago I had six quite good and reliable altos. Five ladies and one man. Now where are we? The one male alto (a very good one too — his business has failed and he has left Hessle). He was in the seed and bulb line, quite a good business, but the war has killed it off altogether. One of the good ladies is a teacher and has gone evacuating. Another good girl was married last summer and now, of course, she has to retire from public life for a period. Two of the others seem to have deserted, staying away altogether. Blackout business too much for them, I suppose, anyhow they have given up coming. One alto left and that is the ever faithful K.C. So I am faced with the trouble I have not had for 25 years, lack of good altos. I have lost eight men, tenors and basses and all of them young ones too; just left with the old stock. And here is Easter coming on and the parsons expect their sung masses with processionals and vestments and graduals and heaven knows what, to which the general bulk of the congregation do not come, and then the Hessle Church people, those who fill the offertory boxes, want their full sung matins and I have got to shift between the two and it is no good going to the parson for any advice because I know I should not get any. I should get nothing but empty and useless talk. Parsons don't give up their glorified mass. So where am I? Phil.

B.S.16 27th March 1940

This very early Easter has come and gone and I am thankful to get it over. Katie always says that I get unduly alarmed at these church festivals. I feel so afraid that the choir will let me down. I believe it always happens the same way — I am always nervous and anxious and then the choir always do well. Katie just laughs at me but she can never laugh away my anxiety. I doubt if any choir in the neighbourhood did better than Hessle choir both on Palm Sunday and on Easter Day, together with a beautiful and quiet little service on Good Friday evening. But I get tired of church going and hymn playing in Holy Week. Every night during that week there is a service. On Good Friday at 10.30 we had matins — *O come and mourn with me awhile* — eight verses and a play over, total nine. At noon the three hours service began with the same hymn, eight verses and a play over. Total number of times I had to play that tune through — 18 — and so on and so on. I just get tired of it all. Easter at Hessle is not what it was thirty and more years ago. In Bishop Blunt's time the Easter Offering always amounted to over £100. On Tuesday I counted all the cash collected on Easter Day and paid it into Barclay's Bank (this is one of my jobs, as you know). The amount was just over £35. Times have changed.

On the Saturday before Easter I spent the afternoon at the Hull Chess Club and I played my last game in the Hull Club's annual tournament. This last game was against the vicar of Christ Church, Hull [Rev. Horace James Mundy]. Mr. Mundy and I are very great chess enthusiasts. We are all good friends at chess and there is a great mix up in our club room on a chess night. We have now a Berlin magistrate (fled from the country), a Polish doctor, two young German Jews, Hull men of all sorts of businesses and professions. Such a mix up, but at chess we are all good friends. So I played my last tournament game on Saturday (a draw), and I am the very first to finish. I have not done so badly but nothing to boast about. I have played 17 games, won 10, drawn 2, lost 5. I expect I shall end up about fifth. The Hull club is very strong just now; they have won the Yorkshire Championship for match play on the last two occasions that the competition has been held, and the Woodhouse Cup is still in our possession, although there is no competition for it this season. Our club gatherings have been very happy times for me, Monday evenings and Saturday afternoons.

Henry continues to send us interesting letters from Palestine. The Hull A.R.P. was very much on the alert during Eastertide. They or he or it were, or was, expecting something or other but it never came. Best love, Phil.

B.S.17 9th April 1940

I think the most important item of news that I have to announce this week concerns Trigo. Trigo started work yesterday morning at the office of the Hull Branch of the Commercial Union Assurance Company. If it had not been for the outbreak of war last September, Trigo would still have been a scholar at the Boulevard Secondary School, Hull. Trigo was to all intents and purposes one of the scholarship pupils at the Boulevard, but all the same we had to pay fees for her which amounted to between £4 & £5 a term. That was because the educational board at Beverley considered that we were in a position to pay. That is what they said and we did not go into the matter. All three of our boys got these East Riding Council scholarships and attended school at Hymers College free of fees. We had already had our fair share without counting Trigo. All the same we liked it to be known that Trigo was a scholarship girl and that our noble quartet had broken a Hessle school record — all four of them gaining one of these East Riding Council scholarships — i.e. free tuition at a Hull secondary school and a free bus pass. Well. That is all finished now. A week or so ago Mary Chignell telephoned to tell Trigo there was a vacancy in her office for a girl. Trigo went to Mary's office and the result was she was offered the job. I hear she is to be paid £1 a week to begin with.

John came home for two nights last Friday. He looks the picture of health and good nature; the open air life on the breezy East coast is doing him good. He looks rough and hefty whereas he was born small and has always been on the small side.

About 17 years ago I published what I call the Hessle Versicles. Banks of York printed these for me. We have used them regularly at Hessle ever since they were published, singing them at Evensong all through the Trinity Sundays period. It is rather funny to notice that someone must have introduced these Versicles into Bedfordshire. They have taken on in that district in quite a remarkable manner. I often get orders from vicars or organists down there and nowhere else. Banks printed a thousand copies for me and they just sent me the whole consignment. Now I am sold out and am just wondering if it is worth while to reprint. Best love. Phil.

B.S.18 23rd April 1940 (St. George's Day)

We have now got to the daffodil season in Hessle. It is wonderful and lovely to take a walk round the avenues of Hessle just to see the millions of daffodils that are now in flower in the gardens. I don't think you would find one garden without daffodils. If only it were not for the war anxiety we should all be feeling joyful and happy. The daffies would make us feel like that, I suppose that is what they are there for. This year it almost seems that nobody has the time or the care to look at them. All the same, they cheer me up, even if I do hear the guns roaring out, as I did last night after I had gone to bed. Curse the blue pencil war.

Henry seems to be having the time of his life in Palestine. For some time he was in a camp near Joppa and now he has been moved to somewhere near Haifa. It is beginning to get a bit warm in Palestine and I expect he will find it very hot indeed later on. Phil.

B.S.19. 7th May 1940

Both Madge and Ruth ask me in their latest letters what I propose to do about my letter writing and the increased postage rates. My answer is 'NOWT'. I don't know if this is a term only used in Yorkshire. I have no doubt you will know what it means even if you never use the same word yourself. Perhaps it should be spelt NAWT. I have a bottle of beer every day of my life as near to noon as may be. I call it my Seven Bells because 11.30 a.m. is the earliest moment that I ever permit myself to call for my bowl. Just lately I have had to pay one ha'penny more per day than heretofore. It is the same with the postage, it will cost me more to send my B.S. letters to my four sisters. That won't make any difference. I shall send the letters just the same as before. Like the beer, I cannot give up the B.S. business. Not I. It will go on just the same as ever. The new tax will catch me in the beer department and in the stamp department but where tobacco is concerned I shall escape entirely because I never smoke at all in these days. Not because I disapprove of smoking but just because I have had to give the habit up. It was making me ill.

Our bowls season has begun and we played our first bowls league match on Saturday afternoon. This match was played on the bowling green of the Costello Park, Hull. It was a glorious afternoon and our Hessle Club won the match by 38 points. I just did fairly well, nothing very wonderful and nothing very bad. One of the Hull barrage balloons was right over our heads, very high up. These balloons were all over the place, we could not even count them, it was like trying to count sheep. I had several tries at the counting of them and once I counted up to 51, that was the highest figure I got to. I am told that each one of these balloons has a dozen men to look after it so that gives you some idea of the cost of this little war item. We can see a lot more of these barrage balloons over in Lincolnshire, Grimsby way. They look like flies in the air.

John has had two days off this week and he went to Huddersfield on a visit to Katie's brother and sister-in-law. He came here last night and was off back to Kilnsea early this morning. He looks very well and fit. He has filled out a lot and has roughened a lot as well. He does not now look like a young man employed in an office, he might be a farmer's boy judging by his looks. However, it is no good worrying about this because the young man has just got to do his bit, which at present means just hanging about somewhere near the mouth of the Humber. Now and then he has what he calls 'a spot of fun' and I must just leave you to guess what that means, but on the whole he has a very dull and uninteresting time. I am troubled by the thought that he is just learning, at 23-24 years of age, how to spend his days doing nothing in particular. I learned that game when I was 65, and now at 68 I am quite sure I could not unlearn it. I have got to go on for the rest of my life doing nothing in particular. It is that thought that makes me worried about John.

Henry's letters are full of the life and sights of Egypt. He is having a grand time. I don't suppose that even he wants to be told that he is in Egypt because the British Government thinks he deserves a jolly good holiday. So far, that is what it has been for him and for his many Hull pals. Now we stop. With best love. Phil.

B.S.20 21st May 1940

We have now come to the very best time of all the year. During the last week or two of May and the first week or two of June, Hessle becomes a place of

NAMES AND TOUR NUMBERS

OF

PRINCIPALS, CHORUS & FRIENDS.

1	Dr. Henry Coward	50	M
2	Miss Jenny Taggart	50
3	„ Gertrude Lonsdale	201
4	„ Maude Willby	202
5	Mr. Henry Turnpenney	203
6	„ Wilfrid Virgo	204
7	„ Robert Charlesworth	5 205
8	„ J. E. Hodgson	5 206
9	„ Robert Chignell	58 207
10	„ P. Chignell	59 207a
11	„ Fredk. A. Smith	60 208
12	Mrs. Fredk. A. Smith	61 209
14	Mr. Horace Harrison	62 210
14a	Mrs. Horace Harrison	63 211
15	Mr. Geo. S. Wilford	64 212
16	Mrs. Geo. S. Wilford	65 213
17	Miss Ice. T. King	66 214

Radcliffe
Mr. E. A. Whitham
„ E. A. Armitage
Mrs. J. W. Beal
„ W. J. Pullon
Miss H. R. Netherwood
„ K. Hodgson
„ G. M. Gaskell
„ E. Wareing
Viscount S. Campden
Lady Norah Noel
Mr. Tom Smith
Mrs. Tom Smith
Miss Mabel Smith
„ Elsie Smith
Mr. Thos. Davage
„ Frank Scott

From the programme of the Sheffield Choir world tour, 1911, during which Philip Chignell (10) met his future wife, Miss Katie Netherwood (205).

radiant beauty. I suppose it is the same at other places. I don't know, I am always at Hessle at this period of the year. The summer seems to open out to us almost without warning. I have never forgotten the train ride through the Rocky Mountains that I had in 1911: go to bed on the train in wintry weather, snow and ice, wake up on a Sabbath morning to see lilac, laburnum, roses and full summer. Oh, but Hessle is glorious just now. It is a sheer delight to walk about the roads of Hessle just to see all the flowers — lilac, laburnum, chestnut, apple blossom, iris, tulips, and ever so many more. If you go beyond the houses you will find the May trees and hedges in full flower and the fields are golden with buttercups. There is one field, down near the river, where the buttercups are so large that you might almost call them Kingcups. We have this day two large bowls of these buttercups, one in our front room and one in the back room, and they give the house a summer warmth that helps to drive away the anxiety and care that we all are suffering from just at present.

You know, perhaps, that there is a war on, a war that seems to get nearer and nearer to us every day. These are sad and anxious days. Many young men that we know quite well, the friends of our boys and sons of our neighbours, have just vanished into the maelstrom over in France and Belgium. Nobody knows where they are or what they are doing. No news of them comes to hand. You can imagine the anxiety there is in their homes. Best love, Phil.

B.S.21 4th June 1940

We are living through a strange and historic period. In my early manhood when the world seemed settled and happy none of us ever dreamed that we should come to times like these. June is always a lovely month in England; this year it seems more beautiful than ever. On Sunday morning I went down to the river quite early, long before anybody else was about. It was just glorious down there, not a cloud in the sky anywhere, nothing to be seen above but blue sky, a mid-summer sun and a large company of barrage balloons. For the best part of an hour I sat on the river beach and just let my thoughts drift. A lovely way of spending time. Before returning to my waiting bicycle I gathered a bunch of gelder roses, growing wild down there, and returned home, ready for the sung eucharist and the rest of the choir duties.

I suppose England is now full of soldiers returned from Flanders in the great evacuation or retreat. Every returned soldier will have his own story to tell and there will be few of them who cannot stir your sympathy and admiration. On Sunday I spoke to three such young men. Two of them old choir boys of mine and the third, one of the youngest members of our Bowls Club, I could tell you their stories, wonderful stories, only I know you will hear the same stories and they are all of the same nature. One or two of the young men we know have not come back. Alas. One young man I heard of, but did not see, Eric Briggs by name, has come back with a crowd from the neighbourhood of Dunkirk, when we thought he was in Palestine with Henry. Henry told us of Eric's illness, how he was in hospital and later on how he was well again and going about his job as usual. Certainly Henry has not mentioned him in recent letters and now he turns up, direct from France. Well. I suppose they will have to go on with this bloody business until all the ammunition gets blown up and then there will be a halt for a certain number of years, that is until another store of war material has been accumulated and then we shall have the same thing all over again. It seems that mankind will have to put up with this sort of thing every twenty years or so in the future. I have seen it once, I have seen it twice, and that is my fair share of this idiotic and senseless game. This is my last turn, anyhow, and I shall not worry to quit life, the life that is hardly worth having nowadays because it has to be lived with such a lot of ingenious devils who have, by their ingenuity in manufacturing machines of destruction, made life not worth the living. I, for one, shall be glad to be quit of it and I don't mind how soon, so please note.

Queerly enough, here in Hull and district we seem to have obtained some little relief. With all this terrible imbroglio going on just over there everybody is too busy to worry about the Humber and the Port of Hull where everything is at a deadlock. Just at the present we are not worth worrying about . However. It is a strange war and one never knows. The roads all round about us are mined and guarded by troops and guns and barricades. Don't you try to pass one of these places without your identity card in your pocket. At our bowling club we have a big board at the entrance which faces the Boothferry Road, the exit road from Hull to the West Riding, a new main road made some ten years ago. This notice said on it — Hessle Bowling Club —. Now it says ——- - - - - - Bowling Club. If a German parachutist drops anywhere near about and wants a game of bowls at any rate he won't know that he is in Hessle unless one of us is foolish enough to tell him where he is. The word Hessle was expurgated by order of the military authority. Best love, Phil.

B.S.22 18th June 1940

Yes. Yes. Yes. The fall of Paris. I know all about it. And is this not Waterloo Day. Of course it is, but have you heard about a nice funeral last week. I had a talk with the four bearers afterwards. Nice men, all in dismal black. They left the coffin in the church whilst the friends were taken back home, to the top of Southfield, for refreshments, I suppose. Then they were coming back to fetch the dear deceased J.P. to take him off to Bradford to be buried. The four hired bearers were the only ones who remained to hear Chopin's *Funeral March*, also by request, and I was surprised to receive their unanimous and nicely expressed appreciation of my playing. The coffin, the four bearers and me, and a lovely old church filled with sunshine at midday on a June morning. And there's a picture for you.

I had a visitor the other day, one of my old choirboys Geoffrey Wilson. He was one of the leading boys in Hessle Choir in 1911. The headmaster of our Hessle Church Schools is now resigning and a new man has to be appointed. G.W. is after the job. He called on me to solicit my help with the managers of the school, who have to make the new appointment. The idea of a Church School under Government control seems queer to me. They have to pay a lot out of church funds and don't get anything back that I can see. All the same they have the choice of a new headmaster. Such a funny lot, too. Of course the vicar, who is one of the most unbusiness-like men that I know. There are five others, every one of whom was in Hessle before I came here, nearly forty years ago. Two old and wealthy spinsters who can be relied upon to hold up their hands at the vicar's direction. Billy Coulson, a retired churchwarden, who lives all by himself. Then there is old Tommy Appleton, an old boy getting on for 90, who has been scared away from this district by the threat of air raids. I don't know where he has gone to but he certainly won't come home just to vote about the new headmaster. There is also an ancient solicitor who, for his own peace, would vote exactly as the vicar told him to. It is a funny sort of committee. I suppose it was elected thirty or forty years ago and has always been re-elected en bloc, year after year. Canon Lenton will have the matter in his pocket. I told G.W. this but

I promised I would do what I could in the matter. I had a talk with Canon Lenton on Friday and I soon learned how things stood. I should say G.W. has not the slightest chance. The vicar does not know him and he has already made up his mind. It is no concern of mine but I would have liked to see G.W. and his wife back in Hessle.

Trigo and Stephen cycled over to Kilnsea on Sunday to see John. I think that most people would say that Spurn Point is not far from Hull. Kilnsea is 4 miles from Spurn, but even then it meant about 33 miles there and 33 miles back. That's a good long run for Trigo at least. They saw John and had the afternoon with him. It was nice for John, I hear he was very glad to see them, but there was nowhere to go when you got to Kilnsea, just the sea and the beach. Trigo looked like a boiled lobster when she returned home at 9.30 p.m. Katie and I were sad and lonely, not one of the four of them home for Sunday dinner. Best love, Phil.

B.S.23 2nd July 1940

I was in church yesterday morning, in the vestry. I was the only person in the church on a fine sunny morning. I was counting up the cash from the Sunday's offertories, a thing I always do on Monday mornings, getting it all made up and ready for Barclay's Bank. I had in front of me a table full of loose silver and copper and I was making it up in £5 and 5/- bags. Bang went an anti-aircraft gun. Not very far away, either. Costello Park, I reckoned, 1 mile from Hessle. It made my heart go thump and I stopped counting the money to listen. There were several more bangs. It sounded as though several guns were firing at an aeroplane. I stopped to think what I should do. Run to a shelter? Run home? I know the church is reckoned to be a place of danger in the case of a raid, I have thought that out for myself. Should I run into the churchyard and shelter behind the largest tombstone I could see? That seemed rather like anticipating things. So I just went on with my money counting. A pale-faced woman opened the vestry door: 'Where is Leslie (the young newly-married verger)?' 'I don't know.' 'Didn't you hear the guns?' 'Yes, but what can I do?' Thereupon the face disappeared. It was Leslie's mother-in-law. A dead silence fell over Hessle, like the two minutes Armistice Day's silence, and then an immense chatter broke out. As I walked to the bank with the cash, all the women in Hessle were standing at their doors and telling each other what had happened. July 1st is a busy day for bankers. Barclay's Bank was full of customers, all talking, cashiers and clerks and all. Just one jolly big chattering party. I came home. Katie, when she heard the gunfire, went into the garden. Naughty girl. She saw the shelling of the German aeroplane and she saw it either dive for safety or drop quickly, disabled. After that I went to the Darley Arms and had 'one'. Another talking party. It was funny how many people knew all about it and just where the plane had fallen. Half a dozen different places, by the way.

Stephen, when he came home to dinner, said that he had heard that it had fallen in Hessle.

There was another uproar about 5.30. Somebody got something in Hull. I went to the bowling green and there was a fire in Hull, the result of a raid, I suppose. Big clouds of black smoke curling up and drifting away, fortunately for us and our game, not in our direction. Ominous and threatening all the same. Later on still and after listening to a Sibelius symphony on the wireless and after getting into bed, the raid warning siren piped out again and made us all get up and go to our shelters. I think we have had these warnings every night for the past fortnight.

The war does not seem very funny 'nowanights', as I might say. If the sirens have not sounded on one or two of our recent nights it has been, not because there was no need for them to sound, but because the people must have some rest and chance it rather than spend the nights chattering and shivering in their garden dugouts. Bah! It's a silly war as ever was. I'm tired of it.

This summer of 1940 has been pilfered from me. When I think of all the good things that mid-summer means to me in an ordinary year and then how very few, if any more, summers I can hope to see, my eyes fill with tears to think of this one that is now passing away in such agony. All the joy and happiness has gone out of it. We live in constant dread of attack from the air and the sooner the long, clear days of summer have gone, the better. The sooner we get back to the short days of winter and the long dark nights and the snow and the frost and cold, the greater will be our chance of living our lives in quiet and without the menace which now haunts us day and night. Oh! It is a fond and silly war, as ever was. Best love, Phil.

B.S.24 16th July 1940

We are getting so used to air raid alarms that we don't seem to take much notice of them now. Last night the siren sounded just as I had gone off to sleep at 11.0 precisely. Katie had not given up her novel for she has a quiet hour at night whereas I get the quiet hour early in the morning, a little arrangement that seems to work very well. I never got out of my bed for the darned row of the siren (a terrible shrieking row, only a few doors away from us, a row that nobody could escape from, not even a deaf man). I just stayed where I was and waited for the two minutes' yelling to cease and then I turned over and pretended I should soon be asleep again.

We have had these alarms so frequently lately that one cannot keep count of them. They come at all times of the day and night. Noon, midnight, dinner time, tea time, and in between times. I don't think there is any one hour of the twenty-four hours of the clock that we have not had at least one alarm. Last Thursday we had four alarms, 1.00 a.m. 8.00 a.m. 11.00 a.m. and 5.30 p.m. Four in one day is a record. So far. You know the story of

Wolf, Wolf. Well, it is getting like that. One day perhaps he will really get at us, so far it has been all noise and frightening.

Two years ago, just at this very time, Katie and I sat on the big lock gates at Harlingen in Holland. We sat there and had our lunch, made up for us at the hotel in Amsterdam. We watched a boat pass through the lock and then we went into the little cafe close by and had some jolly good coffee. In the cafe were two or three young men playing bagatelle or some such game and one of these young men left the game and made our coffee. The coffee was absurdly cheap, tuppence or threepence, and it was excellent and very much to our liking. These young Dutchmen were just fine, they all knew just a tiny bit of English and we had a most amusing chatter, all of us laughing together. I remember that incident so well. Yesterday, on the wireless, we heard that an English bomber had wrecked the lock gates at Harlingen. What about my nice Dutch friends? And an English bomber, too. My God, isn't it damnable? All the Dutch people we met two years ago spoke about their BIG BROTHER (England) and here is the BIG BROTHER dropping bombs on the LITTLE BROTHER. Damnable, isn't it? I am not arguing as to the necessity of this. Just remarking on it and the sadness of the times.

We have not heard from Henry for weeks. He was in Palestine the last time we heard from him. John now comes home once a fortnight. He gets eight hours' leave, half of which is occupied in getting here and getting back but he does enjoy a dinner with us and then an hour or two slacking about with the wireless, and the early cup of tea before he goes off back again. John can tell a few yarns too. Very funny. Best love, Phil.

B.S.25 30th July 1940

You would not go to the Psalms to find humour, would you? But sometimes I come across it unexpectedly. I know the Psalms by heart from the beginning to the end. The Psalms for the 9th Sunday after Trinity - - 44 and 45 - - I once wrote to Novello, the publisher of the Psalter we use, and suggested that they should use the ordinary figures in giving the numbers of the Psalms and not the Roman figures which the choirboys never seem to understand. It was no good, Novellos would have none of it. So for 44 & 45 we get xliv & xlv. In Psalm xliv there is a section reminds me of Mussolini. 'For they gat not the land in possession through their own sword: neither was it their own arm that helped them.' Rather far fetched I suppose but I am hinting at Italy's war declaration on France after our late ally had been beaten down by Germany.

Yesterday afternoon I played at the funeral service of Luther Stromberg. I wonder if the name means anything to you. The vicar and churchwardens of Hessle Church in 1901 selected me as the new organist of Hessle Church out of over one hundred applicants. Mr. Stromberg was one of the churchwardens at that time. He was in Government employ, something to do with the shipping in Hull. In 1914 when the war broke out, L.S. suddenly appeared in uniform and adopted the title of Commander. He gave up his third class railway pass and took out one for first class. He got too big a man for me and I dropped out of the keen friendship that had existed between us. For some years he was on the Urban District Council of Hessle and became its Chairman. Alas, he grew too old for this work, and at one election he was discarded. That was about five years ago. Since then little has been heard of him. He seems to have been forgotten. A few of the oldest inhabitants came to his funeral service. Had he died twenty years ago there would have been a very great ceremony.

We continue to have our air raid alarms, night after night generally about 11.45p.m. to midnight. Last week we had three nights in succession without any disturbance and everybody was talking about it, how nice it was to go through the night peacefully. It's an ill wind etc. The other day, when an air raid warning came during the day, Stephen went into a shelter with others and had a game of cards. He won tuppence. That was during business hours, too.

We have heard from Henry for the first time for six weeks. The letter was written on June 16th. Delivered here on July 25th. I wonder by what route the letter came. Letter from Isabel took eight weeks from Australia to Hessle. Also I wonder which way that letter came. What a disturbed world we are living in now. Will it ever calm down? Best love to all, P.

B.S 26 13th August 1940

It seems strange to think that we are in the middle of the usual holiday month and yet nobody talks about holidays or thinks about them. We had no Bank Holiday on the first Monday of the month. All the seaside resorts are deserted by visitors and there is no holiday traffic on the railways and motor roads.

We have had many air raid warnings lately, two last night and two the night before. Last week we had a little holiday from them because there was a gale of wind blowing and Jerry [the slang word for the Germans] did not seem to like that sort of weather. Stephen tells me he has kept count of these warnings and that the number is now over forty. You would think that Jerry would have done us some injury after warning us over forty times that he was coming for us. When these air raid warnings pipe up we can hear at least another dozen sirens, all more or less alike, besides our darned Hessle shrieker which is almost at our door. When the Hessle siren is singing the row is so great that every other sound is wiped out. They don't all go off together and we usually hear many of the others before we hear the Hessle one. A shrieking jargon or medley of abominable noise.

On Thursday of last week Katie had a women's bridge party in our house. I have only one dislike of these card parties that Katie gives every now and then, or of those she goes out for, and that is that they carry on too long and I dislike Mrs. C. coming to bed perhaps an hour and a half or more after I have gone off to sleep. On Thursday I went to bed at 10.30, but not to sleep. The card party was in the front room just under my bedroom and I could hear all that went on there. I don't profess to be a judge of women's parties but, to me, it seems that when four women get together to play bridge they all talk all the time and altogether. It sounds to me like that, especially when I am curled up in bed just overhead. I said to myself, 'I wish to goodness they would close down and let a poor fellow get to sleep.' In common justice I should state that they were using the front room at my request, I wanted the back room, our drawing room, for the wireless and a good concert earlier on. Suddenly my bedroom was filled with white light and I sat up and had a look round. All the searchlights in this district were out , flashing round and searching for a raider. I could hear the beggar somewhere overhead, very high up and not far from our district. Soon I heard the Hull siren sing out and I knew that our local one would follow suit very quickly. The dear people downstairs could not see the searchlights and they were too busy chattering to hear the distant sirens. I just waited events that I knew were bound to happen. Ah! there goes our Hessle siren, shrieking up and down in its usual horrible manner! There was a sudden skirmish down below and our house was clear of visitors in less than thirty seconds. I never heard who was winning or how the stakes were settled. Next morning when I came down to hear the Norwegian news (6.45) I found the front room just as the ladies had left it, cards, scorers, chairs, etc. all hurriedly thrown down and deserted. So sometimes I can say 'Thank you' to the air raid siren. Phil.

B.S.27 27th August 1940

I was in the church this morning on my usual Monday morning business of tidying up. Two Hessle workmen that I knew quite well were knocking a hole in the north transept. 'Hullo, Alec,' I said. 'What are you up to?' I did not doubt that he was up to some set task but I could not imagine why he was knocking the church about like that. He held up a golden coloured vase with a label attached. With a bit of a laugh he said, 'We're just putting old Brickie away.' 'Alas , poor Yorick. I knew him well.' About a fortnight ago I met him on one of my Humberside excursions. I then had a long talk with him. He was very tall. Nearly seven feet, one of the tallest men I have ever seen. He had the oddest falsetto voice imaginable. He was a good sort. Not married. A retired Hull Corporation official. A long modern avenue in Hull (N.W.) is named after him, Bricknell Avenue. If you live in that avenue then you are a man of standing and position. And for a moment I held the golden vase that contained all B's remains. I never once saw him in Hessle Church, or ever heard of him being interested in any church work or ever giving anything to the church funds. It seems strange to me that they should brick up his ashes into the walls of the old church which did not attract him in any way during his lifetime. But it is a queer world. Queerer than ever just now.

Last night we had our sixtieth air raid warning, a jolly long one too, the warning siren at 9 p.m. and the relief at 4.20 a.m. — seven hours and twenty minutes. All sorts of funny things going on most of the time. All sorts of funny bangs and dull thuds and whirring aeroplane engines. Searchlights by the score twisting and twirling about all over the dark skies. A funny little moon coming up very late on, just to have a peep to see what further follies these men are up to. Here in Hessle we have at last experienced the trials of an actual air raid. Early Friday morning, August 16th, 1940, records the date of the first air raid ever launched upon Hessle. Fourteen bombs were dropped in the vicinity of the railway station. The idea seems to have been to blot out the searchlight operating close by. The light was not hit. Three bombs gouged up big holes in the adjacent field, two more fell on the railway, the damage to which was repaired in an hour or two by a couple of men. Other bombs fell among the houses and gardens of Southfield. One house was completely wrecked. There were three people in this house, all friends of mine. Two were in the cellar and the other, the only man, had gone back to his bed. Not one of the three were injured although they all had to wait for a rescue party to get them away. Other houses were damaged and all the windows round about were broken. One of the queerest things about this attack happened to one of my bowling friends. Mr. Harrison had made a specialty of his garden, especially a rock garden in the front. A bomb fell on the rock garden and just demolished it. When I saw it, it was just a heap of brown clay. Another bomb fell in the back garden and yet the house remained untouched. I think there was one pane of glass smashed and that was all.

Our house is about half a mile way, a little less perhaps. When this attack was made, three of the bombs seemed to fly screeching past our house. Katie and Stephen and I were in the front bedroom and this unearthly shriek made us all drop straight onto the floor. Katie rolled under the bed and Stephen and I rolled over to the wall of the room. We did that instinctively. It seems funny enough now but it did not seem very funny at the time. On the following Monday night the second attack came on Hessle. After throwing out a basket of bright parachute flares that lit up the place like daylight, Jerry proceeded to bomb a big chalk pit to the north west of Hessle. Here again three or four bombs were dropped in an adjacent field and the rest fell into the pit, where, I should think, they greatly helped in the excavation work (chalk) that goes on there every day. On Saturday night (Aug 24th) we had four air raid alarms during the night. At one time Jerry dived suddenly over Hessle and released a wonderful curiosity that burst in mid air with a noise like the breaking of a glass palace. I am told it was a bomb of mixed glass and concrete. The contents were thrown all over the place but nobody seems to have suffered any injury. In the first raid one old lady died of shock. She was in a shelter that partly collapsed. That was the only casualty of the three raids. Goodbye, Phil.

B.S.28 10th September 1940

I have just had my early morning cup of tea and heard the early morning news, first in Norwegian and then in English. I don't pretend I can follow all that is said in Norwegian, but, listening to the Norwegian broadcast every morning as I do, I can at least follow the gist of it and prepare my mind for what is to follow in my own language. I only wish this opportunity of picking up another language had come to me earlier on in life and not when I have nearly finished with it. Sometimes I wish I had finished with it.

At our bowling club last Saturday we had a bowls drive. Twenty to thirty people there and all very well entertained and happy with thoughts of war and air raids far enough away. Yes. Bowls is a fine antidote. In the middle of it all our Hessle siren shrieked at us and a dozen other local sirens, some fairly near and some far away, took up the strain — 'Danger, danger, danger, fly to your shelters, and tremble and tremble and tremble. Hoots, away with you all and dread the mighty Hitler and all the horrible things he has in store for you.' Well, it just didn't come off. We all went on with our bowls in the good old Francis Drake style. I never heard any suggestion that we should break off. A minute or so before the siren sounded I had heard gun fire or bombs coming from the South East and I thought, if anything comes it will come from the South East and I shall just shelter under that fence close by. However, nothing came and our game went on, and, if it is not too egotistical, I may add that I came home with the first prize in my pocket. The raid warnings of last night bring our total up to 84 as recorded by Stephen, and duly entered in his air raid ledger. 84 raid warnings and one actual attack on Hessle.

Last week I had four days' holiday. I had no summer holiday during 1939 and I did my work at Hessle Church for 70 successive Sundays up to the 1st of this month. Then at that weekend I went off with Stephen to Owston Ferry, a little village on the banks of the Trent, which I have visited several times in recent years and have got to love. Stephen and I went by train to Goole (the first time I have travelled by train for over a year) and from Goole we cycled through Swinefleet, Eastoft, Crowle, Belton and Epworth to Owston Ferry. I give the names of these villages because I think the very names are interesting. I timed our visit to Owston with the new moon because I wanted to see some of the Trent eagres again. On Tuesday, (Sept 3rd) I went west, through Haxey and Wroot, a little out-of-the-world village on the edge of Thorne Waste. At the little pub in Wroot I seem to have been entirely unexpected, and, when I ordered a bottle of beer, my order seemed to be also quite unexpected. 'Terrible price is this bottled beer!' the old man said to me. I said, 'Well! somebody has got to pay for all these aeroplanes.' I thought it would be a ninepenny touch. I received 6d. change out of a shilling. When I finally retire I think I will go to live at Wroot. Good beer at 6d. per half pint is not so bad. Nobody would ever find me at Wroot. It looks as though it is a village completely forgotten and overlooked.

Whilst I was typing the last page we had our 85th air raid alarm. Now the 85th release has just sounded. Bah. Silly game that! On Wednesday I came home, riding along the Trent bank through West Butterwick, Althorp, Gorthorpe, Adlingfleet and Ousefleet — I wish I had the job of the lighthouse keeper at Ousefleet. Best love. Phil.

B.S.29 23rd September 1940

Last Friday night (20th) we had a calm and peaceful night's rest. I woke on Saturday morning at 5.45 having slept six solid hours without any interruptions. I was surprised to notice that it was daylight and to see the hands of the clock very nearly pointing to the hour when I usually get up. For 27 nights previous to this we have had air raid alarms, sometimes once only, sometimes twice or three times and now and then the number has been four. Every time we get this alarm the siren at Hessle Town Hall shrieks at us. For 27 nights in succession it has yelled at us, one or more times every night. It used to be two minutes in alarming us and two minutes in relieving us. Now the first period has been cut down to one minute and that is some little relief from this trouble. We had a second peaceful night The following night, Sunday, I felt quite optimistic about these night calls and the blessed old Hessle siren. Would it ever trouble us again? The answer soon came. Before I was asleep the first warning sounded and then through the night the old Hessle siren and all his neighbouring friends kept up a babel of calls and releases. Five of them, and that is a record for one night. That means ten siren blasts. I just stay put and in bed. If a bomb comes it comes and that is just the end of the matter. We were not very far off such an event on Wednesday night. We had, that night in Hessle, our second serious raid. I am told that fifteen bombs were dropped all over the place and also some ignition bombs. In this house we were all suddenly wakened by a jolly old bang. It turned out that we had only heard the last few bars, so to speak. The early notes of the symphony, or whatever you like to call it, did not wake us up. It was the devil of a bang that did the trick. Half an hour afterwards an A.R.P. warden called to our open bedroom window and told us that the bomb had fallen at the tennis club. Our bowling green is at the north west corner of this club and I felt a bit alarmed. It takes many months to make a bowling green. One of Jerry's bombs on our bowling green and we are finished for some time to come.

I went up to see the damage next morning before breakfast. The tennis court at the extreme opposite corner of the ground to our bowling green was just a heap of muck. The bomb had just gone right into it and gouged it out. It had become a big, muddy crater. All the boundary netting and palings had been thrown over and broken. Close to this tennis court is the last house in Oaklands Drive. So far as I could see, there was not one pane of glass broken, although a small green house in the gardens was broken to pieces. It so happens that the gentleman who lives in this house is deaf. He never heard the bomb and knew nothing about it until he was called by one of the wardens. All the same, he was within thirty yards of pretty certain death. Other bombs fell on both sides of the club grounds. One did not explode but dug a 20-foot hole in a back garden of a house also in Oaklands Drive. It is a miracle that no lives were lost in that raid.

Since the war started we have had 111 air raid warnings. Two real attacks on Hessle, two more very partial attacks. That means 107 warnings without anything to follow, so far as Hessle is concerned. No lives lost, two people slightly injured and one old lady, over 80 years of age, died of shock. So we have been lucky in Hessle and I am sure I hope we may continue to be so until the end of the war. It is an ill wind etc. etc. Last Wednesday night when we had that nasty air raid, Stephen won Spiller's sweep: he guessed correctly the hour the siren would sound that night. Phil.

B.S.30 8th October 1940

Goodbye to Bowls. Every year and every summer the same thing happens as the days shorten. We all have to say goodbye to our cricket, our tennis, our bowls. This summer we came to a very sudden and unexpected closing down. On Saturday afternoon, September 28th, the entrance of the bowling and tennis club was barred and a notice was written up — 'No play today. Danger. Unexploded bomb.' Day after day this notice remained up and the courts and bowling green remained deserted. The days went on shortening. The season was over. Never had the last day, the end of the season, come like that. The unexploded bomb was in a garden just a few yards away from the south side of the club. This garden bomb was not at first discovered. A local man was looking about in his jolly little garden, possibly picking a rose or two for home decoration, when he found a hole close to an apple tree. This was reported to the police. A time bomb? Every home round about was evacuated very speedily. Those who had to find temporary homes included the little, unmusical curate we now suffer at Hessle Church. Also the very tiny man who is my assistant organist, E.F.Ross, Esq. And don't forget the esquire. A very useful little man, all the same. Not much idea of time and less of choirboys but he knows the difference between F sharp and B flat and that's something in these days.

But where was I? Oh yes. The unexploded bomb and our closed bowling green. Some of us had the audacity and temerity to dodge the barrier and to creep into our club house where there is a billiard table. We had a few games of billiards but there was the unexploded bomb not so very far off. You can't play billiards with a time bomb just outside the door. I went round to the garden and had a look at things. The garden had been dug up completely, one or two fruit trees were lying uprooted, the fruit still on the branches. The whole garden was a mass of mud and clay. Half a dozen soldiers were sitting down on any old lump of soil or roots of trees or garden rockery stones. They were having their dinners, just as though they had not been playing about with a live bomb. The thing had gone 25 feet into the soft soil. There was water down there and, as they dug down, the bomb went down lower and lower. It had not gone straight down either, it had burrowed like a mole, sideways. I tell you that beggar took some getting out. I wonder they did not just cover it up, bury it and let it stop there. Anyhow they got it up. When I paid my visit, the bomb was waiting to be removed. It was lying on the ground close to the house. A great big thing as long as the body of a well-grown boy. It made me sad to think that men can do such things. I am sorry for that man and his garden but I expect he does not feel sorry for himself. With the three air raid warnings we had last night, our number is now 141.

We have had three letters from Henry in Palestine, the last of which was dated August 28th. Up to that day he was quite happy and well. These letters of his were sent by air mail and there were stamps on each of them to the value of l/3d. but nevertheless they took about six weeks to get here. We have never put more than 1d. stamp on any letter we have sent to him. I wonder how long they are taking to get to him.

In an empty house just opposite to No, 19 a small gang of soldiers have been billeted. They are a rum lot, mostly from the Cambridge district. We have given them a free invitation to come over to No 19, two or three at a time and whenever they like. George and Arthur, who were the first to nibble at our invitation, enjoyed themselves so much that they came several nights in succession, playing table tennis with Stephen and Trigo and some of their pals, or playing cards or dominos in the front room. It was the nice warm fire that seemed to please them most. Arthur had been over in France and come through a very bad time there. Poor chap, he seems absolutely worn out and tired to death. He said to me one night as he went out (they have to be back in their opposite house at 10 p.m. to the minute), 'I have never enjoyed myself in all my life so much as I have tonight.' Then one day the whole gang of them had moved off somewhere or other and we have seen no more of George and Arthur. I renewed my invitation to the newcomers who appeared on Saturday morning but so far none of them have ventured to accept. Best love, Phil.

B.S.31 23rd October 1940

And so we go on. Our air raid number is now 168. Last Sunday night was a bad one. We had had a warning at dinner time on that day. Jerry seems to like upsetting our Sunday dinner hour, he has done this on several occasions, or at least he has tried to do so. As a matter of fact we don't take any notice of the warning but just go on with the dinner, it would be a pity not to eat it when it is all ready. During the Sunday night we had four alerts (as they now call these raid warnings) and four reliefs. The wretched siren seemed to be going on all through the night. Nothing came our way. On Monday night we were shaken out of our beds at 2 a.m., a jolly old bang somewhere or other. It seemed pretty near and we took what cover we could immediately. Mrs. Mary Hebblethwaite, my niece, can tell you more about this big bang than I can. The biggest noise she has ever heard in all her life. I can well believe that remark. We were five and a half miles away, she was one or two blocks away. As I say, it made us jump out of bed all that distance away. One poor girl killed and half a dozen other people taken off to hospital. Goodness knows how many houses had their windows blown out and other damage. Life is a bit trying in these days. We are an armed camp here just now. It is nice on Sunday to have our church very well filled, a great portion of the congregation being young men in uniform. Voluntary attendance too, no sort of church parade. And such a nice padre too. He comes along and takes the sung eucharist at 9.45. Such a nice, young and fresh voice. Very different from our curate who is, alas, one of the most unmusical people on earth. He makes me groan, he is so horribly unmusical. So it is nice to have this young padre helping us at Hessle Church. We had a letter from Henry yesterday, written on September 11th. He told a good story of the whole place where he is, you know, civvies as well as soldiers running for shelter when an alert was sounded. A flock of geese flew over the town. The watch had mistaken these birds, flying in formation, for an aeroplane, and gave the alarm accordingly. This occurred in the middle of breakfast. P.

B.S.32 5th November 1940

There will be no fireworks in 1940. Never a suggestion of one. Gunpowder treason and plot is quite forgot. I need hardly refer to the reason why it is forgot. He who wrote that rhyme could never have guessed that one day gunpowder treason and plot would really be forgot. Well. Let it go. Good bye, Guy Fawkes, your fame is now quite eclipsed.

Our instructions, given verbally and from the pulpit, are that in the case of an alert (air raid warning) about service time: if during the service, we should close down as quickly as possible, if the alert came before the service hour, the service would not be held.

Sunday, October 27th also Sunday, November 3rd. The sirens sounded just half an hour before service time. On the first of these occasions I, remembering instructions, remained at home, reading in front of a cheerful fire. To me it seemed rather a nice way of spending a Sunday evening. Just

Hessle Church choir, 1919.

Philip Chignell — sitting between the vicar, Canon C. H. Lenton, and the churchwarden, Mr. Hole. His sons, John — middle boy, second row of choirboys, Henry — fourth boy from left, second row of choirboys, Stephen — end right, second row of choirboys. Katie Chignell — second lady from left, back row.

a nice quiet, easy way. No organ, no sermon, no choirboys, no hymns and psalms. Rather a nice change. Five minutes before the fixed hour for the service (6 p.m.) a sudden impulse came over me. I jumped up and was down at the church as quickly as my legs would carry me. My friends at home told me that it was no good for me to go to church, there would be nobody there. That is what I really thought myself, but the impulse took me there almost without knowing why. I got to the vestry just on time. The vicar and the curate were waiting there, all ready robed for the service. Four members of the choir, ditto. A congregation of about fifty. We held the service. The relief sounded just as the last hymn was being sung. The vicar said to me afterwards, 'I am most grateful to you for coming to the church. Had you not arrived we could not have held the service and I could not have blamed you in any way after what I had given out.'

John was at home Thursday and Friday last week. He tells us his commanding officer has recommended him for a commission. He went to York yesterday to be interviewed. I have not yet heard the result. Somehow I don't feel very keen about this although I am glad to know that John's work is appreciated at Headquarters. I don't think John is very keen, either, and I don't think he is very hopeful, judging by some other cases he knows of.

Yesterday afternoon I played the organ at the funeral of Clifford Gooderick, aged 22. Clifford was Henry's contemporary and the two were great friends. He was an old Hessle choirboy and more recently a server at the church. I have no particulars. He travelled abroad once too often and that was the end. I think he crashed somewhere in Lincolnshire. Poor boy. Goodbye, Phil.

B.S.33 19th November 1940

How the years roll on and the anniversaries come and go. It is now 58 years since I went to Windsor to begin my five years as a chorister at St. George's Chapel in Windsor Castle. Even to this day I am often reminded of that interesting period of my life, from the time I was ten years old to fifteen. In these days I wonder what a church congregation would say to a building lit only by candle light. At St. George's we had no other light, only candles. One candle would last two services and the candle end was the perquisite of the nearest choirboy. I do not remember what we did with the ends but we used to play marbles and pay for our losses with the ends of chapel candles. Many a game of marbles on these terms have I had with [Sir] Walford Davies who was contemporary with me for three of my five years.

Once I talked to the Prime Minister, W.E.Gladstone, just before one morning service. I found him deaf and uninteresting. Another time I met and talked to the Crown Prince Frederick of Prussia, the father of Kaiser William. He was a tall and handsome man with a long beard. He was

*Philip Chignell, choirboy at St. George's Chapel, Windsor, 1887, the year of
Queen Victoria's Golden Jubilee.*

interested in the music to be sung in the chapel that day. Another morning I had an interview with Prince Leopold, Duke of Albany, Queen Victoria's youngest son, and Alphonso XXII, King of Spain. They were visiting the chapel at the time, I was putting out the music for the morning service. Although both young men at this time they both died within a year or so. I was present at the funeral of Prince Leopold on which occasion I stood close to the Queen and saw that she was crying. The Prince of Wales, afterwards Edward VII, supported her and comforted her. I stood by and saw her approach, and look through a window in the head of the coffin. The Duke died in France and the body was brought to Windsor for burial. On that same day I heard the Duke of Cambridge, the Queen's cousin, swear at some of the Highland soldiers who acted as bearers of the coffin. I could hardly believe my ears. At that time of my life, the use of the word 'dam', seemed a terrible sin. Certainly it was not quite in order at a royal funeral and in the sacred building dedicated to St. George.

I also met Princess Christian many times. This lady, one of Queen Victoria's daughters, lived in the Great Park and was keenly interested in the musical societies in Windsor. She would drive to Windsor in a tiny trap in which no more than two persons could travel. She would drive to the choir school and ask for the services of a chorister for a couple of hours. The chosen boy had to look after her horse when the Princess did her shopping or paid her calls on her friends. It was half a crown easily earned. I have never driven about with a princess since then and I have not forgotten those afternoons.

We came off badly for schooling at Windsor. Try as they might to give us good instruction, the Dean and Chapter could not make up for the hours we gave daily to the services at the chapel. An hour's practice every morning and another practice every afternoon and two hours devoted to the chapel services. Four hours gone every day of our lives before any schooling or recreation could be considered. No wonder I left St. George's shortly after the 1887 Jubilee with a very poor outlook for anything but music. In the matter of holidays we also came off very badly compared with the average schoolboy or schoolgirl. We were given a fortnight's holiday in the year and only one boy could be away from Windsor at any given time. It is true we had periods when there was no schooling to be done and our time was our own except for the hours of practices and services, but we could only get away from the chapel for the allotted fortnight.

I used to spend my fortnight at Wimbledon Camp with Father, who was a well-known rifle shooter. Consequently I hardly ever went home to New Barnet where we lived. In fact, when I left Windsor for good and had a long period at home, I found myself a complete stranger there, many of my parent's friends not even knowing of my existence.

Other Windsor memories concern the clergy. I was present at the installation services of two deans, Dean O'Connor and Dean Davidson. The former died very soon after his induction. His successor afterwards became Primate of All England. Once I sat on the shoulders of Dean Davidson at a Deanery party. The two of us made up a giant in a charade. I was the head, and from the neck a long cloak descended, hiding the Dean's very genial face. At another Deanery party I acted the part of Humpty Dumpty and had to sit inside a large egg-shaped apparatus on top of a book shelf. The Dean's butler stood behind the improvised wall and at the critical moment, when the fall was timed to occur, he had to touch my back so that I could fall with the certainty that he was there to catch me and prevent any accident. I remember that the party who was responsible for the crash of broken glass which should have coincided with my fall was a second or two late and everybody roared with laughter. The egg seemed a tough one and not so easily broken. Still it had to be broken or there was no point in the rest of the story which concerns King's horses and King's men.

We had our annual Armistice Service on the 10th. The church was quite full (3 p.m.) although we had a raid warning fifteen minutes before the service was timed to commence. However, the relief sounded just as we were going to sing a hymn. I transposed the tune from G to G flat to avoid the nasty clash with the B flat and D flat of the siren. The siren sounds to be entirely in the key of G flat, so that was all right. I made it blend with our music instead of being the annoyance and horror that it is supposed to be. The choir do not robe at this Armistice Service because the nonconformist choirs are invited (very few accept the invitation) to come along and sing. We have several soldiers of the Norfolk Regiment stationed in Hessle who help in the choir now.

I suppose you have heard of Howard Marshall (a well known B.B.C. announcer). We have in our choir two basses, one is Mr. Howard and the other is Mr. Marshall. Mr. Marshall is the best bass I have got, a really useful man. Phil.

B.S.34 3rd December 1940

The weary winter wanders on.

I was up this morning 2 hours before the law of this country permitted me to draw back the window blinds and to admit the small amount of daylight allotted to us during this mid-winter period. I am not disposed to quarrel with the new regulation by which the clock is to be kept one hour ahead of the true time all through the year. It is such an advantage to have the extra hour of daylight somewhere about tea time that I can put up with the long delay in the early morning. To tell you the truth, I have a quiet happiness in beginning every day: a nice big fire going in the kitchen, two cups of tea and a biscuit, various jobs, such as boot cleaning, attending to the flowers etc. The early morning news on the wireless, first of all trying to puzzle it out in Norwegian and then hearing it all over again in English, an interesting way of getting hold of a language; all this time the blackout goes on and I am entirely indifferent to the outside world. It may be raining, it may be foggy, it may be cold, it does not matter to me. The morning paper comes, the postman drops a letter or two through the letter box. I can spend a couple of hours quite easily, entirely on my own. Somewhere about 8.0 other members of this household turn up. I then retreat to this little attic study, for I don't desire to hear the wireless news all over again. When I think the news is over, I go down to the kitchen to have my breakfast, and by the time I have finished the law will permit me to draw back the blinds. Today, for instance, we can open up at 8.32. In 8 hours' time the blinds will have to go up again and not a wee shaft of light may be allowed to filter out to the world beyond. It's a funny state of affairs.

We have now had three whole days and nights without any air raid alarms. The quiet and peace of these past three days and more so the nights, has been just lovely. Of course, we know that we have this quiet at the expense of the southern towns that have suffered badly. There it is. Only on one day during November, and that the very last day, did we escape the blasting siren. From October 22nd to November 29th we had these sirens shrieking at us day and night. Six times in one day on one occasion, five times in one day on four other occasions. 85 times in all during the period mentioned. (Grand total up to date, 259). With all this row and racket nothing whatever has happened in Hessle during the period mentioned. Nobody takes any notice of the alarms now. Once or twice they have come on Sundays during the hours of service, twice in the middle of the vicar's sermon. Nobody moved, the vicar just went on talking, although the siren almost drowned his voice. Twice we have been disturbed during our weekly Friday night practices. We just go on and stay put.

It is a sad world just now. Last Thursday morning I went off with my old sack, riding on my old bicycle and clothed in my oldest garments as I have done many, many times on Thursday mornings. I go off to get a sack full of good wood to keep the home fires going. It is an excellent habit or hobby. I enjoy the two hours spent in the fresh air in the morning and I have found a place where the supply is absolutely unlimited. I found this place a long time ago. It is two miles west of Hessle, down by the side of the railway where the line follows the course of the Humber for several miles. It is a small wood cut off and isolated completely from the outside world. It is only approachable by anyone who is prepared to trespass across the four double lines of the North Eastern Railway. Not many people care to do that. I do, however, and I always get as much firewood as I can carry home and my depredations never seem to make the least impression on the harvest. In crossing the lines I am always very careful to watch the signals. If one signal is down, I sit on the fence and look out across the Humber and wait until the train has passed and nearly always exchange a hand wave with the engine driver. Last Thursday there was a small gang of plate-layers working just where I wanted to trespass. I know all these men, I have often seen them and always waved hands, or, if close enough, exchanged a word or two with one or other of them. On Thursday they were just where I wanted to cross. I asked one of them if he would just look the other way for a minute. He laughed back at me and said something about being careful with the trains. After having been in the wood for half an hour or so I retraced my steps and noticed that the men had moved along the line, fifty yards or so. That was just about noon. The 2 p.m. express from Hull to Leeds ran into this gang of men, killed two of them, badly injured a third, and the last member of the gang went into the witness box at the inquest. His evidence was accepted and a verdict of accidental death was passed. I wonder which of those four men it was that told me to be careful about the trains.

B.S.35 18th December 1940

Here we are, a week off Christmas, nearly a year since we last saw Henry. He left us last Christmas Day at break of dawn and we have not seen him since. Talking about Henry, we had two letters from him on Monday, the later of the two came along by the help of Egyptian stamps and that was the only clue we had to his whereabouts because he said nothing much about his doings in his letter.

This is going to be a strange Christmas, the strangest I have ever known. We are living in a war zone in this district. We often hear bombs and guns going off. Last Sunday night, as ever was, we had a crowd in this house. I don't know how many, ten or a dozen. Three soldiers, very nice young men who come and grace our choir at least with their very comely presence and youth even if they are not much help musically. After our 3.30 p.m. evensong they get an invitation to tea. John turns up quite unexpectedly, he just rushed home for a couple of hours, two bob bus fare return to Hull and 7d. from Hull to Hessle, just to come and have tea and a short chat with us all, then back to his job for an all-night watch over the cold, cold sea. Then there are Stephen's pals, Trigo's pals, they just come along in the early evening. We call them the GANG. One night they are all at No. 19, another night Stephen and Trigo disappear and we have the house to ourselves, sometimes I am absolutely alone and then I know the GANG has a meeting somewhere else. So I seldom know if the house is to be full or empty. On Sunday it was full, quite full. Part of the GANG upstairs playing table tennis and part of it downstairs playing a card game. And then the guns all round us begin firing. Such a din for a few minutes. What a strange world. The gang members just laugh at the gun firing. John gives expert advice for he knows something about this business. He can tell you all about gun firing and bombs and he knows the tang, or whatever you call it, of the enemy aeroplane. And Sunday night, mark you.

The police have constrained us to give up our six p.m. evensong. We have to hold the service at 3.30. Not a bad idea from my point of view. Nothing to do after tea but read and listen to the guns and so on. Twelve and sixpence in the offertory last Sunday. Won't keep the church in cats' meat. Air raid warnings have calmed down lately. Since my last B.S. eight and fifteen are the figures for the two weeks. In the second of these we had six warnings in one night which equals the record. Total up to date, 286.

This is an extract from a railway holiday book for 1940, although I cannot imagine why it was ever published. Here it is — 'Where to go? Try the Isle of Wight — Ryde — Carefree holiday is assured ... England's safety zone. Write for information ...' Another side of the story. A few days ago Miss Ida Samuelson, who still lives in Hessle and is a great church worker and a lady generally useful (same as Ruth at Findon), received a telegram from Ryde — 'Bombed out, Ella in hospital'. So much for the railway holiday book. Best love, Phil.

John, 'Trigo' (Ruth), Henry, and Stephen Chignell, 1932.

1941

B.S.36 1st January 1941

I don't think any of us will regret the passing away of the year 1940. Good riddance to it. Soon after our tea the sirens started with their melancholy strains, Hitler's signature tune. This brings our score up to 301. We got to the 300 level two days before Christmas and so we have had eight complete days and nights without any alarm. This has been a great relief to all of us who live in this district. It meant that we had a fairly happy Christmas. We do not deceive ourselves that all danger has now gone by. I was in Hull on Monday afternoon and it was very obvious that everyone in Hull is expecting an air raid on a large scale, such as other cities and towns have experienced. But then, Hull people expected an attack immediately on the outbreak of war. Such attack never came this way. All that Hull has suffered so far has come from night attacks made by single bombers and not very much damage has been done. No really important building wrecked and at Hessle we have only had one serious raid and only one casualty up to the present time. So we have not had much to worry about. We get so used to hearing the sirens that we take hardly any notice of them. Now the all clear is sounding for the first time in 1941.

As I type these figures, 1941, I am reminded of father. I have been so thankful that he is no longer at the Charterhouse. I have not heard anything about that lovely old place, if it has been damaged or what has become of the old men living there. It must be a very anxious time for all of them and also for those who look after them.

John has now left Kilnsea for good. He spent 16 months there. It was a deadly dull place, miles from anywhere, as you can see if you look it up on the map. Just at present he is in Lincolnshire, I don't know exactly where. He crossed the Humber in a motor launch and only just escaped being seasick, so he says. I told him that I went all round the world in 1911 and was on the sea twelve weeks and was never once seasick. I should have fainted with shock had I been told that one of my sons was seasick in crossing the Humber, even if that noble river is two or three miles wide down that way.

I broke off there to listen to Schubert's C major Symphony on our wireless. If I ever reach the Land of Promise I shall not ask for a harp, I shall ask to be allowed to play the bass trombone in this Schubert Symphony. Not the cello but the bass trombone.

Trigo has got a RISE. Five bob a week beginning with the New Year. John is now Lance Bombardier, he has had to wait a long time for even this slight promotion. Goodbye and Happy New Year to all, Phil.

B.S.37 14th January 1941

I was in the free library in Hull yesterday morning just before noon. I pay a small subscription because I am not a resident in Hull and I am permitted to take five books from the library at any time, not more than two of which may be novels. I very seldom read novels but I read all sorts of other books and I pay weekly visits to the Hull Library, which is a very big institution and wonderfully well organised. Well. I was at the library yesterday when the Hull sirens began yelling at us. It was really very amusing to see what happened. There were about a dozen girls running the show and perhaps about fifty people roaming about the bookshelves just as I was. I had just picked out a book I thought I would like to see when the alert sounded. One of the girls pointed to a corner of the library where there was a spiral stairway going into the basement and she told me to go down there. I went. I found a nice warm compartment fitted up with chairs and tables with a lot of magazines and newspapers. I had my new book and just sat down and read it for half an hour or so. Everyone else did the same, more or less. There was no talking, everybody was reading. I quite enjoyed the quiet and peaceful time, right in the middle of the day and right in the middle of a rather noisy city. The relief sounded and everybody got up and returned to normal life. The book I had picked up I returned to its place as I did not care for what I had read and I went on and chose something else.

All the same this book set my thoughts roaming on the subject of a man's head gear. Nowadays it has become the custom for all young men to roam our streets hatless. A custom rather bad for the makers and sellers of hats but good for the man. It gives his hair a chance to grow and it saves his pocket from constant expense. In my Windsor days I was compelled by the school rules to wear a square college cap with a button and tassel on its top. It was by this article of dress that I was recognised as a chapel chorister whenever I went into the streets of Windsor. Later on in life, at the age of fifteen to sixteen I was compelled by another school rule, at Magdalen College School, Oxford, to wear a topper. That was on Sundays only. Consequently I just loathed the Sabbath day throughout the year I spent at that school. Fancy boys of fifteen or so being compelled to spend their Sunday afternoon balancing a topper on their heads. The top hat was in those days the mark of a gentleman, anything in the bowler line was decidedly low class and a soft trilby or a cap was the last word in bad taste. So the topper ruled mankind of that period.

Henry is somewhere in Greece. Yesterday we received a big parcel from him. It was evidently sent off at a time when he was clearing out of Palestine. He sent garments he did not want to lose or to take with him: a camera, some miniature scores and many curios from Palestine and Egypt. The parcel came safely. It must have been packed by a professional packer. One of our soldier friends has failed us. He borrowed a pair of dance shoes belonging to Henry. This man had been in the Dunkirk trouble and we did our best to cheer him up. He was a constant visitor in our house and accepted our hospitality scores of times. He has gone off now with a new pair of shoes. Good luck to him and his dancing. Phil.

B.S.38 28th January 1941

On Sunday morning I was up early as usual, about 6.30, and you must remember that Summer Time is still going on. We are not allowed to draw back our blinds until 8.45 a.m. and until I went to church at 9.0 I had hardly looked outside. When I opened our front door I found the whole of the porch blocked with snow as high as my head. I had to retreat and go out of the back door. Even then it was a struggle to get down to the church, the untrampled snow was feet deep in many places. It was, however, possible to pick out a route by dodging round drifts so that I got to the church all right and soon shook away the snow from my feet and trousers and comforted myself by the side of a radiator. One choirboy turned up for the Sung Eucharist, three ladies, one tenor and two basses. Of the six adults, three came from this house. It says much for their musical ability that the choral service was quite well rendered and it just seemed to match the tiny congregation of about one dozen. It took me two hours on Monday morning to clear the stuff away from our doors and paths. I have not seen so much snow on the ground since I was in Montreal in 1911. Fortunately a thaw set in on Tuesday and a good deal of snow disappeared.

Our head bell ringer, Will Speck, a man I have known and respected ever since I first came to Hessle, popped off, I won't say for a warmer climate, although I would not wish him a colder one. That is a point somebody else will have to decide. Another old friend of mine passed away during the very cold weather. Harry Heslop, one of my bowling friends and often my partner in matches for Hessle Club. He was a strange mixture, a gardener by trade, a Methodist by conviction. He greatly disapproved of our Sunday afternoon play. At the same time he could give you a tip on any coming horse race and a good deal of his pocket money found its way to a local working man's bookie. You know I won the club's championship in 1939. As it was not played for last season I still hold the little silver cup and my name is the last to be engraved on it. Harry Heslop's name is on this cup — 1937. So we go on. I never thought my name would ever get into such a famous place.

I went down to the Humber this morning, the first time for a fortnight or so. I still love the riverside even if the wind is hard and biting. I did not intend to go sticking but I took my usual paraphernalia, the old bicycle, a small box on the carrier, an old potato sack and a bit of strong rope and a few pieces of cord. The south wind brings the drift wood to our side of the river. I came home with my box and sack full, and with two long floor boards over my handle bars. The whole load nicely tied up and balanced, so that I only had to walk easily, holding on to one handlebar. The floor boards mean enough fire wood for a month, and the rest of the consignment can go on the fire as mere fuel. People of Hessle are so used to seeing the organist-tramp coming back from one of his sticking expeditions that nobody raises an eyebrow now. They used to laugh at me but in these queer days they may think I am not such a fool after all. And then, doesn't a glass of beer taste nice after all that cold wind, crisp air and the exertion of getting the wood home? I can tell you it does. So I shall be off again tomorrow about 11 a.m. if the weather holds up. I wonder other people don't think of the same game. Perhaps they do but have not the time. Best love, P.

B.S.39 12th February 1941

No. 230 of our alerts has just blown off, so I can get to work in comfort. Mr. Platt (the chap who works our Hessle siren) was fairly busy last week, 16 performances, that means 32 siren performances. 16 on and 16 off, including one fine effort on February 5th, six alerts on that day. Seven in one day remains our present record, but six means a pretty lively time all round.

I was reminded of my St. George's Days (1882 — 1887) by an article in the London *Times*, one day last week. February 10th was the hundredth anniversary of the birth of Sir Walter Parratt. Sir Walter, or Mr. Parratt as he was in my time, was organist at St. George's Chapel, Windsor Castle, all the time I was a chorister there. I remember the first time I ever saw W.P. and that was one day in October, 1882, when my father took me down to Windsor to show me off to W.P. I remember standing in front of a big map which hung on the wall of W.P.'s study while he and Father settled my fate. I was to go to Windsor Castle as a choirboy. W.P. had only been at Windsor a few months and I was the first boy that he selected for his famous choir. The article in the *Times* suggests that Sir Walford Davies, known by that title nowadays, was the first choice made by W.P. but that is not correct. Davies joined the choir early in 1882 (or late 1881) and was almost the last boy chosen and appointed by old Sir George Elvey, Sir Walter Parratt's predecessor. W.P. was not liked at St. George's. He had a very sarcastic and biting tongue. Once or twice there were actual strikes among the layclerks. I can understand that the old-fashioned singing men in any cathedral choir became almost moribund with the constant repetition of the two daily services. When I went to St. George's W.P. was just introducing a lot of modern music which these old men resented and would not sing with any heart. Stanford's famous *Te Deum* in B flat was quite a new idea and these old choirmen just hated it. By the way, the oldest of these choirmen, or layclerks as they were called there, was John Mitchell who had sung at the funeral of George III (1820).

At Oxford W.P. became friendly with Leopold, Queen Victoria's youngest son. So when old Sir George Elvey displeased Queen Victoria by marrying for the fourth time (You perhaps remember how the old Queen cherished the memory of her consort right to the end of her life) — he was politely told to send in his resignation. Through young Leopold's influence W.P. went to St. George's. He was a brilliant organist. His feats of memory were extraordinary. In those days the chapel was lit only by candle light. W.P. would never, or very seldom, have any light at the organ. He played almost everything from memory and usually transposed everything a semitone down as he objected to the high pitch of the old organ that was there in my time. It is said that he played the whole of Bach's 48 *Preludes* and *Fugues* from memory. He was one of England's best chess players and when

19, The Weir, Hessle, the Chignell family home.

he was available he took part in some of the biggest chess matches of that day. The love I possess for chess, and have possessed all my life, I owe in some measure to W.P.

In 1887, when my voice broke, that was after the Jubilee Service of that year, my father and mother were anxious that I should return to St. George's as an organ pupil, and, had I done so, I would have followed close on the heels of Walford Davies, another musical genius, such as W.P. I never knew why Father and W.P. did not come to terms. I have always had it in the back of my head that W.P. thought little enough of my musical abilities. No. It was not to be. I went elsewhere, to Norwich, as you know.

There are six shops and our one little private house (No.19) in this row of houses in The Weir, Hessle. We have to do this fire watching business as ordered by some high authority. I believe it is obligatory. At any rate No. 19 has to supply one watcher who has to turn out in his turn (two nights a week) if an alert has sounded. The little café at the corner is kept by a woman whose husband is a chauffeur. Then comes a grocer's shop, then our butcher's shop, Dodson's, quite a good bowler and a friend of mine. Dodson lives in a nice house near the station, and I don't blame him. Next door to us is Miss Craft, who has a milliner's business on a small line. She locks the shop up every night and goes elsewhere to sleep, her shop and house are empty at night. Two other shops to the south of us make up the seven, between us we have to supply two watchers whenever there is a night warning. I am rather old for this job especially on really cold nights. Stephen said he would take it on. His first turn came on Monday night. Mr. Platt blew up at 7.30 that night. Stephen and the chauffeur husband turned out, as per rota. It was 1.45 a.m. before Mr. Platt blew off. Long before that time the chauffeur and Stephen got sick of it and went off to their beds. At 4.30 a.m. (three hours later) Mr. P. blew on again. Stephen stayed in bed. We called him, he still stopped in bed. We went and roused him up. I got up too. I went downstairs, lit a fire and made some tea.

B.S.40 25th February 1941 (Shrove Tuesday)

And this is Pancake Day. I dare not remind my beloved of this day. Pancakes. I wonder how many people will think about pancakes today. I wonder how many people will seek absolution today. That is what Shrove Tuesday is intended for, is it not? This year I think we might be excused all Lenten penances. Tomorrow is Ash Wednesday and we shall begin the forty days of dismal hymn singing, at least that is how it appears to me, a church organist, very tired of *Forty Days and Forty Nights* etc. etc. I think times are trying enough without any of this Lenten stuff.

I was round our Hessle Station way yesterday afternoon and saw a big crowd of stranded railway passengers. The railway was at a standstill. No trains running either way. From what I gathered elsewhere, not at the station, there is an unexploded bomb somewhere on or near the line between Hessle and Hull. The trains dare not run by it for fear of exploding it. We had two jolly bad nights on Saturday and Sunday. Cold and frosty and perfectly clear, just the sort of night that Jerry loves. Katie and I were invited out for an evening's bridge to a house in Barrow Lane. We were on our way there about 7.30 when the siren blew on (No. 366). In the early days of the war we should have turned again home and sought shelter in our own house. Nowadays we have become hardened both in body and soul to all this siren shrieking. So on Saturday night we just went on to our friends in Barrow Lane, ten minutes' walk from our house.

We soon sat down to the card table and when the bangs began soon afterwards we just went on with the game. However, there was one jolly big old bang that made us all jump up and stopped our little game for a bit. It was about the biggest crack that I have heard recently. It seemed right overhead and the crack was accompanied by a splitting sound, like glass breaking. After that row, we resumed our game. I had a bad evening, kings and queens would not come my way, to say nothing of aces. I had to make the most of the few knaves that favoured me. Actually I lost 6d. at the rate of a penny a hundred. It was a melancholy night, taking it altogether. Trigo was in Hull at a cinema. It was clear to us that this noble city was being attacked and we were rather anxious about our one and only daughter. Stephen was doing a turn at night watching. It was his night for duty and he was therefore patrolling about The Weir. He told us afterwards that he had seen what happened when the big crack, of which I have already spoken, alarmed us all. There was a big explosion in the air over Hessle, north-west. The whole place was lit up brilliantly for some ten seconds and the air was filled with falling fragments of some kind or other. Stephen was convinced that a Jerry had been hit by anti-aircraft guns and had exploded in mid-air.

When the relief sounded, Katie telephoned home and found that Trigo had come home and Stephen had been relieved from his night watching business. After last week and beginning with tonight Stephen will be on duty, that is if the siren blows on, every Tuesday night. If there is an alarm on a Tuesday night I am going to get up just to keep Stephen company. To keep a fire going and perhaps to make a cup of tea for anyone who is doing out-of-door watching, perhaps to take a turn myself and so relieve Stephen who, after all, has to do a day's work on a Wednesday whereas I can stay in bed all day and nobody would miss me very much. We had another rotten night on Sunday, the night following the Big Crack night. From about 8.0 to 10.0 there was one long series of bangs and explosions. Once or twice I went and had a look out. I saw any number of shells going off in the sky and one long series of flashes coming from all over the place. It was impossible to form any opinion of what was going on and it was certainly not very wise to stand at the front door, however interesting the show might be. All these shells that are shot into the air are bound to fall somewhere or other, either whole or in pieces. Anyhow it is as well to have the roof of one's house over one's head, when all this firing is going on. From what I hear Hull has had rather a bad time of it during the two nights of which I speak. So many different yarns are heard, it is difficult to sum things up. I just tell you what I know. I certainly think we might give up Lent this year. I am not going to confess my sins and feel sorry for myself. I'll have none of that sort of stuff this year. But I wish we could have those pancakes. Best love, Phil.

B.S.41 11th March 1941

Every day in March seems to be an anniversary with me. Today is Stephen's 19th birthday. It should be a festival and a happy event. We try to pretend it is that way. The sinister shadow of war hangs over our heads and nobody wants to be told that at the age of 19 a young man is considered ripe for army service. When I was 19 there was never any suggestion or even prospect of any big war. It never entered my head, when I was a young man, that perhaps one of those days I should find myself in uniform. My youth was lived in days of peace. I feel sorry for my three sons that they should have been born in an age of war and strife. It is their bad luck and my sorrow. However, it is no good to anticipate things. Stephen is still at home and there is no immediate prospect of him getting marching orders. But he is 19 years old today.

That chap Alphonso who died in Rome last week. I seem to have an especial interest in him. First of all I was present at the wedding of his mother-in-law, Princess Beatrice. That was before, although not necessarily before, he came into the world. That wedding took place in the Isle of Wight in the summer of 1885. Somewhere about that very same time I met and talked to Alphonso's father who was known as Alphonso XII. I did not know who I was talking to at the time although I knew he was not English. I was in St. George's Chapel (I may have told this story before, it was the only time in my life that I have ever talked with a king) getting the choir books ready for the service. This young man, for he was quite young when he died, came up to me and asked me some questions about the service and the choir and the music to be sung, etc. Afterwards one of the vergers came to me and told me I had been talking to the King of Spain. Alphonso XII must have died very soon after this because I remember how he was succeeded by his eldest daughter, a minor, who was nominally Queen of Spain for but a few months. She was no longer Queen when her posthumous brother was born in 1886. Alphonso XIII, who has just died. A curious bit of history. What a strange and dangerous life he led. I have always felt interested in him. Those must have been rather happy days in Spain, before the times of dictators and civil wars. So much for my friend Alphonso XIII.

I went to bed last night just about my usual time, 11.0 p.m. Nicely in bed when bang went a couple of guns. I may say that an air raid warning had blown on at 9 p.m. Number 387 of the present series. We don't take much notice of these sirens now. It was that way last night. I went to bed and just forgot that the warning was on. Bang went the guns and then a series of window rattlings and door shakings went on. Heaven only knows what they were up to. I don't know. I never got out of bed. Just stayed put, as they say. Katie came up to bed about twenty minutes later and she just undressed and turned in and seemed quite indifferent to the noise going on outside. Somewhere about midnight an aeroplane buzzed over us, flying very fast and low. Is he going to drop an egg? I wonder. 'In durance vile, here must I wake and weep.' (Burns, if you want to know.) And then at 1.0 a.m. the siren blew off. Beastly row. And we rolled over and went off to sleep. Nobody mentioned the disturbance at this morning's breakfast table.

Last Sunday we went back to evensong at 6 p.m. instead of 3.30. The afternoon hour during the past three or four months has proved a complete failure. Congregations dwindling down to a score or so. Choir just as bad. No good to anybody. We were glad to get back to 6 p.m. but the change back was marked by terrible weather. Heavy and wet snow, and nobody went to church. An entirely miserable affair. I don't know where I should be with my choir were it not for the valuable help given by the three remaining members of my own family. They never fail me. Goodbye everybody, Phil.

B.S.42 25th March 1941

You will have noticed in the newspapers the announcement of the death of Sir Walford Davies, the well-known music lecturer for the B.B.C. You will doubtless know that he was one of my old school fellows at St.George's Chapel, Windsor. At the very first choir practice that I attended I was placed next to Davies who was told to put me through the ropes. One of the things we practised that first morning was Mendelssohn's *I praise Thee, O Lord, my God* (St.Paul) and I remember being astonished at the beauty of Davies' singing as he stood next to me. Hal, as we called him, had joined the choir rather later in age than most choristers. His was a very special case. He was a beautiful singer and was very much in request by members of the Royal Family whenever they attended the services at St.George's. The arranged music for the services was constantly changed at a moment's notice just for this single reason — Princess So-and-so wanted to hear Davies sing. Hal was a very good pianist. He would sit down to the old Bord piano in the choir school and play from memory, generally Mendelssohn's *Songs without Words*. I used to wonder how he did it. I met Hal many times after I left Windsor. The last occasion was in 1911, by my suggestion, he came to Hull to conduct some of his orchestral works at a concert given by the Hull Philharmonic Society. This idea was not quite a success. Hal was such a crank. The Society was made up rather largely of amateurs and Davies' music was difficult and written for professionals. One way or another my idea was not very successful and the member of the Committee who entertained him found the job rather difficult, as I heard afterwards. I could never listen to Sir Walford on the wireless. As my boys used to say, he was too cissy. However, he was greatly liked by a certain class of listener and so I don't wish to belittle him. I had a letter from him not so very long ago which I did not destroy.

Oh, yes. We have had rather a nasty time in the blitzing line lately. The worst raid Hull has had so far came to us on Thursday, March 13th, the unlucky number. We had an eight-hour siren business, from 9 p.m. to 5 a.m. Guns firing nearly all the time without any cessation. Another 'do' the following night, not quite so noisy but quite bad enough to be going on with.

No damage came our way at Hessle but the Hull Charterhouse was badly knocked about, including the chapel which had its windows knocked out, including the stained glass one over the altar. The place was set on fire but this was successfully dealt with, so the damage was not so serious as it might have been. We did not escape at Hessle on Tuesday night, March 18th. You would be surprised if I took you to where the three or four Hessle bombs fell and saw all the damage and then to be told that nobody was injured. Two great craters in a garden close to the wall and a road, the road entirely closed by two or three big fallen trees which were uprooted by the bomb. A small house close by entirely demolished, hundreds of windows smashed in all directions and not one person even injured. So I am told. Hessle's luck continues. 395 air raid warnings, one casualty. Other bombs fell in open ground in the Northfield district and did no great damage. Trigo was at the cinema which is actually next door to the garden where the damage was done. Near enough to make one think. Katie was at a soldiers' canteen not a hundred yards away and Stephen was out on his fire watching duty. At the time the bomb fell I was playing chess with a friend who had come out from Hull to give me a game. We had the usual alarm but had not taken much notice of it. Then came the sudden shriek of a falling bomb, a jolly big crack, somewhere quite close. Stephen ran in and then my friend, Alfred Hole, took refuge in our house. He was covered with dust, etc. He had fallen down against a wall to get some sort of protection from the bomb. And so we go on. Let's give up these bomb stories. Goodbye, Phil.

B.S.43 8th April 1941

I will begin this week's letter with two stories about chess: On Saturday night (April 5th) I was alone in this house. Everybody else had gone out for the evening — Plaza Cinema — I was just settling down to a long and solitary evening with books and wireless — a much nicer way of spending a few hours than footling off to see some American film star pretending to be beautiful and very clever. A knock at the front door — a soldier whose face I remembered but could not place. Home on leave for a few days, Allen, a member of the Hull Chess Club, a sporting but not very great player, had come out to Hessle from Hull to see someone. Not at home, so he remembered that I lived in Hessle and he came round to see me. We spent the whole evening playing chess. Much better than going to the Plaza. Allen told me that he had lately been doing sentry-go at a concentration camp. One of the internees is a certain Dr. S., a German by birth, also a member of the Hull Chess Club. A very good player indeed and quite a nice old fellow as far as my knowledge of him goes. Both Dr. S. and Allen were most regular members, never missing an evening, they were always at the club and often opposed to each other. The sentry and the interned doctor are not permitted to speak to each other. Curtain.

I went to the Kardomah cafe in Hull on Friday last for some lunch and a game or two of chess. Half a dozen chess maniacs were sitting at a small table with a chess position set up — King and four pawns or so to each colour. There was a laugh when I appeared and I looked at the board to see what was interesting the party. One of the men said 'Here, Mr. Chignell, see what you make of this. Which side wins on adjudication?' I looked it over and then I said I thought the game was a draw. Blackburn (a famous chess master in his day) says it is a win for white. An old newspaper was produced and the game was played through from the beginning. It did not seem to me a very wonderful game nor anything like modern chess that one sees in the *British Chess Magazine* every month but I was interested in it. One of the men read the game over from the journal and the other one made the moves. Then the joke came out. It was a game that I myself had played 34 years ago in a match between Sheffield and Hull.

It was only the other night (March 31st) that we had our front door blown open, the lock smashed, and the fan light over the door smashed all to pieces by a nearby bomb explosion. Also smashed, a window in our front bedroom. We were having supper in the kitchen when the smash came and because of the blackout regulations we were unable to clean up the mess until daylight came eight or nine hours later. Even then we were lucky. Of the seven shops on either side of us in The Weir, six of them had their front windows blown out although some of them were protected by wood covers. Our front windows were not damaged. There were two bombs that fell close together not far from the Plaza, the cinema that only just escaped a week or so ago, and these bombs did an immense amount of damage, especially to windows and house property, and about 200 people had to spend the night in the local Town Hall. Hessle's luck still holds. Not one single casualty. An extraordinary thing considering the vast amount of damage done to property. Hull did not escape so lightly but that is another story. That was No. 406 of our Hitler Series.

I suppose you remember the centenary [of his father's birth] a week ago last Sunday. I am glad that he did not live to be 100 years old. I am sorry for any old people in these days. I am even sorry for myself and my 69 years. Old age should bring peace and not war.

John goes from Plymouth to Llandudno this weekend to continue his course for a commission. He will not be a stranger to Llandudno as he has been at Plymouth. I wonder what comes after that. We heard from Henry yesterday, a letter dated February 14th. He is still at Athens and seeing life as none of us has ever seen it. I wonder what he is doing now, for things are moving quickly in that part of the world. With best love, Phil.

B.S.44 22nd April 1941

We last saw Henry on Christmas Day, 1939. Since that day he has spent his life in Palestine, Egypt or Greece. It has been a wonderful time for him. He has lived cheaply, seen the world and saved quite a nice little bit of money. All this time he has had the very uncertain future to think about. It is quite clear that his turn has now arrived. He is no longer having a jolly old holiday at his country's expense. We had a telegram from him a few days ago. A birthday message for two of us. Where he sent it from was not mentioned and the date was not clear. I think it was April 6th, if one can so judge the figure 64 which appears on the telegram form. I have just listened to my wireless talking about a big air battle over Athens. I wonder. It is an anxious time. So far as I know, John has met more danger in Plymouth than Henry has in Greece. John had a very narrow escape in one of the Plymouth air raids. Life is very cheap just now.

We are by no means without danger in Hessle. Air raid warnings up to date — 428. Mercifully we had three nights quite calm, Good Friday, Easter Sunday and the intervening Saturday. which, as you know, was my birthday. I am sure I was thankful for that alleviation. The days could not have been better chosen, the nights, I should have said, for the little peaceful holiday. I have survived another Easter. The services at Hessle Church were just the same as usual and I was kept as busy as ever. Our fine old church was very lucky the other night when literally thousands of Hessle windows were smashed, the Wesleyan Chapel windows blown out completely, the stained glass windows of our church were damaged here and there but nothing very serious. I feel very anxious for this old church. In these sad days or nights it can be destroyed so easily, as many a good and ancient church has already been destroyed. So far it stands safe and almost untouched. Who knows? Tonight? Tomorrow night? What sad times these are. P.

B.S.45 5th May 1941

I say. I am in a terrible fix about a wedding I have to play at next Saturday, May 10th. Of course I know a lot of things may happen between now, Monday night, and next Saturday, and I am hoping for the best. Somebody may rescue me from the dilemma in which I seem to be placed at this moment. A request has come to me from the prospective bride that I should play *You walk beside me.* I am a little confused now as to the correctitude of this title. Did she ask me for *I walk beside you?* Maybe that is what she said. To my mind these two little titles imply the same sentiment. I mean, it cannot really matter which of the two I play, that is, if there are two to choose from, because it is perfectly obvious that if you are walking beside me, then I must be walking beside you. Q.E.D. There is more in this than meets the eye. I am not acquainted with this particular song or air or whatever it calls itself. The longer I go in ignorance the less time have I to practise up my part and earn my guinea in a fair and square manner. I can still reckon on four whole days. As I have nothing very much to do in these four days except to play bowls or snooker, according to the weather, I am hoping that, by some means or other, I shall fall across a copy of this much desired piece of music. At the moment I have no idea where to look for one. A dilemma means the choice between two objectionable courses. That's just my case. Choice No.1. Go to the bride, confess my ignorance and beg either for a copy of the item or for release from the request. Choice No.2. To play Handel's *Where 'ere you walk* and, if questioned afterwards, pretend that I understood that lovely air to be the one that was asked for. The wedding would be over by that time and there would be no having it over again because of my little mistake. They would be all having their photos 'took', and I would slip off and all would be quickly forgiven and forgotten. Brides are funny things. If only they knew what they were in for maybe they would not be so funny.

I have had to begin this letter by trying to be funny. Often enough a little humour will pierce through a lot of sorrow and trouble and make things easier to bear. We are certainly very anxious about Henry. Where is he? The latest news of him came in a telegram which I think I mentioned in my last B.S. That did not tell us where he was but only that he was safe and well on, as I read the telegram, April 6th. From the early part of this year he has been in Athens. A letter received this morning and written in mid-March gives us the impression that he has moved out of Athens to elsewhere. No place is named. You all know what has happened in Greece and Athens during the past week or two. I am sure you can see how anxious we are for news of the boy. We just hope that he is now in Cairo. Perhaps by the time I write another B.S. we shall know the best (or worst); as it is we must just go on feeling worried and anxious about him.

We have had some very noisy nights lately. Last night, Sunday May 4th, nobody could get any sleep until 4 a.m. (No. 439 of the series). It was one of the noisiest nights we have ever had. All the same, I have not heard of any serious trouble round about here. It was just a beastly noise and that was all. Goodbye, Phil.

B.S.46 13th May 1941

My dear ones — I have written these B.S. letters every fortnight, on a Tuesday morning, ever since the war started. They are now a more or less good record of the war as it has affected our domestic life. It is interesting to look back to May of 1940, the time of beautiful gardens and flowers. Nobody can help being moved with the sweetness of Hessle gardens from mid-May to the end of June. Last year, at this time, I spoke of the five air raid warnings we had had up to then. Had anyone told me on that day that a year hence I should give the number as 446, I think I should have been rather astonished. Lately the general rule seems to be just the one warning per day, or I should say per night, because it is very seldom now that we get any warning during the hours of daylight. The one warning comes just after we have gone to bed and it lasts all through the night until about 5.0 in the morning. For instance, the last ten nights have been exactly to the apparent rule, 11.0 p.m. to 5.0 a.m. In this house we have got so tired of being disturbed that we just go to bed or stay in bed and take no notice of all the row going on outside. Last Wednesday night (May 7th) the row got a little too much for us all. It was quite obvious about midnight that Hull was in for a bad raid.

There was a huge fire blazing somewhere in the city, it lit up the whole of Hessle and the church spire was brilliantly illuminated. Shells from anti-aircraft guns were bursting all over the place and it is dangerous to be looking out of the windows, especially in the direction of the firing. All the same, every now and then we had a look out, and we could see this immense fire blazing away. After the raid had died down we went back to bed, wondering what part of Hull had been attacked. Soon after 6.0 a.m. our telephone bell rang. It was Bessie ringing from an A.R.P. station to say they had been badly hit at the Charterhouse and asking if she might come out to us. Of course, we said, 'Yes'. Later on she arrived here and she has been with us ever since then.

As it happened Katie had sent the mattress of our front bedroom into Hull to be re-made and so we are just at present a little bit short of bed accommodation. The place where the mattress was sent has just gone up with hundreds of other Hull establishments. Well. So Bessie went into Trigo's bed and Trigo went to the place that I generally occupy at nights and I went into the boys' room, using a bed which is kept ready for John at any time. 'In going to my lonely bed' I vowed no amount of noise would get me out of it. This was Thursday night. There was another big air raid and another big fire that night, but I saw nothing of it, I just remained in my bed, but even Stephen got up and went downstairs, which seems to be the correct thing to do in a raid.

I went into Hull on Friday morning and I saw what had happened. The raid attack had hit the centre of the city very badly. It looked just as though an earthquake had occurred. Houses down in every direction. Streets blocked with masses of stones, bricks and girders and goodness knows what else. I never thought I would live to see such a sight. I went in on my bicycle. Time after time I was turned off my road and sent up bye streets to get to my destination how I liked, so long as I did not go along the particular road the policeman or the soldier was guarding. I remembered that Katie had bought a new coat for Trigo, price £3.17.6, at Hammond's, the large emporium, near Hull Station. That place was completely burnt out, every scrap of it, and I remembered that the coat has yet to be delivered. Eventually I got to the Charterhouse and found that ancient establishment in a sorry condition. It was not actually in ruins like so many of the other

ALLANSON HICK

The Charterhouse — Hull.

The three Chignell brothers in the Hull Charterhouse garden c.1930: (left to right) Rev. Arthur, Philip, Norman.

places I saw, but I should say it has been so badly damaged that it will never be used again. I am talking of the whole place, Master's House, the Chapel and all the little rooms the inmates lived in. Everything and every place is damaged and blasted. Broken windows, broken doors, dirt and soot all over the place, the roofs all shattered, with red tiles hurled all over the garden and flower beds. That institution will never be used again. It would take months to repair it and it is now in quite the wrong part of the city. Arthur is now living the life of a troglodyte if you know what that means. He has his bed in an underground dugout, where he keeps his books and his wireless. He is safe enough there from anything but a direct hit, no amount of blasting can touch him. After all, this dugout of his, which we have so often laughed at, has proved its worth. He is safe and sound at the present moment and he has a fairly safe bed to sleep in and that is more than even I can say. What he is to do in the future is a bit of a problem. If I were one of the Charterhouse trustees I should suggest that a small pension would meet the case and let the whole place stand as it is at the present, just a ruin. The old people can be paid an allowance in lieu of their raided quarters. So there you are. Arthur is living in a ruin and Bessie is with us in Hessle.

I had a cup of tea with Arthur in front of the kitchen fire, and every window was broken and out and every door open and uncloseable and half the ceiling down on the floor. Just the same in every room, broken pictures, broken furniture and glass lying about everywhere, things crack under your feet as you walk about and all the time you feel that the house is going to tumble down on top of you. Whilst we were having tea an unexploded bomb or a workman's blast went off quite close and the whole place rocked. Just over the gardens' wall is St. Philip's Church, the Rectory belonging to this church, and the Alexandra Theatre, all close together. A bomb smashed the lot up, the theatre with its big spiral tower fell right over the vicarage. Canon Sedgwick, the vicar and a friend of mine, has not been heard of up to now, Mrs. Sedgwick was rescued from the wreckage. It is only a few days ago that I stood at this very corner talking to Canon and Mrs. Sedgwick. A barrage balloon had broken away from close by and the trailing wire rope had fouled the Canon's telephone wire so that he was cut off from using his instrument. He and Mrs Sedgwick were examining the damaged wires as I passed on my way to see Arthur. Canon Sedgwick then told me that he had just returned from burying six people who had lost their lives in one of the Hull air raids. Well. Whose turn next? This is just what it amounts to . Broken glass in Sykes Street cut through my bicycle tyre and I had to return to the Charterhouse to mend it. Next time I tried Sykes Street I walked. A little old woman picked me up and began talking to me. In such times as these everybody talks to strangers ad lib. The little old lady told me of a wrecked home she had just visited. Then I found out that she was the cousin of my very old friend, William Burwell. We parted and I came back home by way of the Old Town and roads down by the docks. I thought I should be clear of soldiers and bobbies that route. The big Holy Trinity Church had its east windows wrecked. Buildings all around the church were down and most of them smouldering. One could hardly breathe because of the smoke. At one place there was a water burst in the midst of ruins, and a torrent of water squirted across the road and rushed down the gutters. There were ruined houses and craters down along the dock roads and even in that district I was pushed about from one road to another, avoiding wreckage or unexploded bombs. Hessle seems a place of repose after seeing Hull, but we are now swarmed out with refugees, such a scruffy, dirty and untidy lot. I spoke about the flowers of Hessle in May. This May it is soldiers and refugees and very little else. I say. What is there to live for now?

Phil. B.S.47 27th May 1941

Old Charlie had a bomb at his front door the other night. I am not speaking about my vicar but of an old retired sea-going man who now lives in a small boat drawn up on the Humber Bank which the water reaches only at the spring tides. I have often talked to old Charlie, he is a most interesting old man. The other day he gave me a vivid account of a steamer going through the Panama canal. Charlie was a watchman in Hull on the blitz night, May 7th. His burnt clothes testify to this fact. Some nights after this raid Jerry came round our way. Not far from Charlie's little boat is an old derelict river steamer lying on the river bank, practically a wreck. Jerry evidently spotted this larger boat, had a shot at it, missed and nearly sent Charlie to kingdom come. The bomb dropped in the Humber mud between Charlie's little house boat and the river. It sent tons of mud into the river and left a big round crater-like gash in the Humber bank. Succeeding tides are gradually putting this disfigurement right and Charlie still sits on his boat side, calmly smoking the pipe of contentment. A miss is as good as a mile.

Not far from Charlie and his old boat is my favourite summer resort, the little wood just over the railway line. Just now the bluebells are out, the wild cherry is just over, the ground is full of celandines and ground ivy. The gorse is in flower and one can fill up a sack with firewood in next to no time. I don't know who owns this little wood but nobody seems to trouble anything about it. To all intents and purposes it might belong to me.

Since the time that I was a little boy and was a little afraid of Hell if I should happen to tell a fib or say something rude to Auntie Polly, I have not given much consideration to the eternal punishment of fire threatened to all living people. That thought has not worried me much. Now we are jolly near Hell in this part of the world. The latest idea seems to be to drop a parachute; it does not matter very much where it drops so long as it drops somewhere. As soon as it touches the ground or anything in the way of a building there is a devil of an explosion and every house in the vicinity is wrecked. A tank of oil is released and at once ignites and if that is not Hell my imagination fails me. Some of these wonderful inventions have dropped fairly close to us already. You never know when they are coming and that adds considerably to their devilish schemes. On the night of the Hull blitz some of these inventions of the devil were dropped in Hessle. The marvellous part of the story is that nobody was killed although the number of houses damaged was immense. One of these wonderful machines, or eggs as you might call them, dropped into the river. The big explosion occurred even if the contact was made with water. Those who saw this event say that the water was thrown up as high as the church spire.

Poor old Hull. It is a sorry spectacle to see the ruins of so many fine buildings in Hull. It is also sad to see the rows of small houses wrecked by the wonderful inventions of men. I am afraid the Master and his Charterhouse have come to an end. There is no possibility of putting that old establishment back in its old place. It is all ruined beyond repair. I paid a visit there last Friday. The Master is still hanging on to the old house and sleeping in his famous old dugout. The roof of the house is wrecked, most of the red tiles are on the garden path or on the lawn, those that still remain up above are all out of order and broken. There is hardly a window in the house that has not been smashed and most of the doors are broken and out of order. The furniture has just been tossed about and broken and most of the pictures have come down. There is not a room that is habitable. Most of the ceilings have fallen, especially in the centre of each room. My word, it is a sorry sight. In every direction from the Charterhouse other houses are in ruins. I don't suppose there is one habitable house in that district.

Some day Hull will recover and live again. Just now it has received a knock-out blow. This sort of thing was rather expected at the beginning of the war. When it did not come we all began to think it never would come. Well. The same thing cannot exactly happen again. We are never likely to see the city burning again as it did that night, May 7th. There is not the stuff to burn. I think I told you we lost a new coat ordered and paid for, for Ruth (£3.17.6) but not delivered. The old mattress came back all in order. It had escaped the blitz and the fire. The loss of a pound or two in cash is nothing. What about the hundreds who lost their lives and the thousands who lost their homes? Phil.

B.S.48 3rd June 1941

The name June seems quite wrong. Here I am sitting in front of a log fire and thankful to be indoors and finished for the day. We have had a keen north-east wind since the month commenced and some time before that and it chills us all to the bone. It is extraordinary how cold May and June can be when the wind gets round to the nor'east.

On Sunday last, which was Whit Sunday I completed forty years service as organist at Hessle Church. That is a good time for any organist to be in one job and I feel pretty sure it will be a record at Hessle. I suppose I was cut out for some bigger job, a cathedral or some big city church, if you consider the training I went through. Well. It is not for me to pass a verdict on my own doing. I do know one thing and that is that I have been very happy in Hessle. Hessle is a place I really love and cannot imagine myself being happy anywhere else. Just fancy how I should miss my dear old friend, the Old Man River (Humber) that I visit practically every day of my life. No. No. No. Maybe I should have done much more than I have done. Others must judge of that. Hessle is quite a small place, although it has grown ever so much in recent years, but, come and see the gardens in Hessle just at this time of the year. Talk about a flower show, and there is no charge for admission.

Alas. I never dreamed that I should see such sights as I have seen in Hessle and the neighbourhood or that life would be so hard and trying to live. Last night, Whit Monday, we had our 455th air raid warning. It was a daylight one although fairly late, about 10.30 p.m. Of course, you know our clocks are now two hours ahead of normal time. It is daylight up to midnight just at present. At 11.30 we all went to bed and everything seemed quiet enough. At 12.30 the all-clear sounded and we were thankful for that and prepared to go to sleep. Then, to our surprise, two bombs dropped somewhere or other from goodness knows where. That was a bit of a surprise and we waited in suspense to hear the siren sound the alert once more. Nothing more happened and the hours of darkness, few though they are just now, passed away quietly. This morning we hear that a single Jerry was being pursued by English and Polish aeroplanes. They got him all right and brought him down. As he passed over this district he chucked them out, his rotten eggs I mean, and, before he and his crew were killed, he managed to murder a few innocent people in our nearby city and wreck several houses. That is the sort of thing we have to put up with nowadays. How plucky we all are, some people say, especially those who live thousands of miles away. But just you tell me where I can find peace and quiet without forsaking my work, such as it is, and I will be off. The other fellows can have the medals. I don't want them. Yes. I'll be off. But just tell me where I am to go.

I went into the Hull City Hall last Friday afternoon. I saw that hall built something more than thirty years ago. I saw the whole business, the ugly old houses and streets that were pulled down and blotted out in order to make space for the hall and the big open square named after Queen Victoria. I used to watch them pulling down the houses. Then I saw the City Hall rise up layer by layer until it was completed. A grand building. It was one of the best concert halls in England. The big organ was built by my old friend, Philip Henry Selfe (Forster and Andrews). It was his masterpiece. I spent many hours with P.H.S. in the City Hall when the organ was going up. I have never had such another opportunity of learning about organ

The
London Symphony Orchestra

•

PROGRAMME

THE NATIONAL ANTHEM

Overture   -   "Der Freischütz"   -   WEBER

Pianoforte Concerto No. 4 in G major BEETHOVEN

INTERVAL

Symphony No. 7 in C major   -   SCHUBERT

Conductor :

BASIL CAMERON

Solo Pianoforte :

MYRA HESS

Leader of the Orchestra : GEORGE STRATTON

Secretary : W. G. WOOD, 14 Edgeworth Crescent, N.W.4

Concert Tour Direction : IBBS & TILLETT, LONDON

Programme of the last concert at the City Hall, Hull, 6 May 1941, before it was bombed.

construction as I had then. In December 1910 (31 years ago) I managed the first big concert that was given in that new hall. I was then the secretary of the Hull Philharmonic Society and that society was the first of the three big musical organisations to give concerts in the new hall. I remember what a job it was, everybody new to the work, doormen, stewards, programme sellers, refreshment caterers, orchestra, audience — a new experience for everybody. Seating arrangements, numbering of the seats, placing of the orchestra — everything new. I wonder that I survived the task. An excitable little French woman was the soloist that night. The doormen refused her admission because she had not got a ticket and her cab driver drove round and round the hall, not knowing which was the artistes' door. Alice Verlet missed her first appearance, she was in her cab outside, wandering round and round, nobody to meet her or to gush over her. I came in for something warm, in French, when she did at last manage to evade the keen doorman. I wonder how many concerts I have been to since then, generally accompanied by my old 'cello. All the musical events of the past thirty years took place in the City Hall. Dances, social events, mayors' and sheriffs' receptions. And so on.

A certain Mr. Chapman, an old soldier, was appointed caretaker in 1910. I made friends with him in that year and he has remained my friend ever since. Last Friday I stood with him inside this hall and lamented with him at the scene of destruction that surrounded us. There was a concert in the City Hall on Tuesday, May 6th. The London Symphony Orchestra with Myra Hess playing a Beethoven concerto and Basil Cameron conducting. I was there. The last concert I shall ever attend in that hall. A case of alpha and omega with me. I was at the first and also the last concert in that hall. The débris walls of the hall remain, the roof has fallen in, the floor is a mass of débris, broken and half burned beams, charred seats, broken glass, muck and filth everywhere. A sorry sight. The grand piano used by Myra Hess the night before the blitz had not been removed. It will never sound again. Myra Hess's playing will not be forgotten by the hundreds who were present. The next night the blitz came and, although escaping the flames and utter destruction, the piano had its back broken by a fall from the roof and the beautiful ivory keys were black with dirt and dust and looked as though some evil giant had hit them here and there with a big hammer.

The console of the organ was worse than the piano. It was not burned, or only very slightly, but it looked as though a dustman had come along and emptied his cart of refuse over the four rows of the keyboard. Another filthy dirty mess, enough to make you weep. Mr. Selfe had a funny little habit of carving the form of an elephant on any organ he built. It was like a signature tune with him. On the City Hall organ the elephant is under the keyboard and would be near to a player's knees. On Friday I happened to notice this elephant and I remembered Philip Henry Selfe and his old friendship for me. I am glad that he has not lived to know of the calamity that has befallen his masterpiece. As a matter of a fact the City Hall came out of the blitz better than the surrounding offices, shops, buildings etc. Nearly everything in this part of the city came down completely. This is the district that was built up about forty years ago when Hull was completely changed and rebuilt. The old part of Hull, Whitefriargate, escaped and is now doing roaring business once more. It is an ill wind etc.

I should have commenced this letter with the news that we have had a cable from Henry. He was in Greece on April 20th. That we know for certain. Greece was evacuated on April 24th, 25th. We had no further news of Henry until May 30th when his cable arrived. We did not know where it came from but we are very relieved to know that he is well and safe. Next please. Phil.

B.S.49 10th June 1941

The very hairs of your head are numbered. So it was said many years ago but I have never believed that statement until quite recently. I should say that my hairs could now be numbered without much difficulty. For this very reason I resent having to go periodically to a barber to have my hairs attended to and my head tidied up so that I appear to be a benevolent old gentleman instead of a tramp, which I really am by nature. A tramp. Yes, a tramp and no more. All the same, I have to go to the barber's now and then. I tried a Hull barber on the day in the week that I always visit Hull, Friday. Quite a nice place where I used to go when I worked for the Savings Bank. I couldn't find the darned place. There was just a heap of bricks where I used to spend my eightpence. I used to go up a little alley, in between other houses, to get to the barber's place. Well. Now there is nothing but a big heap of rubbish. So I went on until I came to the posh, shilling a cut, barber. I might have known all about that place. It was under the big Prudential building , in King Edward Street. Every business in that street came down in the blitz of May 7th. Gone completely is Mr. MacKenzies's magnificent barber's shop. His magnificently dressed half dozen assistants, where are they now? So I went off to lunch and to meet my chess friends. We sit at one table and play one game of chess, two of us looking on and commenting in the usual cafe manner. I tell my tale of woe about the blitzed barbers and Leppington tells me of a new place and a very good one too. After lunch I go along to this new place in Silver Street. Up another alley and I open the glass door. What a sight meets my eyes. A long row of comfortable armchairs, all filled with patients. A long row of seats and benches for waiting customers, every seat full up, every man reading a newspaper and smoking a pipe or cigarette. No thank you. Not for me. I don't like the tobacco and I don't want to waste an hour or so of my precious time, seeing that it is a Friday and I have a church choir practice at 8.0 p.m. So I just come home and get a large pair of scissors and trim myself up a bit in front of my wife's wardrobe looking mirror. Anyway I have saved about a shilling and nobody seems to have noticed anything peculiar about my appearance.

John came home on Saturday for a week. He has finished his training for a commission and is now a full blown 2nd Lieut. I must admit I felt delighted to see him in his new uniform. He is on the small side but he looks wiry and fit. He has been at Llandudno for the past month, where he has many friends, including his Aunt Maude. His next move is to Hunstanton where he is due on Saturday next. I have carefully taught him that he must call this place 'Hunstan'. I think that is how Norfolk people speak of it and he may as well frame up to that at once and before he goes there. John tells me that he has had an allowance of £35 towards his outfit. That seems to me to be rather a large amount. I mean I could keep myself in all the clothes I could possibly want for a very long time for that amount.

I weep for this month of June. So far we have had nothing but north-east winds and sirens. The lilac and laburnum are now in flower, apple blossom too, but everything is nipped by the cold. There is no inducement to go to the bowling green. Those who do go up to the club to see if there is anything doing end up on the billiard table. The bowling green is deserted. Nobody wants bowls with a north-east wind blowing, and our green is open to that quarter. Will the summer never come?

On the last day of May I played in a bowls match on the bowling green at Pearson Park, Hull. It is a very prettily situated green and it is very popular with Hull bowlers. In a recent raid Jerry managed to drop two of his bad eggs on the bowling green. We had to play our match with these two craters on view all the time. Two rinks, then a crater; two more rinks, then another crater, and then another two rinks further on. To talk to your pals on the adjacent rink you had to talk over the crater. The house of my old tennis partner (Evelyn Saxelbye) overlooks this bowling green. Evelyn now lives in Ipswich. A good job too. Her old house is in a sorry plight. All the windows smashed, the roof nothing but a mass of broken slates. The garden just a dirty mass of broken glass and other refuse. The flowers all in disorder but growing, nevertheless. The grass long and uncut. I walked into the house . There was nothing to stop me. A few old pictures on the wall and that was about all. All the furniture had been removed. I used to have tea with Evelyn and her old mother in that very room. Ruins, ruins, ruins. I still possess a photograph of myself taken by Evelyn, in part of this house, one Sunday afternoon, the day after we had done well together at a Hull tournament and I had ridden over from Hessle to talk it all over. That was very long ago. 35 years or so. More than that perhaps.

We have no further news of Henry. We just know that he got away from Greece at the time of the evacuation from that country. Now we are wondering if he went to Crete. If he did go there, has he got away from that place? What a life he is leading and when will he ever come home again? We have not been bothered much with sirens lately. There was a daylight one yesterday (458), but nobody took any notice and nothing happened. Phil.

B.S.50 24th June 1941 (Midsummer Day)

Yes. And very nice it is, too. Last night I came home from the bowling green at 10.15. The sun was well above the north-west horizon and the day seemed as if it would go on for ever. We are now using time that is two hours ahead of Greenwich time. This arrangement suits me all right. It means that we do not use any artificial light at all. We go to bed by daylight and sleep through the very few short hours of twilight so that we never get any darkness at all, unless Jerry disturbs us too violently as he has done once or twice lately. Just now we are having nightly alerts, we had another again last night, or early this morning, 1.20 a.m. (472.) This one did not worry me very much, the all clear woke me about 3.30 and nobody seems any the worse. Stephen did not even know that the siren had sounded. So we go on.

Talking about strange things we see these days and nights. I was cycling in Hull last Friday, riding along George Street, when I was held up by a very excitable policeman who stopped all the traffic and forced it back as much as he could. It was just as well he took this action for the whole side of a four-storied house came tumbling down on to the roadway, which it blocked so effectively that all the road traffic had to turn into a side street and continue its course as best it could by another route. I went back the way I had come, from the old Charterhouse, and passed along the street where the Alexandra Theatre used to stand — vanished completely — nothing but a heap of ruins.

Opposite our house is the military prison, or whatever they call it. We have often been amused to see the three or four poor fellows who are undergoing punishment for some military breach. There was always a corporal in charge. He would line his three or four men up on the roadside and with loud command he would march them off to breakfast. Those who were in prison seemed to spend the whole of the evening in cleaning windows and whistling to any young women that happened to be passing along The Weir unescorted. Now there has been a change over, new prisoners and new corporal. The corporal is a musician. He spends all his leisure hours and some of his working ones in singing. Jolly good voice too. True as a needle. As I was tidying up our front garden I listened to this man's singing. It began with *Jerusalem*, every note of it, two verses. Then it went on to the *Londonderry Air. On the bonny, bonny banks of Loch Lomond.* Then came *You walk beside me I walk beside you* (I still do not know which way it is although I now know the tune), and then he came out from the front door and stood at the garden gate and looked around him. I put down my spade and walked over to have a chat. Such a fine young man, handsome and cheerful and all that is nice in a healthy young Englishman. He told me he had been solo choirboy in Southsea parish church but had not done anything in the music line since his voice broke. If I had a voice like that with my knowledge of music I should have been a little more than a Corporal Caruso.

We saw John leave Paragon Station for Llandudno. A wedding I was playing for was badly delayed — some hitch about the banns certificate — I played from 2.15 to 3.20 and then had had enough of it. I just bolted and caught a bus into Hull to see John off. Phil.

B.S.51 7th July 1941

On Saturday morning I was informed by telephone that there was to be a church parade at 11.0 on Sunday and that the band would play the voluntaries, the hymns, the psalms, and the *Te Deum*. I asked the padre who telephoned me from the vicarage if he would arrange a rehearsal and I offered to go to the church at any time during the Saturday. I heard no more about it but I wondered how the band would manage the psalms and the *Te Deum*, for obviously the choice of music for these was with me. However, I am not too particular. These church parades are very good even if the music is a bit on the rough side. It is lovely to see hundreds of healthy and nice-looking young men trooping into the church. Our choral eucharist went on until 10.45 and the church parade started at 11.0. Just a quarter of an hour to fix everything up. Of course, we have to use hymns that the band can play and we have to sing these hymns in the keys the band can play them, and of course, the congregation and the choir have to keep up with the band as best they can. The band cannot coax and help things along as the organ does as a general rule. However, everybody likes this band business, and I include myself in this remark. I just have to do the best I can to make things go along easily.

The choirboys get a bit excited when they hear the band approaching the church and I have to give them a little rope. The little dears must go and have a look at the soldiers coming in. You can see it is a bit of a job to get everything going exactly to time. I have lately taught the choirboys to march up the centre aisle in slow step. As a rule these little beggars are undisciplined. They are more or less voluntary and just come to church if they like and stop away if they don't like. They seem to enjoy this new idea of marching up. I expect they look upon it as playing at soldiers. Anyhow, I like to see about eighteen boys, all in surplices etc. just marching slowly up the church.

How I miss the cricket news in the daily newspapers. I long to see a county cricket match or even a local league game. Henry, before the war, was coming along nicely as a cricketer and had already made quite a name for himself as a bowler of the Wilfred Rhodes type. I am often asked how my cricketer son is getting on, where he has got to and if he gets any cricket, etc. etc. We fancy he is in Crete.

An old diary I possess reminds me of some interesting cricket I saw many years ago. On May 29th, 1888, I was at Lord's and saw every ball that was bowled that day in the match between the Gentlemen of England and the Australians who were touring this country. What a feast of cricket I had that day. W.W.Read 109 and W.G.Grace 165 for England. G.Bonnor 119 for the Australians. The great Australian hard-hitter knocked one ball out of the ground, right over the pavilion. I never knew that any man could hit a ball like that. P.

B.S.52 22nd July 1941

This is the one and only letter I received last Friday morning — (July 18th). 'Sir — I regret to inform you that a report has been received from the War Office that S/78551 — S/Sgt. Henry CHIGNELL. R.A.S.C. was reported as missing on the 2nd June 1941.' From 1.30 to 3.30 that same morning there was a very violent air raid going on in this district, about the noisiest we have had. (486). It was two hours of incessant noise — bombs — gunfire — shells — searchlights — floating lights, forty or fifty at a time — a continual roar of aeroplanes overhead. Nobody could possibly remain in bed with all that disturbance going on. Two big fires over in the Hull district blazed away and lit up the whole city. It was a terrible night. As daylight began to come the noise died down and by 4 a.m. we all went back to our beds. It is not easy to sleep after such a noise and I was up again soon after 6.0, drinking tea and reading something or other and then the postman dropped the little light brown slip of paper through the letter box. It was a shock to me and I sat and thought about it until it was time to call Stephen. I told him the news and then I went into Katie's room and told her. You can guess what our feelings are like. Since that moment we have hardly spoken on this subject. There are plenty of our friends to do the talking. You know all the possibilities of the case just as well as I know them. There is nothing more to be said. Henry was last at home on Christmas Day, 1939, we have not seen him since then. I notice by my church choir register that he was in the Hessle church choir on Christmas Eve, 1939, which was a Sunday. That was the last time he helped me with his very useful bass voice. One day we hope he will come back to his old place in the choir seats.

Henry was born in September, 1918. At that time I was acting as manager of the Holderness Road Branch of the Hull Savings Bank, commonly known as the East Branch. Some time during business hours I had a telephone message that told me of Henry's arrival. It was a great surprise to me at the moment, for two or three hours earlier I had left Katie doing her usual homework. When I returned home at teatime I found everything going along happily, but that is wandering from my story. In the blitz over Hull on Friday morning the East Branch of the Hull Savings Bank was completely knocked out and gutted. Nothing left of it at all. Nothing but a ruinous heap of bricks and stones. It was a dirty old bank, one of the first two branches built by the Hull Savings Bank. It was entirely too small and inadequate for the very thickly populated district of East Hull. The Savings Bank people had long ago considered the idea of entirely rebuilding the place. The old bank had no dignity or fine feature about it, it was just an ill-constructed shop. In recent years the Savings Bank has opened other branches all over the place and these buildings are quite noble and attractive, mostly built in fine Aberdeen stone. Jerry did this East Branch job thoroughly. He knocked the place down absolutely and completely. There was a small house built over the bank but it was so small and uncomfortable that no member of the staff ever wanted to live in it. The last occupant of this house that I know of was one of the bank porters but I think it has been empty for some long time. I am told that the safes stood up to their job. Although the contents were soiled, there was no actual cash lost. All the workings has been duplicated and the Savings Bank was able to carry on almost immediately at another branch in the same district.

Another place that was knocked out on Friday morning was Spiller's head office in Cleveland Street, where Henry was employed when he left school and until the time he was called up. So, on the whole, Friday seems to be devoted to Henry and his life. My sister-in-law, Maude Netherwood, turned up quite unexpectedly on Saturday night. She had travelled over from Llandudno. It was surprising how her arrival cheered up Katie. It did her a world of good.

I played at two weddings, Saturday and Sunday, the latter being a choral wedding immediately after matins. That meant I had a good long spell of organ playing and services. Choral eucharist, matins and the wedding. There were special hymn papers printed for the wedding, brought down in a parcel to the church by the best man, ten minutes before the service was timed to begin. Knowing what funny things they do at weddings I asked to see one of the papers and I saw at once that a verse had been omitted from *The voice that breathed o'er Eden — For dower of blessed children* etc. Omitted. Don't want 'em. I had to prime the choirboys not to sing verse 3. Just leave it out. Such a lot of people there too. But I have played at weddings before and know what to expect. It is nice to have a wedding group 'took' in front of the fine old church porch even if you and yours never go into church, year in, year out. It looks well in the newspapers, anyhow. Here is a quotation from the local journal giving an account of the wedding, — 'The *s*eremony was *dondult*ed by Canon Lenton'. I wonder how you *dondult* a wedding *s*eremony?

I must have failed to touch wood when I wrote my last B.S. and said that we were enjoying a spell of quiet nights. We have had eleven noisy nights out of the last fourteen, three of them very noisy indeed. Always beginning at about the same time, 1.30, and ending any time between 2.30 and 4.0. Total 488. Getting on for 500.

Missing. *O Absalom, my son, my son.* Is it all a dream? Surely it is not true. The world has gone wrong. Life has gone wrong. I loved Germany and the

German people. Their music is noble and wonderful and glorious. It cannot be true. *O Absalom, my son, my son.* MISSING. Phil.

B.S.53 August Bank Holiday (Aug 4th) 1941

My memory takes me back to many August Bank Holidays of past years. I think the one I remember the best was about ten years ago. I was then working at the Hull Savings Bank and a Bank Holiday was a very acceptable break. A day's complete holiday without any loss of pay. That particular Bank Holiday Katie and the two youngest members of our family were in North Wales. John and Henry were at home but they went off very early indeed to spend the day at Filey, by invitation of their uncle, Law Netherwood. At 7 a.m. I was alone in the house. It rained all day long. I never saw a soul, nobody called at this house, nobody came to see me and that was before the days of our wireless. It was the most solitary day that I remember. I went to bed before the boys returned and I thoroughly enjoyed myself. The quiet did me good. Very different from the August Bank Holidays I spent at Beverley, playing the tennis tournaments. Noisy and vigorous affairs. This time all is very quiet. Nothing much going on. I hope to be on our bowling green all afternoon and that is about all.

On Saturday night we had our usual tuning up of the sirens at about 1.30 a.m. (Sunday morning). Those Hessle people who live in the north-west district of Hessle can hear the Spring Head alarm more easily than they hear the siren at our Hessle Town Hall. The Spring Head alarm is not a siren but a hooter. The hooter gives broken blasts for the alarm and a continuous hoot for the relief. On Sunday morning it got out of order and it could not give the broken blasts but it had to go on in one continuous sound until shut off altogether. Everybody in the district heard this sound and they concluded that it was the relief and that they had been asleep and missed the warning. So the whole district stayed in bed and went off to sleep again. Two hours later the actual relief sounded and again the people thought they had missed a second alarm and were now hearing the second relief. They were lucky because they got a good night's rest. We, who live close to our Hessle siren, were not so lucky. We cannot fail to hear it every time it sounds. (496). It is taking a long time to get to 500. Business was slow last week, only two alarms.

I must ask to be excused from answering letters I have received about Henry and the news that he is missing. I thank everyone who has written to me. I know Katie and I have your sympathy but I shall be glad to be spared replying to those letters. I will merely say 'Thank you'. We have no further news. Just missing. For my own part I fancy he is still in Crete. I think that is where he was when he sent us a photographed letter dated May 14th.

I was away from home last Thursday night (July 31st) for the first time for a whole year. I went to a place called Hayton on a visit to the vicar of that place. Parson Mundy is a very good chess player and that is how I know him. Until recently he was vicar of Christ Church, Hull. Two or three years ago Hull Corporation began to clear out most of the houses in his parish. It was an ancient part of Hull, the houses had at one time been quite good and fashionable ones but, somehow or other, they became slums. The people that lived in them were of the poorest class that a sea port can produce. Lately Jerry has made a speciality of bombing this district and has settled the whole question of general clearance. Christ Church, though not actually destroyed, has been put out of going order and I doubt if it will ever be rebuilt. Somehow or other Parson Mundy has managed to get another living and he is now quite comfortably settled in a quiet and old country vicarage, three miles from Pocklington. I had six games of chess with him, honours even. I enjoyed my short visit to Hayton and I returned by train from Pocklington to Hull (I went to Hayton by the Hull to York bus) and that was the first time I have been in a train for a whole year. It was quite an exciting experience. When I got back to Hull on Friday morning I had quite a long hunt to find a bottle of beer. Most of the pubs were closed. No beer. However, I got what I wanted at the Queen's Hotel and then went on to see Arthur at the Charterhouse. There had been heavy rain on Thursday and that was why I went to Hayton by bus instead of cycling there. The rain had made a sad mess of the poor old ruined Charterhouse. The roof is all broken up and the rain comes straight through into the bedrooms of the house and from those bedrooms it just pours down to the basement. The whole place was flooded out when I saw it on Friday. More of the ceilings had fallen and there was hardly a dry corner anywhere. Arthur seems quite cheerful. He had a big fire going in the old kitchen and he seemed to be going along as though nothing had happened. However, it is obvious that he cannot go on living like that during the winter. There are no windows, or hardly any, in the house. Half the ceilings are down. It is dangerous to go upstairs and the three tall chimneys look as though they may fall at any moment or at the next blast of bomb or thunder storm. Well, it is not my business to tell the worthy Master what he should do. He goes his own way but I feel anxious about him.

From what I hear Stephen will be off to join H.M. Forces in two or three weeks' time. And then? P.

B.S.54 19th August 1941

'Our little systems have their day; they have their day and cease to be.' Yes. It seems to be that the system of life that I have known for well over sixty years, is now passing away, never to return again. The things I lived for: my home, my family, Hessle church with its constant round of choir practices, men, boys and girls. Good old fashioned English church music. The whole system of our music at Hessle church has passed away except so far as the singing of simple psalm chants and hymn tunes. The rest, the more glorified and complicated music, anthems etc. finished for the present. Indeed I think soon it will come to a complete turn out and then some day we can make a complete change, a new start with something in the music line, I know not what, I shall not be there to make this new change over, but it will come, I have no doubt.

Early yesterday morning, at 2.15 a.m. to be exact, Jerry dropped two totally unexpected bombs in Hessle. No warning had been sounded and everybody was in bed and asleep. The din of the bomb exploding woke us all up , shook our house and caused all the windows in the neighbourhood to rattle. It was like an earthquake. This time the bombs dropped, one on Hessle Golf Course and the other between the road and the course. Two big trees were brought down and one of the golf greens was put out of working order, or perhaps I should have said, 'playing order'. At that unearthly hour it was not to be expected that any golfers were putting-out on that green nor were there any mischievous boys climbing up the two trees that will never again grace the high road between Hessle and Ferriby. No. 502 of the air raid series. You will observe that after a long period of anticipation we have reached the fifth century.

We had one other warning last week and that was on Friday afternoon at 3.30. I was in Hull at the time and I was attending a concert given by the London Philharmonic Orchestra, one of a series of twelve concerts given by that organisation in Hull last week. I went to three of them and enjoyed them immensely. When the sirens sounded on Friday afternoon nobody took the slightest notice of them and the concert continued up to the interval. During the interval the relief sounded and nobody was one penny the worse. All the same one cannot help thinking just a little bit. The Little Theatre where the concerts were given has escaped the many Hull blitzes in a wonderful way. There are ruined shops and houses and churches and factories all round it. One has to pass up a ruined street, Albion Street, to get to the theatre, but the theatre itself has escaped all injury. It is just a matter of luck

When the social life of Hull revives, when the musical societies of Hull again resume concerts and when all the other big functions get going again, I wonder what they will do for hall accommodation. I have no doubt the fine City Hall will be rebuilt and will rise again with many modern improvements but it will be a long time and nothing will be done towards this end until the end of the war.

Several churches in Hull have been knocked out completely, St. Philip's, Christ Church and others.I don't think these two churches will ever be rebuilt. Most of the houses round about these churches are now in ruins, the people that lived in them have all disappeared, goodness knows where. I should say the Charterhouse, too, will be cleared away and put up somewhere else. The whole of that district could be set up again on an entirely new line. It could be made into a fine shopping or industrial centre, whereas before it was a conglomeration of old houses, arranged just anyhow and without any preconceived regularity. Hull will then one day find that some good has come out of the dreadful blitzes that it has now to endure. [St. Philip's has been demolished. Services were held in the gallery in Christ Church until 1952. The church was demolished in 1962. The Charterhouse has been restored on the same site.]

The same thing can be said of the High Street district. When I first came to Hessle, I used to go into Hull and spend the whole morning or afternoon roaming about the streets of the city, picking up the geography of the place. I made a point of never asking my way or making any inquiry. I remember that I was puzzled because I knew there was a HIGH STREET in Hull but I never seemed able to find it. Such a name seems to imply a central street, close to the big station and a street where buses and trams were to be found and all the best shops of the whole city. One day I was wandering along a slum street which did not keep a straight line for more than twenty yards and twisted about here, there and everywhere with all sorts of dirty old warehouses and offices on each side, all in a higggledy-piggledy order, that is no order at all. A street so narrow that two vehicles could not pass each other; if they met, one would have to withdraw into a yard or side road to allow the other to pass by. And then I found out that I was in HIGH STREET, HULL. The strange manner of twisting about just anywhere was caused, I found, because it followed the line of the river Hull which flows into the Humber hereabouts.

High Street has been badly blitzed. It will have to be rebuilt and I have no doubt the opportunity will be seized to make a good fine job of the rebuilding. Yes. One day when all the sores have been healed and casualties forgotten, the citizens of Hull will not be so very sorry that the old and ungainly places like High Street were blitzed and cleared out in the 1939-? war. The city will revive and live again but not in my time, I'm afraid. No news of Henry. I am going to Owston Ferry this next week and hoping to see the Trent eagre once more. Stephen is coming with me. Best love, Phil.

B.S.55 2nd September 1941

Today is John's 25th birthday. The very typing of the date sets my thoughts back to the night of September 2nd, 1916. There was a Zeppelin air raid over Hull that night. I was staying at a house in Marlborough Avenue, Hull, with a friend, Athol Gregson. John was born at Huddersfield and our Hessle home was closed for the time being. I had just heard the news of John's arrival by a telegram sent to the Hull Savings Bank. It was a strange evening. A.G. and I sat up playing chess. We did not go to bed because of the air raid warning. In the middle of our chess, a Zeppelin air ship went right across Hull and dropped its bad eggs at various points. We stood in the garden and

Postcard from Henry Chignell, prisoner-of-war.

> 26 Jun 41
>
> Dear Folks,
>
> I am a "Prisoner of War" in German custody.
>
> I am unwounded and quite well.
>
> Please do not write to me until you hear from me again as I am at present only in a Transit Camp
>
> Love
> Henry

heard it pass over our heads but could not see it because of low clouds. It seems strange now to talk of Zeppelins. That was 25 years ago. Here we are at the same sort of game again. In those days an occasional air raid warning was all we had, one every now and then, and they gave us a good deal of worry and anxiety. I think the total for the four years' war was 54. This war has gone on for just two years. Last night's warning was No. 522, according to my reckoning.

Stephen and I went to Owston Ferry on August 23rd for a brief holiday. There I had the joy of three nights undisturbed sleep in a comfortable bedroom overlooking the Trent. I can tell you what a pleasure, a comfort and a joy these three nights were to me. It was the best part of my little holiday to turn over in my bed and know that I should not be disturbed by the yelling of a vicious siren. Stephen went off yesterday morning to join the army and we have the good news that Henry is at least alive and well.

I had to go to the Hull Charterhouse on Friday (Aug 29th) to hear that news had been received from Henry. Henry was reported as missing on June 2nd. We received official information of this on July 18th. Since which date no further news was forthcoming. I came to the conclusion that Henry had probably gone from Athens to Crete and had failed to get away from Crete when that island was evacuated. There were many other possibilities, of course, but my guess seems to have been pretty correct. On Friday,

Henry's friend, Len Gambie, who lives near Ferriby, received a postcard, obviously from Henry, although the correct name and army number were not given. The date of this postcard was July 18th which is the same date as mentioned just above. July 18th was the same date that Spillers in Hull was blitzed. The news about Henry soon got the round of our friends and we were kept busy answering the telephone and writing letters of thanks etc. I am afraid that I soon got rather tired of telling the story and of how Henry got the news to us. As I say, I was at the Charterhouse when I heard that Henry was safe. I had gone to Hull before Len Gambie telephoned. Trigo followed me into Hull, on her bicycle, tried to find me at the Hull Library but failed, then went to the Charterhouse, saw the Master and gave him the news. I called later and got a very vague story of a mysterious postcard. It was good enough for me. I knew it meant that Henry had sent a message. That is what we have waited for for weeks. So far we have had no direct message from him. I think that he has written to us but his card has not come through the censor. This would be the censor in a German prisoner of war camp.

Stephen went off to Nottingham yesterday morning. The time has come for him to join up. I think he was really glad to go. For one thing I am sure he will be thankful to get away from a district of everlasting sirens and night air raids. Yes. I think Stephen is quite glad to be off. It is as well that he feels like this because he had to go whatever his feelings were. He had a house party on Sunday night. I don't know how many of his friends came in to play table tennis. There must have been a dozen of them. The sirens failed to stop the progress of a lively tournament that was tabulated and arranged in the usual Chignell manner. It went on gaily, even the new curate who called to say goodbye joined in the fray and seemed to have been pretty successful. I found the unfinished table of matches played when I went into the table tennis room (the attic) on Monday morning. Soon after the siren call, gun firing started, which developed into a regular and noisy blitz. This put an end to the tennis tournament. The visitors all vanished and it was 2 a.m. Monday morning before the noise subsided and we were able to get a little sleep. That was Stephen's last night at home as a civilian. He was off into Hull soon after 8 a.m. on Monday. He did not seem to be overburdened with luggage. In fact he had none at all, just his gas mask hung over his shoulder, not even a raincoat or anything to carry in his hand. I understood he put on his very oldest suit and was prepared to discard everything he wore as soon as he got to the camp near Nottingham where he has been sent.

This house seems deadly quiet since his departure. I have now five bicycles of the male persuasion in my garden outhouse. Two of my own and one each belonging to the three boys. At the present time these are all rideable and I am going to try to keep them all in good running order. On Saturday afternoon I went to West Park in Hull to play in a bowls match. The military authorities came down upon us and we were called upon to produce our identity cards. I had mine all right but two of my pals failed and several of the Hull players. P.

B.S.56 16th September 1941

I played at another wedding yesterday afternoon. That was the 17th so far this year. That means that from January 1st, 1939, I have played at 66 weddings. Really it is not much to boast about to say I can play Mendelssohn's *Wedding March* from memory. Our new curate came to me at the organ and asked me what I though* about singing *The voice that breathed o'er Eden* and verse 3 in particular, 'For dower of happy children'. They were a middle-aged couple marrying more or less for companionship. It seems nonsense to sing verse 3 over their heads. So we just left it out, also the three next verses, including the one that always makes me laugh — 'Be present, awful Father, to give away this bride'. I am positively certain that if ever Trigo gets married we won't have that hymn. I object to that 4th verse. So today we just skipped from verse 2 to verse 7, with a nonsensical disregard for any meaning. However, the congregation sang out all right and the photos were 'took' at the usual porch and the fees paid up on the nail, so I have nothing to grumble about. It is all a bit of business, though. I have now got quite callous on the subject. I don't go to any weddings unless I am paid to go. So please don't invite me unless you want me in a professional manner.

I have something to say about our new curate, [Rev. Thomas Clement Broadbery] Wilkes. He has now been in Hessle for about six weeks. He knows nothing whatever about music but he has a grand voice and his diction is charming. I listen to every word he preaches. Oh Boy! That is a high compliment, I can tell you. He sings the priest part at our sung eucharist exceedingly well. It could not be done better. You could hardly imagine that anyone with such a nice voice cannot sing either a tenor or bass part of the simplest hymn tune or chant. He may learn to do this and get some knowledge of music into his noddle for he is quite anxious to learn and comes to our choir practices.

Well. No sooner had Stephen gone away to join His Majesty's forces than I received a form from a local billeting officer asking for information about my bedroom and house accommodation. There are five rooms in this house that can be called bedrooms, including this little attic room where I am now and which I honour with the name of 'my study'. Five bedrooms and we now use two. What are we to expect? On Sunday I heard that the curate was looking for new lodgings and I said, more in fun than anything else, that he should come to live with us at 19, The Weir. He jumped at the notion like a fish taking bait and I invited him to come in after evensong and we would see what Katie had to say about it. I mentioned it to Katie and Trigo at our dinner table and in the afternoon I went off to play a bowls match, our Hessle club against the staff of the *Hull Daily Mail*. When I came home again I found the curate having tea with the family and everything fixed up, including the 35/- per week that he is to pay. I have not had much to say about it either but I have already been told two or three times, 'Well. You suggested it.'

I am just wondering who is going to clean the curate's boots and make his bed. You may not know that I make the beds as often as not in this house, and why shouldn't I? And I always do all the fires in the morning long before anybody else gets up. Who is going to do the curate's fire? I wonder. There are many other questions such as the use of the telephone and the wireless, I have no doubt a curate likes to hear the nine o'clock news. I wonder if the 35/- includes these amenities. I couldn't say for certain, although I don't get either of them for nothing, although the junior members of our little family have always seemed to regard them as two of the necessities of life, supplied as a matter of course by the head of the family. I wonder if curates expect the same. Anyhow we are going to give the scheme a run and see how it works. One thing we are all agreed upon and that is that he is a nice curate and if any difficulties arise I dare say we shall all be sensible enough to get along without any bickering. I don't want any lodger but if we must have them, well, we should like to have some sort of a choice. I will tell you in my next B.S. how the dodge works. I may say that he has matrimony in prospect, his girl lives in Retford, and so he is not likely to fall for Trigo. That is just a point that may cross your thoughts and it is as well to know how we stand in this matter. P.

B.S.57 30th September 1941

And now a talk about funerals. Chopin's *Funeral March*. The first time I ever heard it I stood in the Albert Memorial Chapel, Windsor, with other members of St.George's Chapel Choir waiting for the service to start. Minute guns were firing in the Long Walk. I counted the seconds between each bang, trying to get my timing exactly right. Then, far away, I could hear the slow strain of the melody. The body of the Queen's youngest son, Prince Leopold, came by train to Windsor, South Western Station, down below the castle on the north side. The procession came up Thames Street. We lost the strain but the gun firing went on. Then we heard the band once more. The same tune. Under the Henry VIII Gateway and up to the chapel. I always think of that royal funeral when I play the Chopin *March*.

At Clewer, in 1883, I sang at the funeral of the last surviving officer from the Battle of Waterloo. I forget his name. The old man had survived the battle by 68 years.

The lodger business seems to work all right. This morning Katie handed me 35/- towards the housekeeping expenses. So far I have nothing but pleasure in the company of our curate lodger. I have just done a little extra work in the fire-lighting department and have just once, that was this morning, cleaned his boots. I don't know that I have suffered much by these acts. What about the chap that washed the beggar's feet? Perhaps that is not the correct story, but you see what I mean. I don't suppose the curate will have any less respect for me at the church because he knows I clean his boots.

I played at a funeral yesterday. Miss Dorothy Cooper. Dorothy was one of the very first pupils I had in Hessle. I remember her quite well as a very pleasant girl. She was one of the few pupils that I liked to teach. Most of my music pupils bored me stiff. Some of them agonised me. Just the very few pleased me. Dorothy Cooper was one of those that I enjoyed teaching. She was an only child of wealthy parents. I remember once she made me dance as I never danced before and never since. She just got me round my waist and she made me hop it. I wondered at that because I was a fool at dancing, but Dorothy made me dance. When both her parents died she was left with a very nice house in Southfield, Hessle, and plenty of cash to carry on. She became quite a rich woman. I wonder that not one of our long succession of Hessle curates did not walk off with her. She was devoted to church work and did ever so much for the G.F.S. and the Mothers' Union in this parish. She was most regular at Sunday services and almost every Saturday morning I would find her busy, polishing up the brass candlesticks or dusting round, getting the church nice for the Sunday. Yes. Dorothy Cooper was a nice and good woman. She will be missed. Well. I played at her funeral yesterday morning. I wonder where her money goes to. Best love, Phil.

Total number up to date is 549. Generally just one every night. You know what I mean. We take very little notice nowadays.

B.S.58 14th October 1941

I suppose you know the parable of the ten virgins. I was thinking about that pretty story last night. The facts are these: soon after the hour of blackout had come and gone (about 6.45 p.m.) I had curled myself into an armchair in front of a log fire and thought how nice and good it was to have the whole evening in front of me. I had one of Galsworthy's books with me, the *British Chess Magazine* for October 1941 and no visitors expected. Trigo, with a boy friend, viz. Peter Geraghty, was going to the local cinema. Nobody but the curate to fear, it was possible that he would come into my room and want to talk and I am not fond of talking just as an entertainment. I had the wireless close to my chair, I could turn it on without getting up. This was about 7 p.m. and I had a good four hours of peace and happiness to look forward to. These sit-at-home winters have their pleasures as well as their advantages. I am not so sure that this armchair and my own fireside are not better even than the chess club.

Hardly had the evening started when that damnable Hessle siren shrieked at me. Down and up, down and up, down and up. 'Shut up your damned row, for heaven's sake!' No. 565. I continued reading but my ears were like a 'moke's' ears, twisted round to hear something round the corner. Another few minutes and all the electric lights in the house failed. 'Whoops!' said I to myself. 'Somebody's gone and blown up something.' I know so little about electricity that I could not guess what had happened but I quite naturally connected the siren with the electricity failure. This is where my parable comes in. I am quite pleased with my foresight. For many months I have kept an oil lamp, a very good one, trimmed and ready for use if necessity arose. It did not take me long to get this lamp down from my attic study, dust it down a bit, trim it and light it. Very soon I had a sweet soft light glowing in my comfortable sitting room, I am not sure that I do not prefer oil lamp to electricity. In days and nights gone by we used to be in fear that the boys, in their romping, might upset the lamp. They never did and now they never can, so why may not I use this dear old lamp once more.

How does the parable go on? 'Depart from me, I never knew you', something of that kind. Katie gave up her kitchen ironing, the curate gave up the love letter he was writing and very soon Trigo and Peter turned up, the cinema show having closed down for lack of light. My evening, the calm and peaceful evening I was expecting, vanished. Phil.

B.S.59 28th October 1941

Do you believe in ghosts ? I do not, nevertheless I am fighting a ghost at the present time and so far I have not been able to dispose of him. It comes about like this: Henry Chignell had the misfortune to be captured by the Germans in Crete on June 1st and since that date he has been a prisoner of war. We are now receiving definite news of him for he is allowed to send one card or letter a week and so far we have received four communications from him. The prisoners' camps in Germany are all numbered and we now know the number of Henry's camp and we have a very good idea as to where that camp is. It is in a part of Germany that I have visited and where I received every possible hospitality and kindness. Well. About this ghost. According to the War Office and the Red Cross people a certain Henry Chisnell was posted as missing on June 2nd. This same sergeant was later on reported to be a prisoner of war in a camp in Crete and now he is reported to be in a prisoners' camp in Germany, the same camp that we know Henry Chignell to be in. The very curious point about this Chisnell chap is that his father and next-of-kin is called Philip Chisnell and the address is the same as mine, 19, The Weir, Hessle. A postman calls with two registered letters for No.19. One for Philip Chignell and the other for Philip Chisnell. The two envelopes contain exactly the same things — 40 clothing coupons in case either of the Philips want to send clothes to either of the sergeants, and also half a dozen other documents telling me or the other Philip, the chap I have not yet met, how to send parcels, what may and what may not be sent etc. etc. Twice I have carefully replied to the Chisnell communications and tried to expunge the poor old ghost from the War Office list and to have his number cancelled but up to the present he is still officially alive and his wants and troubles must be attended to. Good old Red Cross Society. You have softened this shock that has come to us and we feel really grateful for your kindness and good advice but there really is no reason why you should be worried by a ghost. I should scorn to take advantage of the double ration coupons etc. that I have received. So there you are. So much for Sergeant Chisnell.

The sirens are at the old game. No. 579 this time. Will they never cease to worry us? Best love Phil.

B.S.60 10th November 1941

I have often talked to you about weddings. I seem to be mixed up with weddings, not from any choice of mine. It just happens this way because I am the man that can play Mendelssohn's tune as the happy pair leave the altar as man and wife. Last week one of the brides called and asked me if I would play *Ave Maria* at her wedding. 'Certainly,' I said and did not think much more about it. I just made a note to that effect in my pocket book. The next day Bride No.2 called — Would I please play the *Ave Maria* at her wedding. 'Certainly,' I said and then began to think about it. I presumed these two brides, who very probably were friends and had compared notes, wanted the Bach-Gounod *Ave Maria*, although Gounod has not a monopoly on this title. I hunted all through my organ and violoncello music with no result. Then I went through Trigo's violin and piano music with no better result. I got my copy of Bach's immortal 48. You know, of course, that the *Ave Maria* is founded on the *First Prelude* in the 48. I could play this prelude and sing the melody super-imposed by Gounod but I could not trust myself to fake a wedding performance with nothing but Bach in front of me. I was in Hull and so called at a shop where they sell dance music, cheap crooners' songs and strange-looking musical instruments, the very names of which I do not know. I asked a young woman who served at the counter, could she supply me with a copy of the *Ave Maria* She just slid one hand under the counter without looking to see what she was doing and produced the required music — price sixpence. But my story is only just beginning, I am so long winded, that is why the young generation of today won't read Dickens.

On the following Sunday there was a Church Parade at Hessle Church. Fifteen minutes before the hour of the service several hundred men were sitting in long rows in the side aisles looking rather bored and not daring even to whisper to one another. I said to myself, 'I will try to cheer these fellows up a bit.' I detailed someone else to look after the choirboys and went up to the organ, switched on the electric blower and picked up the first thing that came to hand — *The Ave Maria*, left on the organ desk from the No.2

wedding. I had got very deeply into the melody when I heard a quiet humming tone going round the church. These men, or many of them, knew the tune and they were singing it sub-consciously, quietly and reverently. They grew bolder as I went on with the melody, and when I repeated it, playing it for the second time in a somewhat different tone colour, the men rose to me and helped me to a really fine performance. I was pleased about that and I am now trying to think of something I can give them the next time they come to our service so that they shall not feel bored or sad in having to wait fifteen minutes or so, sitting on a rather hard and uncomfortable bench. I suppose I should have said 'pew'.

I don't get many music thrills in these days but I have had another one. Recently Trigo and I started playing through Mozart's *Sonatas for Violin and Piano*. One or two of them she has studied with her teacher, Evelyn Alexander, but most of them she played at sight. A very good thing for her and interesting to me because I have never had much to do with violin classics. We got as far as No. 11. *A Sonata in G major*, and we have not got past that one. Every time we sit down to study Mozart we both want to play No. 11 again. We cannot go beyond No. 11 we like it so much. Fancy, at my time of life, finding something new and beautiful in Mozart.

We had a talk with John by telephone last night. He is now in Norfolk. It is nice to get in touch with him like that. There was nothing special to talk about. He just wanted a word or two with the Old Folks. I wish we could talk with Henry like that. We must not grumble for we hear from him every few days now. Once a week at least. So far he has not written one word of complaint or any kind of grumble. I wonder how long he will be a lodger at Stalag VIII B. This camp appears to be near Dresden, which fact Henry hinted to us by saying that a certain church service held in the camp finished with the *Dresden Amen*. There does not seem to be much harm in knowing whereabouts a certain Stalag is but we were amused at Henry's way of telling us, something we already knew. Phil.

B.S.61 25th November 1941

It is a funny war. I had reason to write to the firm in London that supply us with surplices and cassocks. I wanted a few more black bows for the choirboys. I asked them to send me a dozen and a few spare studs that go with the bows. The boys have a habit of losing the studs, and the bows are worthless without them. I received an answer that the bows are not now to be had and there will be no further supply until the war is over. I shall have to manage with boys and no bows, which anyhow is better than bows and no boys. It is a queer war.

I was all alone in the church on Sunday morning soon after 9.0. I was putting the choir books out and getting all in readiness for the choral eucharist at 9.45. It was a fine November morning and the soft sunlight was coming through the stained glass windows on the south side. It was beautifully quiet and peaceful. That was the hour that our siren chorus chose for No. 600 air raid alarm. Now we are off towards another century. I wonder how long this will take. We had No. 500 on August 12th. 100 alarms in 103 days. Ha.Ha.

I got my ears clipped the other day. On Sunday I noticed that Trigo was wearing something funny on her head. I should not call it a hat or a cap or a bonnet or anything of the kind. It was a sort of beret like the little bit of cloth I put on my old, bald head in cold weather when I want to do a spell of gardening or wood chopping. This little beret gave Trigo a funny look. It was certainly becoming but it made you laugh just to look at her. I know I laughed when I saw it, but I liked it all the same. On the following day I saw this little beret lying on a table and at the same moment I remembered an item in Katie's weekly accounts that I had just paid. I said to Katie, 'You don't mean to tell me that you paid 12/6 for that little bit of a hat?' I forget exactly what Katie said but I know I ran for shelter. A mere man has no business to interfere with the price of his wife's or his daughter's garments. When I got the chance I looked at Katie's account book once more. This time I noticed the price was 12/11. As I have said before, it is a queer war, but 12/11 for a little twist of coloured cloth like that. This yarn makes me think that I shall have to put up my charges for weddings and funerals, say 10%. Why not?

Talking of Trigo. This young woman and her mother are going to take part in a performance of *The Messiah* some time next month. Of course Katie knows the work backwards but it is new to Trigo, or very nearly so. Music in Hull is just about as dead as a door-nail. Nothing doing at all and the best concert hall in the city knocked out altogether. It is nice to know that a little spark of love for music and for *The Messiah* still lives on. It will all revive again one of these days. I wonder when.

We have a charlady who comes once a week, in fact we have two chars who come once a week, each of them. This is not my department really and I hesitate to talk on the subject. I know that if Mrs. P. could come on both days she would be our one and only char for she is a real good'un. Mrs. W. is what I might call the junior char lady. She arrived with our lodger curate. I don't mean that they drove up in the same car to our house. No. She visits us because the coming of the lodger means some extra work and the money he pays us each Monday helps to pay for this No. 2. char. Well. The other day I found myself and Mrs. W. together in the kitchen. Katie had gone out. Somehow or other I said something about the siren No. 595, and that let go the torrent of a yarn that I might have expected had I only thought for a moment. One night, early on in this year, Mrs. W., her husband, a soldier and his wife, the four of them, were playing cards notwithstanding an air raid warning that had sounded. They just went on with their game just as Katie and I have done many times, taking no notice of all the fuss and noise going on outside. Jerry got them all right, or all wrong, that time. It was all over in a second or two. The whole house came down on the top of them. I did not ask Mrs. W. what happened to the cards. One of the four card players had a bruised back, the other three escaped any injury but they all had to be dug out of the wreckage. It was a long, long story and, I suppose, the time she took in telling it was time which Katie had, or was going, to pay her for working. It is a good idea to be paid for talking, isn't it? I know some people who would quickly make a fortune. Don't you? It was a funny little house too. Very old. When it came down, the whole of Hessle stank of soot for an hour or so. Trigo, in the local cinema, was not 50 yards away from where this bomb fell. What a good job it fell on the little old house and not on the Plaza cinema. So we go on. No fresh news of Henry. He is still at Stalag VIII B. Phil.

B.S.62 9th December 1941

Our next-door neighbours, both sides, have just gone in for air raid shelters. That seems rather strange to me after over 600 warnings. I should have thought if they were going to have a shelter they would have had it before the number got up to 600. One fatal casualty so far and only one. Touch wood. Why, our own army lorries have knocked down more lamp-posts — You just knock one down, look round and laugh and drive on. Later a policeman comes along and stands by the fallen post, chivying choirboys and the like away, until two men come along with spades and a barrow. The post is removed on a sort of bier, the choirboys and the other children following in the cortège. One man remains behind to fill up the hole where the post stood, stamps it down, and tomorrow you would never know that there had ever been a light in that particular spot. It hasn't been lit for years and it may be years before it is wanted again. Goodbye, Phil.

B.S.63 23rd December 1941

Another Christmas Day is upon us. Two days ahead and no more. This makes me think of Henry. Two years ago on Christmas Day since we last saw him. We hear from him pretty regularly now, I am glad to say. He is in Stalag VIII B Prisoner of War Camp in Germany. If he is enduring any kind of hardship beyond actual restraint he does not mention it in his letters, some of which I have copied and sent round. One of his letters arrived here this morning. It is written on the 18th November and it brought with it good wishes for Christmas. It was a well-timed effort. When he wrote Henry had just received a card I sent him via the Red Cross in Geneva. It was the first communication I was able to send off after the news came through that he was in a prison camp. It seems that Henry was without any home news more recent than February until he received this card of mine. He should now be getting letters every week. I wonder how long he will be a prisoner of war.

He is now 23¼ years of age. It seems sad he should be wasting the best part of his life like this. Just marking time. Of course, we should be thankful that he is at least alive and well. Our other two soldier boys have been at home during the past week. They both had a week's leave. Stephen arrived home on Friday 12th. and John on the following Sunday. We were expecting John at 6 p.m. but he turned up at 5.20 a.m. That is a bit early even for me, but I was awake and heard his light call from the front garden. By 5.30 he and I were having tea and rummaging about for anything in the way of supper (? breakfast). Stephen has filled out to an astonishing degree. He is now quite a big man, really big. I never thought I should have a son as big as that. John is quite small compared with him. During the few days they were here together we had some fun out of the fact that John is an officer and Stephen a private. I don't think they ever went out together in uniform. It did not seem quite in order for an officer to tickle the ears of a private. That was an old trick of John's many years ago and it seems he has not forgotten it even in these days of uniforms. Stephen, as a little boy , used to take this treatment as a matter of course. Arthur used to tease me ever so much and I always took his teasing as part of my life, just a nuisance that had to be endured. I should hardly think that a big man such as Stephen likes to have his ears tickled, even by his superior officer. Goodbye, Phil.

1942

B.S.64 6th January 1942

I began this day very pleasantly with an early morning pot of tea, the tea being a Christmas present from Canada — one of two nice little packets of tea, each packet just sufficient for my early morning requirement. Just enough to set me going with the domestic work, lighting the kitchen fire etc. It is a cheerless business these dark mornings when we have to keep our blackout curtains up until 8.51, nine minutes to nine, and I am generally at work about 6.30. Phil.

B.S.65 19th January 1942

My little note book tells me that I have quite a number of things to talk about in B.S. fashion tonight. Which shall I begin with? Let it be chess. I have just commenced another game in a county match. I am playing for Yorkshire v Lancashire. My man lives at Stockport which is, of course, in Cheshire, but I suppose he works in Manchester and is therefore a Lancashire player. We should get along fairly quickly and not have a terribly slow game as I had last year when my opponent lived near Exeter. I am told that I am playing on board No. 1. which I cannot quite understand. When invited to play in this match by Narcross, the Yorkshire secretary, I declined and said I had enough of postal chess. At the same time I said I would fill up any vacancy that might arise at the last moment.

The Duke of Connaught is next. He died last week. It was only a day or two ago that I was talking about Queen Victoria's 1887 Jubilee service, held in Westminster Abbey on June 21st 1887. That is getting on for 55 years ago. I was saying that me and the Duke of Connaught must be very nearly the only survivors from those who attended that wonderful ceremony. It was the most interesting day I have ever lived through in my long seventy years. Here I have an old diary which I kept in those days and I will quote from it: 'No. 5552 — Jubilee Day. Went by 7.30. to Vauxhall and from there walked to Westminster. Had breakfast and went to the Abbey at 9.30. Jubilee service at 12.30. Dinner at 2.0 and home by 4.15. Tennis tournament and aquatic sports. New coinage issued. Yorkshire beat Sussex by ten wickets.' I was a bit puzzled about that number — 5552 — I remember now that in those days I used to count up the days that I had lived on this earth. Perhaps from April 12th 1872 to Queen Victoria's Jubilee Day in 1887 will give that number. I also have a large picture of the ceremony and I still have the ticket of admission that I used on that historic day. My picture shows the Duke of Connaught standing in one of the front seats. I try to point out the choirboy in the picture that represents me but my name is not mentioned in the key to the painting that I also possess. However, I am not very far wrong because in 1887 I was one of the leading boys from St. George's Windsor and all the leading boys from the various choirs were placed in the front row. I was actually in the very front row and saw almost every incident in the ceremony. The memory of that day is still with me. The Duke of Connaught was about 35 or 36 at the time. A young man generally respected and liked by everybody. He was greatly interested in music as were all the members of the Royal Family. At St. George's Chapel I have sung music composed by Prince Albert, the Prince Consort as he was called in his lifetime which ended before my Windsor days. Princess Beatrice also wrote music that was sung in the chapel but I remember nothing about it. I have seen the Duke of Edinburgh playing the violin in the orchestra at a Windsor concert and his sister, Princess Christian, singing in the chorus at the same concert. I never heard that the Duke of Connaught had any practical experience in music but he was certainly a musical enthusiast. So he's gone and there is only me left.

Bicycles is the final topic. I had reason to take my Raleigh to be repaired, a new gear wire and new brake blocks. Mr. Johnson's shop and yard were simply crowded out with old bicycles, there seemed to be hundreds of them. I said something about the government and scrap iron. 'No,' said Mr. J. 'You can have any of those old bicycles for a bob or even a tanner. Anybody who will take them away can have them.' 'But what about the demand for scrap iron?' I asked. 'There isn't any demand,' he said. Well. I just thought there was. P.

B.S.66 3rd February 1942

I suppose the weather is the main topic of conversation in this district just now. We have been just persecuted by snow. Every year seems to be the same in the early months. First of all very cold and biting southerly winds, sometimes intense frost. Then the snow comes, day after day we get the snow and hardly ever any sunshine. Snow, snow, snow. There are no road sweepers or extra hands at work now. Any snow removing has to be done by the individual. Some householders see to it that the snow is cleared away from the paths round about their houses, others do nothing. The snow is left on the footpaths, it gets trodden down and becomes firm ice. I have tried to keep my paths clean and free from snow. However, before I can get to work in the morning people are about and the snow becomes hard and difficult to shift. This job has taken me about an hour each morning lately and I am sick of it. This morning my curate-lodger gave me a bit of help and I was very glad of it. The snow was quite a foot deep all round the house. We hear from Henry nearly every week. Nothing to report. John is now at Llandudno and Stephen is not far from Nottingham. Nothing to report from these two either. 13 siren calls in January. Total to date 636. Phil.

B.S.67 17th February 1942

I have had fifty-two letters returned to me. All of these returned letters were addressed to Henry from this house and they have all been sent back. Nearly all of them came by the same post! A big mail. The postman and the sorters at the post office must have thought things over before they sent this consignment round to No. 19. Yes. And we have thought a bit. All those letters — and the poor lad never got one of them. All that time spent in writing those letters and the time just wasted. All those bright coloured postage stamps and air mail labels. All cancelled and wasted. The letters are dated, some of them, as far back as November 1940 — fifteen months back. The latest of them coincides with the date that we first heard that Henry was missing — mid-July 1941. After mid-July we wrote no more letters until we heard that Henry had been taken prisoner on June 1st. It is, in a way, good to know that we have now got in touch with him once more, although we know nothing of the story of his capture. One day, perhaps, he will be able to tell us all about Crete and what went on there on the days leading up to June 1st. One day, perhaps, he will be able to read all those letters that never found him and have now come back here. There. I have thrown all 52 of them into a drawer labelled 'H', unopened.

Oh yes. About *The Sanctuary of the Heart*. I had been asked to play this song, or whatever it is, at a wedding. It was the first time I had ever even heard the title. All my family say I am very slow in picking up these new tunes and I suppose I am. Well. Now to tell you what happened about *The Sanctuary of the Heart*. I called at the little cheap music shop in Hull and asked for the song. 'Sold out,' the girl told me. A little old man heard me talking to his employee and he came up to me with a bit of music in his hand. 'I suppose this is no use to you?' he said. It was a piano arrangement of the song. 'Just what I want,' I said. I paid half a crown and came away with the music. First chance I got I took it to the organ and it just played itself. I had no trouble whatever with it. It was quite a success at the wedding and I could see the guests were all listening to it. On the following Sunday morning I tried it on as voluntary before matins. There were two or three hundred soldiers sitting there in rows. I made quite a good and long affair of it, keeping it going with various repeats and a little improvisation until the parson was ready to begin the service. This is not the end. On the following morning I was sweeping up the snow in the front of this house, scratching about with a spade and cursing the cold and the ice and the snow, when a lady passed. I don't know who she was and I don't remember that I have ever seen her before. 'What a lovely voluntary that was you gave us yesterday morning, Mr. Chignell!' For the moment I forgot what it was and I just said, 'Thank you. I am glad you liked it.' Then I remembered. That good lady, whoever she was, liked my *Sanctuary of the Heart* voluntary. I never remember anybody saying that they liked my Rheinberger voluntaries. The hash-up of a very simple tune, that is the sort of stuff that everybody likes, and I have fallen for it. It is so easy to earn my salary that way. Who wants my Rheinberger and my Bach? Any offers for my library of classical organ music? I extemporised on *Hearts of Oak* the other Sunday and I have not heard the last of it yet. Phil.

B.S.68 3rd March 1942

I think I told you that at a wedding recently held in Hessle Church the bride had to say all her most important words with the siren chorus going on all the time. They never stopped the wedding and the young woman did her part all right. She will remember that minute all through her life.

I have just seen the end of the month of February and jolly glad I am that it is now a thing of the past. No sunshine. Nothing but cold, grey clouds, ice and snow on the roads. Gardens frost bound and dead. One day last week things brightened up a bit. There was some sunshine and I got me away on my bicycle down to the Humber side and then on to my little and very private wood, three miles away towards Ferriby. The little sunshine had softened the paths and they were slimy and greasy. It is mostly chalk down that district and before I knew where I was I had splashed my bicycle and some of my clothes with dabs of white. My boots, my old boots I should have said, were completely white. Soon cleaned them up when dry at home. What a mess.

If you walk about Hull and Hessle and notice the pubs you will see some of them are shut up altogether, others have notices on the windows — No beer — or — Open on Wednesday next at noon. There was such a notice at THE GRANBY, Hessle's chief pub, last Sunday. There was also a crowd of disappointed pub crawlers reading the notice over and over again. I am afraid all The Granby pub crawlers are well known and they would not be able to mix with the crawlers from other Hessle pubs. They would not get much of a welcome at the DARLEY ARMS say. Phil.

B.S.69 17th March 1942 (St. Patrick's Day)

It was on St. Patrick's Day 31 years ago that I set out on that famous world tour which meant so much to me and to many others. At this time in the morning I was travelling along in the well known L.& Y. through train from Hull to Liverpool. And then the *Victorian* and the sailing away from

Liverpool, and the sight of the south Irish coast the next morning, and seeing the Fastnet lighthouse gradually passing out of sight. And that was just the beginning of the great adventure. So long ago now that it all seems to me but a dream, something that never really happened. In these days when I never travel anywhere, never go in a train and very seldom venture even into Hull. In these days when I just wander about on the banks of the Humber, or sit about at home, or spend an hour at a billiards table with one or two old men about my own age, it seems wonderful to think that I ever had enough energy to pack up my bags and go off on a 6½ months' adventure. John and Stephen are both at home with us today and there is Henry in his Stalag VIII B, Trigo in her office in Hull, Katie bustling about with her morning's house work. Well. That 1911 tour meant a lot for all of them. Didn't it?

I am at present sorting through all my old chess records. Whenever I played chess in a match for the Hull Club or played a tournament game for that club I kept a record of the moves on a specially printed form for chess games. I had a big boxful of these records and lately I have been playing through them on my miniature chess set. I have got a lot of pleasure out of this chess spring cleaning. Some very clever games. Now and then I am astonished at my own brilliance and at other times I am astonished that I could have been so senseless and foolish. Eventually I will burn them all, but what a collection! I could have made up a very interesting chess book just on these games alone. I am sure the book would have been worth a shilling or two and would have had a good sale. I could have written a book about the famous tour but I didn't. Just too lazy, I suppose. I know the verdict on me at the end will be that I might have done a great deal more than I did. I mean this — I know I have had abilities that I have not made the most of. To spend 41 years in such a quiet little place as Hessle, that isn't anything very wonderful. I might have done a good deal better than that. But there — I speak to myself. — Shut up!

We have had but one siren call during the past seven days (No. 661) and that of course came along during the middle of our Friday night choir practice. That was a nice and kind choice of time but I am pleased to say that not even the smallest choirboy took any notice of the beastly noise and nobody wanted to go home. So we have quietened down a lot in this business. I wonder if it will revive with the coming of summer or if we have really come nearly to the end of this particular worry. Our Hessle record of one casualty in 661 alarms is nothing to worry about. I wish I could say the same about our neighbouring city. I feel ill every time I go into that place. It will not revive in my lifetime. I have seen Hull in the heyday of social happiness and I have had a large share in concerts and musical gatherings. These cannot revive in my time. The place has hardly got over the great shock of the May blitzes of last year. It seems a dazed city as though nobody knows what to do next. At present the ruins are being cleared away little by little, leaving some extraordinary gaps just in the very heart of the city. What a rebuilding there will be some day!

Our curate lodger is to be married on April 18th at Retford. We shall not be so very sorry to lose him. We like him very much but I think we shall be glad to have the house to ourselves once more. Best love, Phil.

B.S.70 31st March 1942

We have been spared the shrieking siren just lately. Only seven alerts throughout the whole of March. Thank God for that. There was a noisy one last Thursday when there was some banging going on not far from here. It made our windows rattle a bit but it soon calmed down and, as I say, we have had a very quiet time during March. I wonder if this means we are not to be troubled any more by raids and bombs and land mines and the sharp yapping of anti-aircraft guns. I once saw a traction engine running away downhill. It toppled through a hedge and overturned. The driver was drunk. Fancy driving a traction engine when drunk. And he escaped too, not a scratch. Afterwards that driver went out to the war in France and there he lost his life. Sometimes I go and look at the war memorial in Hessle churchyard and there I see his name, one of some hundreds who died in that last war. And why? And what for? And that particular hero's name should never have been on that memorial, he should have died when he ventured to drive that traction engine at a runaway speed down a steep hill. And now, goodnight. Phil.

B.S.71 14th April 1942

There now — I have got safely round that corner — I was going to call it a 'bunker' but perhaps 'corner' is a better word. I see in front of me a different kind of highway from the one I have been jogging along lately. The new road is not very clear ahead. Quickly enough now I seem to forget the past. I forget people, I forget names, I forget places I have visited. I mix up my dreams with the past realities of my life so that I am not quite sure that what memory I still have is not playing me false.

It was, as you know, my 70th birthday on Sunday. I was in church a good deal all the morning and a part of the evening. I wonder how many times on Sunday verse ten of psalm 90 went through my mind: 'The days of our age are three score years and ten.' I like the long and poetic way of referring to my present age, 'three score years and ten' as in the English psalter. Well. Pass on there. There is no time for meditating old fools now this bloody war is going on and nobody knows how soon he or she may be involved in it. I am not so sure that I want to 'be so strong that I come etc'. I feel sure that the world will not calm down again in ten years from the time the war ceases. It has not ceased yet, so what hope have I of ever living again in times and days of happy prosperity? I can answer my own question — I have no hope of any more cheerful and happy days free from all war's alarms. But please do not think that I cannot extract happy hours from the days that pass along so quickly. I think I make the most of a bad job. Today, for instance. For an hour or two this morning I was wandering round the Humber side with my bicycle. There was a sharp, cold, south-east wind blowing, the wind that makes one hungry in half an hour. There was a strong April sun shining right across the water. There were thousands of newly born daffodils, none of them more than three or four days old. One spot down the river way attracts me every day just now and especially an hour or so before high tide, when the song or surge of the incoming water is in my ears. (I can tell which way the tide is running with my eyes shut.) There is a large house called *The Cliff* standing sideways to the river and in front of this house is a fairly large field and in this field daffodils have been cultivated or allowed to grow by the hundreds. The field is now beautiful beyond imagination. On such a day as this the picture I have described is just about perfect.

We have no wireless in this house. Our instrument is out of order. Strange to say, I rather enjoy this disability. The Mullard radio has been a success in this house and we are all fond of it. It can give us the most delightful music and it can be a beastly and vulgar nuisance. So far as I can see, you cannot have one thing without some, at any rate, of the other, according to the tastes of those living with you in the same house. Now the beggar is silent. There is something good and refreshing about silence. We all get to that point in the end. Perhaps I am glad that the repairer cannot come for another fortnight. Goodbye, P.

P.B.S.72 28th April 1942

I suppose it is the strong east wind that is howling round our house at this moment. It is this wind that makes me feel rattled and unsettled. We have had this wind for several days now and only those who have lived in this north-east part of England can know how annoying it can be, even if it comes in summer or spring. We have had days, such as today, of unclouded sunshine but the east wind has gone on howling day and night. I am just sick of it.

Just lately the siren nuisance has broken out once more. It almost seemed that this trouble or complaint was finished and cured but not so, we have been threatened and persecuted once more. Last night's warning brought the figure up to 673. Not a patch on Malta but quite enough to be going on with.

We have lost our curate-lodger. He was married on April 18th and today I have tasted his wedding cake. We are not sorry that he has gone, although we were all very good friends and his weekly contribution was a help to the house-keeping accounts. Soon after he settled in this house we found out that he just helped himself to a box of matches whenever he wanted one, and he was a big smoker. You cannot buy matches nowadays at threepence for a dozen boxes. Sometimes you cannot buy even one box, they are so scarce. So Katie had a special hiding place for the one and only box in the house. I knew this hiding place. It was behind a large brown jar in the pantry. Every morning I felt behind this jar for the one match to light the kitchen fire. On the day Wilkes went off to be married Katie said to me, 'There will be no need to hide the matches now,' and I agreed with her. On the next morning I went about my usual job of attending to the kitchen fire at the usual time, somewhere about 7 a.m. Do you think I could find a match anywhere? No. I could not. There was no box behind the stone jar nor anywhere else that I could think of. Not one anywhere. I hunted about in the other rooms, hoping that Wilkes might have left an odd match somewhere or other, in a tray or under the clock or even on the floor. No. No luck. It was getting on for 7.30 and I gave up the chase and sat on a chair in front of the unlighted kitchen fire. Providence stepped in. The front door opened and someone walked up the passage and opened the kitchen door. 'Got a match, mate?' I said at once. The match was produced and the kitchen fire soon blazed up. Some time later I asked Katie, 'Where did you put the matches?' 'I told you,' she said. 'Inside the stone jar.' True enough there was a box of matches at the very bottom of this stone jar, but underneath half a dozen other articles. If I had looked inside the jar I would not have seen the matches. Well. What with curates and weddings and matches and hiding places I get a bit dazed. However, I have had no further trouble. It was the Rev. Arthur who paid me that very early visit and a day or so later he sent me a present of a whole box of matches for myself. Selah.

Sometime last year our vicar raised a hue and cry after a lost overcoat. I heard the whole story about it, not once or twice but many times. A very good coat — Could not remember where he had left it — Put a notice in the parish magazine asking for its return — No good — It had just gone — One of those mysterious losses we all suffer from now and then. The last day Wilkes was with us he spent mostly in removing his possessions to his new house in Barrow Lane. At the end of this ceremony a clerical coat remained which he disowned and which was certainly not mine. A letter in one of the pockets gave the clue — It was the vicar's long lost garment. We held a consultation and finally it was decided to say nowt but to put the garment on a peg in the clergy vestry at the church. Wilkes went off to get married and we have not seen him since. The vicar returned from a holiday — went to the church to take a service — couldn't find his best cassock — raised hell — looked about and found his coat — was overjoyed — wore a choir cassock for the service. I heard this story from the verger and, when telling it to Katie, I hear that a very nice and dignified cassock was among the garments in the move from 19, The Weir to 84, Barrow Lane. This problem will doubtless be solved when the honeymoon comes to an end. Goodbye, Phil.

B.S.73 12th May 1942

We have been without our radio for the past few weeks. It was returned to us in good working order yesterday morning. I wonder. Am I glad or sorry that the little box of tricks has come back to us? Well. I don't know. I'm not sure. This week the B.B.C. are making a lot of the centenary of the birth of Arthur Seymour Sullivan. I am interested in that. I knew the gentleman. I saw him many times in my young days. He was slightly younger than my own father. I was a boy when his famous comic operas began to appear and I remember how tremendously popular they were. I am sure I saw all these Gilbert and Sullivan operas, one by one, as they were produced. I remember seeing *Iolanthe* from a box at the Savoy, with quite a family party. All my love for these operas perished when I became a man and put away childish things. The last time I saw one of these operas, *The Mikado*, at a London theatre, I left at the interval, I could not stand any more of it. I was once in the chorus when Sullivan himself conducted a performance of *The Martyr of Antioch*. I remember Sullivan did not seem at all funny when one was face to face with him, indeed he seemed just the opposite, rather cross-grained and sarcastic. The Norwich Chorus did not respond to him very well and I remember his very words spoken at the final rehearsal, spoken to the double bassoon player who was caught napping — 'Mister Knight, you have been brought down to Norwich from London at considerable expense to play about twenty notes, will you please play them.' Dead silence. No laughter. It was too dangerous to laugh at a sarcastic conductor. Phil.

B.S.74 26th May 1942

I have made another very funny discovery lately. I have found a place down the Humber way where I have been able to pick up free coal. Coal lying in the tidal part of the river, I mean where the water comes up at high tide but where there is no water for most hours of the day. I found quite a load of coal tipped into the river and I have been just helping myself to it, bringing home about two scuttle-fulls of coal on each journey. I have almost kept this house in coal in this way for the past fortnight and I am still working the same strain and can go on for some time yet. Trigo and I were down there yesterday and our evening fire was entirely made up of this free coal. I have no idea who has given me this coal or who has thrown it there. There is no road within half a mile of the spot where I found this coal. It is near the railway but I cannot imagine any engine driver stopping his train and clambering over a fence after scrambling down an embankment, and depositing half a ton of unwanted coal into the river. Neither could this coal be seaborne. No boat, even at high tide, could sail through the rushes and over the marshes. Anyhow, there it is. Nobody else seems to have noticed this coal and I have just helped myself to it, day by day and load by load. And at the same time I have come home with a bouquet of wild flowers, wild cherry blossom one day, red campions another and so on. But who put that coal there?

Oh, yes. We had a very bad time here last week. A week ago today. No. 686 was a real bad'un. From 11.45 p.m. to 1.30 a.m. there was the devil of a row going on. You know what I mean. Once, on the night I am speaking of, I really thought the whole house was coming down. It seemed to lift up a bit with an especially nasty blast and then fall back. I waited for it to fall down like a pack of cards. Anyhow, nothing happened our way and when the all clear sounded I just turned over and was soon asleep. They were not so lucky a mile or two away. Poor old Hull. Even if the war stopped today it would take a generation to set Hull going again. A lady friend of mine, one of the Savings Bank staff, had a very bad time. Like me she did not get out of bed when the sirens piped up. The all clear had gone when she was roused by a warden and told to evacuate her house at once. She lives all alone in what was her own house in one of Hull's Avenues. There was an unexploded bomb in her front garden. She went to another house, spent the rest of the night there, had breakfast there and went off to work as usual. I saw her at the Hessle branch the next morning, she was relieving there. In the afternoon of that day she was returning home from work and as she went along the Avenue towards her house the bomb exploded and the whole house was blown up. Everything she possessed gone with it. Selah. Phil.

B.S.75 9th June 1942

SALVAGE. I suppose everybody has used this word a great many times lately. You know what I mean. I have done my share in this business for I have cast out bundle after bundle of music, neatly tied up and handed over to 'DUSTBIN' as John used to call the gentleman who visits us every Thursday morning, a designation that has endured ever since the day that John was a very small child. 'DUSTBIN' is a cheerful and friendly fellow. If I meet him in the street he always seems pleased to see me and I often stop to have a word or two with him. My musical consignments to his collection give cause to an oft-repeated joke — DUSTBIN learns all the music I give him. He takes it home and practises it and every Thursday he is ready for another lesson or two.

Just lately we have had on the wireless an Elgar centenary celebration. I met Elgar three times. The first was at the Worcester Festival in 1899 when George Chignell introduced me to him and we had lunch together. I was present when the *Enigma Variations* were performed practically for the first time (Richter had conducted them in London a week or two before the Worcester Festival) and I remember the pleasure and amusement the work gave. The initials or names given to the several variations hid no secrets for they were all more or less local references. That was in September 1899 and a month later I met Elgar again. This time we were in the old Blackfriars' Hall in Norwich. This hall is an ancient and lovely building adjoining St. Andrew's Hall. The Norwich musical festival was being given in the latter hall. Blackfriars' Hall was being used for cloakrooms and refreshments. There were buffets along the side of the hall and it was there during the concert interval that I met Elgar for the second time. He had just scored an immense success with the production of his *Sea Pieces* especially written for this festival and for Clara Butt, the well-known contralto. I was lucky to have been present at the productions of these two, even now, famous English works. The third and last time I met Elgar was in America in 1911. Elgar travelled with the choir for about three weeks both in Canada and in the U.S.A. and conducted *Gerontius* very many times. One day I travelled in the same railway carriage with him for many hours. I forget where we were travelling to but I remember Elgar talked about Parry's *Blest Pair of Sirens*, a fine work that the Sheffield choir had sung at a concert the night before. Elgar considered that the work could be very much improved if it could be re-scored. He thought that Parry was a poor hand with his orchestration, and he said that if he survived Parry he intended to re-score this work. I think that, when Parry died, Elgar must have forgotten all about this particular remark I heard him make.

I was in Cologne in 1906 and again in 1910. I have just been reading over the two diaries I kept in those years and my impressions of that city. In my innocence in those days I looked upon the idea of a war between Germany and England as something to laugh about and not to be taken seriously. In this diary I wrote many times about the German people and how they were over-ruled and ordered about by men in uniform, soldiers, police, railway officials, etc. etc. It seemed to be the rule of life for the civilian to be humiliated and ordered about by the man in uniform. My pal Carl Hillerns (long since dead) and I suffered several times from this complaint, and I was surprised how C.H. accepted the position of under-dog without a word of protest. He was a German by birth and he had a tremendous love for the country of his birth and everything in it, except he could spit at the sight of a Jew in Germany although he was friendly enough with many wealthy Jews in Hull. I never could understand the difference between Carl Hillerns as a naturalized Englishman and Carl Hillerns as a full-blooded German. But what about Cologne? I for one am glad to hear that the Dom has survived so far.

I was going to remark, but I have exceeded my time already, how nice it is to have all those darned motor cars off our streets and country roads. It is just lovely. I hate the things and I rejoice that there is no petrol to be given to joy motorists. Just now our country is sweet and lovely and one can hear the birds singing and enjoy the flowers and fresh air and notice the calm quiet that has come to us now that petrol is scarce. That is one good thing from the war, anyhow. Phil.

| John | Henry | Stephen |

B.S.76 23rd June 1942

We have had John and Stephen at home on leave for the past week. Stephen has returned to his work but John is still with us. It has been nice for them to come home at the same time. This was a pure chance and not an arranged affair. I walked down to the station on Friday evening to 'set' Stephen on his way back to his camp. As we walked I said to him, 'Stephen, answer me a question, yes or no. — If I said to you now, and had the authority to say it, you can turn round now and go home, you can take off your uniform and tomorrow morning you can return to civilian life and your work at Spillers and you can give up any more thoughts about soldiering, will you turn round now and walk home?' The reply was, 'No. I will return to my military duties.' I shall ask John the same question before he returns to his job but I am jolly certain what his answer will be. John is enjoying life to the full. He is well and happy and jovial, one of the most cheerful beggars on earth. The serious part of life does not seem to concern him in the least. We don't hear very much of the other chap, the lodger at Stalag VIII B. We can do nothing except write to him and try to send him a few things in the hope that he will get them. We can do nothing more.

I must tell you how I survived a very trying ordeal on Thursday last. We have a lay reader at Hessle Church. Quite a good chap at that job. Someone invited him to take up the noble game of bowls. He turned up at the club and immediately set to work. You couldn't keep him off the green, cold or wet, rain or fog, he was for ever on the green trundling his woods up and down to a delivered jack. If you went down early in the evening to get an early game you were bound to find this chap waiting for someone to play with him and in common courtesy you were bound to include him in your party of the first six comers to make up a rink game which he consistently spoiled because the side he played for was bound to lose, he was such a novice. He insisted on keeping all the scores and doing all the measuring, although he was but a novice and a poor hand in both these departments of the game. At the beginning of June entries were invivited for two tournaments, singles and doubles. Although most of our novices are rather shy at entering these tournaments, my friend the lay reader was one of the very first names to go down. He was given a very liberal handicap start. When he played his single game he scored one point and was knocked out by Rotsey, the local ironmonger. He had better luck in the doubles, he was coupled with a good partner, George Bontoft, who managed, almost playing a lone game, to win the round against quite a strong pair. Well. My pal, by the luck of the draw, was Frank White, quite a good player. Well. Frank and I also won our first round and then we had the luck to be drawn against my lay reader friend and George Bontoft. I was really terrified at the idea that perhaps G.B. and his tiro partner might put Frank and me out of this tournament. I was afraid of the vestry talk on the following Sunday morning. I heard it all once when I was but an amused listener and I did not want to hear it all over again and this time to be the victim. The game was played on Thursday evening at 7. When I got to the club there was this chap, at it again, up and down the green with his jack and his woods. That was not a very sporting thing to do. With any other player in the club I should have protested, but no other member would have thought of such a thing. I said to Frank, 'For Heaven's sake be steady, we've got to knock this b— out!' We had to give four handicap in a game of 21 up. Frank and I knocked that four off in the first two ends and the rest was plain sailing. I was sorry for poor old George Bontoft and his bowler hat but it had to be. P.

B.S.77 7th July 1942

Those evening bells — How many a tale their music tells.

On Thursday, June 25th, I was surprised to hear the chimes of the Hessle Church clock ringing out the quarter hours as in the days before the war. When I returned, late one night, from my journey round the world in 1911 I could not sleep for joy at hearing those Hessle bells ringing once again. There are six bells — la,so,fa,mi,ray,do in the key of F sharp. It is a long story and I will try to keep it short. In the olden days the straight road from Hessle to Hull was a mere track across a waste land that was liable to be flooded by Father Humber at spring tides. The story goes that one night a traveller over the short route was saved by hearing the bells of Hessle Church ringing. I daresay this is only a yarn but it is a yarn oft repeated in these days. This good traveller owned a house somewhere in the neighbourhood of Hessle. When he died he left this property to the clerk of Hessle Church on condition that the clerk should ring a bell at Hessle Church 150 times every evening at 7 o'clock, make a pause, and then ring the day of the month on another bell. When I came to Hessle in 1901 I was surprised to hear this bell going every night but I soon learned the story. If ever you troubled to count the 150 strokes you would never find that George had made a mistake and if you were not sure of the day of the month you only had to wait until the deeper toned bell started and you were certain to get the correct information therefrom. Well. The time came when this particular property came into the limelight. The railway company wanted the ground on which it stood, in fact they were bound to get possession of it to enable them to carry out very extensive railway improvements. The money the railway company paid for this property was invested and thereafter, instead of £8 or £10 a year that George used to receive, it became a matter of £75 or thereabouts. George did not make any complaint about that and he went on ringing the bells, year in year out. As George grew older his keenness slackened a bit. It was not always very convenient to be at the church exactly at the hour of 7 p.m. George, in the summer months, was very fond of bowls, and the darned bells made him a late-comer to the club. One could always tell when George was coming to to the bowls club, the 150 strokes on the high bell would be rung off at a terrific speed, so fast that one could hardly count them, and then the switch over to the day-of-the-month bell would be done like lightning and before you could say 'Jack Robinson' George would be on the bowling green, hoping that his chance for a game of bowls would be good. After all, there was not much sense about that bell ringing, especially on a summer's evening when there could not possibly be any lost travellers about. When the present war broke out the bowling season of 1939 was still running its happy course. Almost before a gun was fired George went off to the police or military authority — 'What about the bells?' 'Oh, no. No bells may be rung.' And so George got down to the bowling green in good time and from that day until June 25th 1942, our Hessle bells were silent. The absurd part of the story is that if one walked over to Ferriby, three miles away, one could hear the Ferriby Church bells chiming the quarter hours just as usual, and when I stayed at Owston Ferry last August and the August before, the town hall or village hall clock, striking the quarters, disturbed my night's sleep. But there. The order went forth at Hessle and George was relieved of his work. George died soon after the war commenced, thereupon the vicar, in whose hands the appointment of the clerk rests, appointed his own churchwarden to be the official clerk of the parish church and that gentleman now receives the dividends afore-mentioned. I don't know why the bells have begun ringing again, after all, the war is not finished. If it were out of order to ring the bells in 1939, 1940 and 1941, surely it is out of order now. Perhaps the order to ring again was given to celebrate our 700th air raid alarm which occurred just about the same time. We are now on the road for the next hundred but the rate of advance has slowed down considerably. 1941, Jan to June 177 alarms. July to December 146. 1942, Jan to June 77. May this business continue to slacken is what we all hope. Phil.

B.S.78 21st July 1942

Last night, that is directly after the tea hour, I found myself quite alone, and with every prospect of an evening completely to myself. Katie had gone to Hull to see a Shakespearian play, John is at Brancaster, in Norfolk, Henry, poor lad, is still at Stalag VIII B, Stephen is at Chilwell near Nottingham, Trigo is at Llandudno with her Aunt Maude. 'How passing sweet is solitude.' Perhaps. Perhaps not. At 6.30. I turned on the wireless and with full scores in my hand I followed the programme of a Promenade Concert. A Mozart *Overture* and a Brahms' *Piano*

'Trigo' (Ruth) — taken at Hammond's, Hull, 1940.

Concerto in D minor. Jolly good and most enjoyable and interesting. I spotted the drummer in a slip. After a long rest he came in five bars too soon with a rat-a-tat. Quite an understandable mistake for the music led him to think his drums were wanted five bars before he was really due to come in. I don't often catch these fine orchestral players making mistakes. There is , however, usually some slip or other in every performance of a great work. That is where I find my big collection of miniature scores very useful. Now I had been on the bowling green all afternoon and my appetite for playing games had gone. I would stay at home, perhaps do a bit of gardening after some piano practice. You know Trigo and I have just lately learned together Brahms' *No. 2 Sonata* for violin and piano. It is a grand bit of music and so wonderful for me, at my age, to find something new and beautiful in music. Trigo has gone away for a fortnight and by the time she returns I hope to be able to play the piano part of one of the other Brahms' violin sonatas sufficiently well to make a good show in company with my good lady friend. So I sat down at the piano and began with *Brahms' No. 1.* No good — Couldn't get going. Too much wireless. Too much Promenade Concert. Nobody else in the house. Too quiet and funereal. I suppose I always like to feel that there is someone else in the house even when I practise the piano or type out a B.S. letter.

One of the Yorkshire chess players was killed in the air raid on York some time ago. I suppose his game would be counted 'partie nul'. But what luck. To be killed with a chess board in your hand. I have many times both in this war and in the last studied chess positions with a raid going on not so very far away. I can get ease and distraction that way, but I should like to finish the game all the same. Phil.

B.S.79 4th August 1942

I say. That was a funny sort of Bank Holiday yesterday. It makes me laugh just to think about it — What I had planned to do and what I actually did. The idea was to get out of bed just whenever I felt inclined. Dawdle the morning away in the garden. All sorts of jobs to be done there, of course. Spend the afternoon at the bowling club, taking part in a bowls drive which would last well up to tea time. I intended to listen to the Promenade Concert for an hour 6.30 to 7.30 and then to wander back to the bowling green and get going there until it was time for supper and bed. Well. That is how I proposed to spend my Bank Holiday. I wasted my time in even thinking out a programme. The sirens were after us at 2.30 a.m. and my night's rest was disturbed. At 6 a.m. I was weary of lying in bed and keeping my ears open for the sounds of aeroplanes and sirens and perhaps guns and bombs. At six o'clock I got up, only to see a foul morning with rain, low clouds coming over from due north, altogether a miserable outlook for the holiday. It rained all the morning. The sirens were going, on and off, one alarm after another, so that one lost count and could not tell whether we were supposed to be under warning or had been relieved. I found an indoor job up in my study. About noon Trigo got out her fiddle and we began playing a Mozart *Sonata No. 11 in G*. There was a big uproar outside while we were practising, bombs, guns, aeroplanes that we could not see owing to the low clouds. You cannot play Mozart's sonatas with your house shaking with gunfire, at least I cannot. The game seems to have been of the 'tip-and-run' order. Planes up above the clouds, guns firing at them without seeing them and using sound guides only. I don't know which side won or how many runs were scored but it was a darned row. After dinner I went to the bowls club. Too wet for bowls and so all the members sat in the club house and smoked and talked and watched snooker players on the billiards table, praising good strokes and laughing at bad ones. Twice during the afternoon I took a cue and sometimes gained applause but more often earned humorous and sarcastic criticism. Every now and then the sirens tuned up, we could hear perhaps a dozen of them, but, as I say, we lost count and did not much trouble whether they meant a warning or a relief. Sometimes we could hear planes tearing about over head and above the clouds. Some of the members said these planes were 'Jerries', others said they were 'ours' ,but it didn't matter much, the games of snooker went on all the afternoon and the talking and the smoking and the applause and the sarcasms.

Do you know Katie and I have been married thirty years come Friday, as they say in Yorkshire. Lately I have felt sorry for myself and for Katie. We had two years of happy married life and then war overtook our happiness. We lived and laboured through the long four years war of 1914-18. Our two eldest children were born during the time of this great war. Katie and I had to endure all the troubles and anxieties of those Zeppelin raids. We thought they were bad enough and we were thankful indeed when that war came to an end. We never dreamed that we would have to face the trials of another

Katie and Philip Chignell: photograph sent to Henry in Stalag VIII B, 1943.

war with very more serious air raids and attacks. I know, of course, that what I think or suffer is of no consequence whatsoever. If a bomb dropped on this house and plugged us all there would be a few bricks to clear away and that would not take very long. Nobody would worry very much about my old violoncello or my very nice Marshall and Rose piano or all my books and music and this lovable typewriter. Nobody would worry much about such an event. Only one day last week I was in the east Hull district and I went by a house, or at least where I expected to see a house, that I used to visit many years ago. It had a nice garden at the back and I spent a good deal of time there. Now — nothing — Not even a heap of stones or ruins — nothing. Just a vacant plot of ground on which wild flowers are trying to grow and to adorn a place ravaged and massacred by men. So what does it matter what I think or say?

I wonder what the London Philharmonic Orchestra people thought about Hull. This fine combination gave a series of ten concerts in Hull last week; they must have found sleeping accommodation in the city on five nights. On every one of these nights, soon after 2 a.m., there was an air raid warning, and on the last of the five there was a really serious attack on the city with many casualties. I wonder what the players thought about this. I went to three of the concerts and enjoyed them very much indeed. Katie, Trigo and John also went to several of the concerts. I wonder what Mr. Jean Pougnet thought about Hull and the desolation to be seen all over the place. Well. His beautiful violin playing did not betray his thoughts whatever they may have been.

Yes. Thirty years. I can tell you one thing and that is pretty certain — 'Until Death us do part.' I am afraid I shall have to go first. But we won't talk about it. Thirty years is a good long time. Phil.

B.S.80 18th August 1942

Something went wrong with our Hessle siren the other night. I had a very bad night in consequence. Somewhere about midnight all the Hull sirens and buzzers tuned up in chorus (No.725). I lay awake and listened to this inharmonious chorus, expecting our noisy Hessle siren to shriek out its unpleasant warning at any moment. As a rule we get the Hessle siren going before the Hull sirens have moaned away into silence. This time all the Hull warnings died away before the Hessle began. I lay awake in the greatest anxiety for fear that Hessle should not get the warning. We live quite close to the Hessle Town Hall but other Hessle residents, my friends, are not so fortunate, or unfortunate, as the case may be. Then someone ran along The Weir blowing a little whistle. He must have been running and trying to blow the whistle at the same time. 'You can't do it, my boy', I said without getting out of bed. Then there were one or two more guns or bombs seemingly a little nearer. Then I could hear the spasmodic whistle running up a distant street, and then one or two more whistles sounding out in the night air. I began to think perhaps it was my duty to get up and find an old referee's whistle I have and then go out and run about the streets of Hessle in my pyjamas because, of course, there would be no time to dress, blowing my referee's whistle.

Then I turned over in bed and thought to myself, 'Well, I was too old for the last war and it is perfectly certain I am too old for this one. I can't run about the streets in the dead of night, minus decent clothing and blowing a referee's whistle. There, the guns are at it again. My old woman has gone downstairs and she will be sitting in the kitchen, darning, or doing something of that kind. She is not exactly frightened, only she does not like the gun business. She likes to take it, if it has to be, downstairs and not in bed.' You would be surprised at the words I think of when I hear all this banging. I really did not know that I was good as swearing until this war came along.

After an hour and a half I heard all the Hull sirens and buzzers sounding the relief and I wondered what the Hessle people would do. I almost sat up in bed to listen. You couldn't go whistling again for that would mean the same thing. It would have to be something different. After about half an hour and getting on for dawn time somebody produced a muffin bell and then another muffin bell of a different tone and quality. Then a dinner bell. It's funny where they find these bells at a moment's notice. So now we know. A referee's whistle, and Jerry is coming to see us. A muffin bell and he has gone. I shall not stay awake next time the Hessle siren fails.

I know this month of August is a lovely time of the year, if it were not for the war. Quite early in the morning, 6.30 or so, I get into my garden and have a look round. I gather a lot of fine carnations, 'Redcar' carnations I call them. Have them on the breakfast table in a small bowl. Oh, but they are lovely, and my own garden too. Later on in the day perhaps I shall wander off on my bicycle to the most extraordinary and beautiful place — the Hessle chalk pits. Some years ago I noticed that a few buddleia bushes had settled in these pits. They must have come from Hesslewood gardens which were at one time on the ground that has now vanished. There were fields as well as gardens at the top of the cliff that overlooks the river when I first came to Hessle. The buddleias must have come from the gardens above. Once it got a footing at the low level it spread in all directions. Now there are hundreds and hundreds of buddleia bushes and they are all in full flower just at the present.

John has disappeared. Gone. Goodness knows where. We are not likely to hear of him or from him for a long time. He telephoned one night last week a very short and indefinite message. We took it that he was just intending to say 'goodbye', although he avoided anything like a farewell message. A day or two later we received a letter from him, or at least an envelope containing just a small snapshot of him. No letter. No information as to where or when he was going. I have no doubt he has gone off by now. Hessle Church choir almost came down to zero last Sunday. One choirman, the faithful Len Emerson. We did a choral celebration like that. Lloyd in E flat. In one place there is a canon for bass and alto and we had neither a bass voice nor an alto. Nobody seems to mind and I go on playing the organ and the parson dresses up and the offertories are taken. It doesn't matter. Phil.

B.S.8l 1st September 1942

I notice after one year of war,that was up to September 1st, 1940, we had had 60 air raid warnings. A year later, September 1st, 1941, the number had advanced to almost 500. Today the number stands at 732. I don't know that these figures show anything in particular. We seem to have passed the peak of the trouble but it is not safe to be too confident in these matters.

For the past fortnight we were without news of John. He had just left this country and we had no idea where he had gone to. A day or two ago we had a cable from him. He is now in Gibraltar. He gives us an address there and so it appears that he will be there for some time to come. John has never been out of this country before. It will be his first experience of travelling abroad. Tomorrow will be his 26th birthday. Yesterday we sent him a cable wishing him the usual good wishes. On Sunday night Stephen telephoned to say he was coming home on 'embarkation leave' and he duly turned up in time for dinner yesterday. I wonder what his story will be when it comes to be told. We have not any recent news of Henry. He has now been a prisoner of war for fifteen months. It does seem hard that so many months of the best time of his life should be just wasted but, of course, we know quite well that things might have been worse for him. I wonder when we shall see him at home again. Not for some time, I'm afraid.

The Duke of Kent was one of the five royal persons that I have spoken to at one time or another. Four of them were in my Windsor days. The Duke of Kent was in Hull about fifteen years ago and I spoke to him on that occasion. He seemed a very quiet and nice young man and he was certainly good-looking. It is very sad to think that he had to be one of the victims of this war, one of those lives seemingly thrown away in this country.

There. Since I typed the last line I have been downstairs to play the piano for Trigo. We played two Corelli sonatas and three Handel sonatas, with all due repeats. I get a great deal of pleasure in our evening rehearsals and I have learned a lot of music I knew nothing about until Trigo learned how to play the violin and gave me the incentive to study violin sonatas. I wish someone would find a second-hand copy of César Franck's violin sonata. I want to have a go at that but it is not easy to get in these days. It is a French publication. Goodbye, Phil.

B.S.82 15th September 1942

Do you remember your feelings after your last serious visit to your dentist? I mean the visit when that good gentleman removed all your remaining teeth. One by one he drew them all out and then patched you up as best he could and sent you home to recover from the indignity and onslaught you had endured. I remember my thoughts perfectly well as I walked slowly away from the dentist's house. I thought like this. That beggar can never touch me like that again. That game is finished for ever, so far as I am concerned. The story is just this:

Stephen went off on Sunday afternoon after a fortnight's embarkation leave. You can guess our thoughts at his departure. Now he has gone. There are no more teeth left You cannot have any more because there are no more. You have got the lot. Nothing particular was said at his departure. 'Goodbye, old man!' and I went off to the bowling green. Katie and Trigo went into Hull to see him off at Paragon Station. I have not asked any questions about that farewell. Katie and I hardly talk on this subject. It is now nearly 3 years since we saw Henry. John is now in Gibraltar and we have no idea how long he will be there. Stephen has promised to telephone us as soon as he knows for certain that he is booked for a sea journey. Well. They cannot draw any more of my teeth because I have not got them to be drawn. So that is the end of this little story. You know what I mean and how I feel.

Did you ever hear of a choirboy called 'SPUD-SPUD'? I didn't give him that name and nobody knows who did but there it is. SPUD-SPUD he is and SPUD-SPUD he will probably be for the rest of his life to many of his old friends. Well. SPUD-SPUD is one of the best boys in my choir. He is never absent from anything, service or practice. He always attends both the morning services although the boys are asked to come once on a Sunday morning. SPUD-SPUD comes twice and is usually one of the two leading boys at both services. He has also at various times been one of the two choir monitors, a little office the boys hold in turn, leaving out all scallywags. They get half a crown extra on quarter day and they all like the little honour that goes with the job. SPUD-SPUD is the best boy I have ever had as a monitor. I could not tell you the very many things he finds to do which are a help to me. I could give you a very long list beginning with the moving of the vestry piano into position and ready for choir practice.

Last Wednesday at the boys' practice SPUD-SPUD was in a wild mood. I had to correct him and to warn him. Soon after the warning he tilted up his chair and went head over heels backwards, much to the delight of all the other choirboys. It was a huge joke. SPUD-SPUD's books and music had to be collected and put together by the monitor of the day, Peter Tutty. SPUD-SPUD got marching orders for that evening and the practice was resumed not much the worse for the little interruption. On Friday the boys came again for a practice and I spoke to SPUD-SPUD before practice began

— 'Now SPUD-SPUD, no nonsense tonight, just see if you can behave yourself.' About ten minutes later I was getting along quite nicely with about twenty boys, having quite a good practice, when suddenly there was a crash, SPUD-SPUD was overboard again, head over heels backwards, and his books and music scattered all over the place. Another practice break down, all the boys in roars of laughter, SPUD-SPUD who wears glasses, rubbing his head somewhat sorrowfully. 'Good night, SPUD-SPUD, not wanted on Sunday next.' On Sunday SPUD-SPUD came to all the services as an ordinary member of the congregation. At the sung eucharist at 9.45 he came up at the right time and place to receive the sacrament and in order to do this he had to pass between the two rows of surpliced boys. I am told that he had a broad grin on his spectacled face as he went up to the altar.

Well. I don't bear SPUD-SPUD any ill feeling for this little affair. It struck me as being rather funny. I have no doubt he will be in his old place next Sunday. Until quite recently two of my choirboys were related to each other not as brothers but as uncle and nephew. SPUD-SPUD was the nephew. Kenneth Forster was the uncle.

I seem to get on quite nicely without any watch or timepiece. I get up just the same time every morning by instinct, just about 6.30 and when I go off to the Humber bank on a general prowl round I manage to run home just about correct dinner time. But there I have the trains to help me. I know a good deal about these morning trains and they are as good as a watch to me. Now I must go back to the income tax problems. My word, I never dreamed that I would have to pay over £50 in income tax. I suppose it is right but I shall look into it. The beggars bag my money before I see it. Never mind. Good luck, Phil.

B.S.83 29th September 1942

It was quite like old times to hear the sirens blowing off yesterday afternoon (No.739). We have had but seven calls throughout this month and none at all during the past twelve days. It was quite cheerful to hear them all going again about 4.30 p.m. Nothing seemed to be going off anywhere and nobody seemed to be bothered or surprised and by tea time the relief sounded.

Today is Michaelmas Day. At church last Sunday we were made, by an absent vicar, to celebrate this festival by singing a succession of hymns all about angels. Charlie is away enjoying his summer holiday and he left instructions that the hymns selected were not to be altered or changed in any way. That was the message I received by way of the curate. Now please consider what I had to do in regard to teaching the choirboys to sing these angelic hymns. At the present time it seems to me that the young people are not taught properly. I have boys of eight and nine years of age who cannot read one verse of a psalm or hymn without floundering badly over many of the words. I don't see how little boys can be expected to sing psalms and hymns when they cannot read them. I have practically no men in my choir now. Those old stagers who still come along to the choir, Sunday after Sunday, have long since qualified for the old age pension and do not possess half a dozen good notes between them. Wheezy — I should say. All of them.

But here we are and my twenty Hessle choir lads, reading the hymns through before attempting to sing them — 'Raise the Trisagion ever and ay.' What do you make of that and what do you think little Anthony Irwing, aged eight, thought about it? 'These keep the guard amid Salem's dear bowers; Thrones, Principalities, Virtues and Powers; Where with the Living One's, mystical four, Cherubim, Seraphim bow and adore.' Now Trevor Cleaver just read through that verse. 'Principalities' is a mouthful for that little fellow and I only have three quarters of an hour for practice.

'The angels standing before God's throne
Bright things they see,
Sweet harps they hold, And on their heads are crowns of gold.'
Bah! Silly nonsense. That is what this choirmaster has to say about it. Yet I have to teach this mush to my little boys. Here's another one:

'. . . . the warrior Primate,
Of celestial chivalry,
Michael who in princely virtue,
Cast Abaddon from on high!'

(E.H. 241)

Before I went down to practice I looked up a book of reference about 'Abaddon' in case any questions came up. When we read and practised this hymn the boys were completely disinterested in the whole subject of Michael and Abaddon and the sweet harps and the gold crowns. I wish Michael, if he had any power in these days, would set about Hitler as he did about Abaddon, according to Milton. We might get the whole world going again in a happy and peaceful manner. After all, today is St. Michael's Day. Let us put in a prayer for peace and get on to my next subject.

INCOME TAX. When I was a boy I remember there was a lot of talk about income tax. I don't know who invented this tax or how long it has been going on, but I do remember that fifty or sixty years ago the tax was about 2d. in the pound and there was a very big growl when it went up to 6d. Income tax has never bothered me very much. Occasionally I have had to pay a pound or two but I have generally escaped altogether — a small income, a wife and four children and I have not had much trouble. It comes to me as rather an 'eye-opener' to find that I have been taxed to the amount of £66. If anyone had told me ten or twenty years ago that my income tax was going to be £66 in any one year I should have wondered whatever had brought wealth to me like that. Well. There it is. I don't exactly pay the tax, the money is taken away from me before I ever see it and in a sense I don't miss it and we seem to get along all right without it. Nowadays we don't have holiday trips to Norway, Holland or the Hebrides. About sixpence a day sees me through all personal expenses and I never seem to be in want of new clothes or boots so the tax chap may as well have that £66. It makes me laugh, all the same. A good job I do not smoke. Eh? Phil.

B.S.84 13th October 1942

I had a very narrow squeak last week. It was all my own fault and I need never have run any risk at all. I only just escaped by the skin of my teeth, as sayeth the Prophet Job. Up to the present I have not taken the slightest interest in coupons and all that coupons stand for. I know that once or twice Katie has set me the task of filling up names on coupons and I rather object to being called 'JBFJ No.228'. If I really am a JBFJ I should prefer to be the only one in that class. Some little time ago Katie began worrying about my coupons, the ones you have to use for new clothes etc. It seemed that these coupons had to be used up no later than Saturday last, October 10th. I kept on saying that I would go into Hull with my book of coupons just to see what I could do with them but I kept on postponing my visit. Some days it rained and on other days the bowling green was so attractive that I had to spend my time there, it was absurd to think of going into poor old shattered Hull.

Then Katie began to threaten me — If I were not going to use the coupons she was going to use them herself. I did not think that was playing the game — not within the meaning of the act — so to speak, and I would not agree to that. Eventually I ran into Mr. Needham's, my tailor, (No. 15 The Weir) and had a talk with him. He told me that the last order I had given him was in the spring of 1939. So I asked him if he would like some coupons, just to be going on with. He seemed delighted with the idea. When I handed him my book he was as pleased as Punch and said he had never seen anything like it. I asked him if he was referring to the JBFJ business, but he said it was not that which made him happy, it was the sight of so many coupons all in one book and unattached. I told him just to help himself and with a big pair of tailor's scissors he cut out 26 of my coupons. I asked him what he was going to do with them and he replied that he would send them along to the bank. That sounds a fairly good idea. Before I left the shop, and after talking about our sons and their whereabouts and their military careers, I wondered if there was anything else to be done, for instance, have a look at a bit of cloth, but nothing else transpired and I came home feeling much relieved by the disgorging of the coupons.

Thursday came along and I still had a few coupons left and Katie again said she was going to pinch them if I did not use them and I replied that if she did such a trick as that I would report her to the local manager or inspector, for I suppose somebody looks after this coupon game. When she was quite sure I did not intend to give away my coupons she looked up some list and told me what my remaining coupons would purchase — a pair of walking shoes and a pair of cotton swimming drawers. Off I went into Hull and soon got quite a nice pair of shoes. I suppose it's all right. I gave the young man a couple of pound notes and he gave me back a few shillings and he left me with just one coupon, although I had told him to help himself. He might just as well have cleared me out, seeing that time was so short and the problem of spending just one coupon and no more than one is not so easy to solve. Anyhow, I came home with one coupon and thought no more about it. On Friday I met my tailor at my garden gate when I was sweeping up the leaves which blow on to the grass from all sides of The Weir. I asked him how my coupons were getting on at the bank and he seemed quite pleased to report that they were doing all right but didn't think there would be any interest. Anyhow it is nice to know they are in good hands.

On Saturday afternoon I played at another wedding — that's one of the shoes, anyhow, and, as I have to play at another wedding this afternoon, I have got two new shoes without much trouble and the few shillings change. Well. After Saturday's wedding I went to the bowling green and then came home for tea. Katie frightened me — Oh, gracious! There is that one coupon of yours and Mr. Needham will be closed in five minutes. I handed my book over to her, the one guilty coupon still there. Why had I not thrown it away? Nobody would have found me out. Off she went and I went on with my tea. All's well that ends well. I had to pay out 1/9d and in return Katie presented me with a couple of new handkerchiefs. As a matter of a fact I like a nice new handkerchief, it has a nice smell about it and I enjoy blowing my nose as long as the smell lasts. It is better than scent. So I have had two real good days with new handkerchiefs, Sunday and Monday last.

We had our Harvest Festival last Sunday. When we were all singing 'Come, ye thankful people, come' I wondered how many people there are still living who remember the composer of that hymn tune (St. George). This hymn, always to the same tune, appears in practically every published hymn book and it is sung all over the world. Yes. I remember old George Elvey. I remember him quite well. He had something to do with my coming to Hessle. The vicar of Hessle, in 1901, the year I came to Hessle, was Sir George Elvey's brother-in-law. It is a long story but there it is. I came here because I had a St. George's training as a choirboy. That appealed to Savory, the vicar of Hessle. You will remember where I began the life of an organist. Stephen is now in that city. I wonder what he is doing there. Best love, Phil.

B.S.85 27th October 1942

I suppose it is the general rule in most churches for the curate, the junior curate if there are two or more, to take all the christenings. You cannot imagine an elderly and learned vicar wasting his precious time over babies and christenings. That is the job for the young curate. The curates don't like this view but they just have to put up with it. Well. Just now we have one curate. If you look through the register of baptisms you will see that he has taken practically every christening since he arrived here. You would have to look a long time before you saw the vicar's signature in that record book. Well, one day not so long ago a christening party was late and my friend Wilkes sat in the vestry and, not having anything particular to do, he went on signing his name not only to the record for that day but he went on and on. It was perfectly clear that he was going to christen all the little Hessle babes for many a long day and so he went on signing his name to the blank records, enough to last the Hessle babes for quite a long time. It was like a schoolboy scrawling his name over and over again for mere mischief.

Then Wilkes went off for a bit of a holiday and the vicar had to roll up his shirt sleeves and get to work. Lo and behold, according to the register Wilkes had already christened a good half dozen babes before they were born. I have not heard the end of the story. It is not really in my department. P.

B.S.87 24th November 1942

Those evening bells. How many a tale their music tells. We were told that our church bells could ring once more on Sunday, 15th November. They have been silent ever since the war commenced more than three years ago. There are children in Hessle, including some of the church choirboys, who cannot remember that they have ever heard our Hessle bells. Our curate, Wilkes, has been here for 18 months and has never heard the church bells ringing for a service. We have a very tuneful peal of six bells. You can ring a lot of changes on a peal of six bells but our local ringers were not given to study or to over-work. In fact they were very feeble at the job. They seldom started ringing punctually, i.e. half an hour before the service, and when they did start they were generally one short, sometimes two short or even three. The late comers would drop in and the ringing would change from three to four bells,from four to five and from five to six, as the late comers arrived. They never attempted any Bob Majors or whatever you call them. They would ring six bells in the order of the scale, from La to Do, for a few minutes and then someone would shout an order and there would be a change, Nos. 1 and 2 would reverse, so to speak and Nos. 3 and 4 would do the same. Thus a little variety was obtained but it was a poor effort at its best. The ringers never seemed to take an interest in the service to which they rang an invitation. As the choir trooped into the church the ringers were just going away, putting on their coats and going out by the side door next to the vestry.

I laughed when I heard that we were to hear the church bells once more. They could not ring them when there was no war and it was certain they could not ring them after 3 years without any practising. Also, three of the ringers had died, and two more had left Hessle, leaving one regular ringer and perhaps a couple of reserves. No. There would be no bell ringing at

Hessle Church, whatever might happen elsewhere. At least that was how I decided the case.

Now hear what actually happened on that Sunday, Armistice Sunday, 15th November. I went to church just before 9 a.m. I was passing along the west side of Hessle Square towards the church. A soldier stopped me and asked to be directed to the parish church. That made me laugh. The church was about 50 yards away. Where were his eyes? It was a bit foggy but not enough to hide the church from where we met. I asked Tommy what he wanted at the church ¾ of an hour before the next service. He said he was going to help with the bells. Lo and behold, when I got to the church I found at least a dozen soldiers playing with the bell ropes under the tower. A very large and smart sergeant seemed to be in charge of the party, one man to each rope and one, or even two reserves to stand by each ringer. The boss was giving instructions for something they could not possibly have rehearsed together, namely, how to ring Hessle Church bells.

I was alone in the vestry when the 'pulling up' process began. And then somehow or other I had a bad attack of emotion. The ringing of the bells, just the irregular preliminaries, upset me and I sat down on a chair and had a gentle weep. 'That's queer,' said I to myself. 'How silly and ridiculous.' Then off the bells went. My choirboy monitor, Owen Andrews, turned up to give me a hand with the books and hymn numbers etc. and I recovered my equilibrium and the day's work began and the bells went on ringing and everybody rejoiced and I was quite wrong in thinking that Hessle Church bells could not be rung.

A day or two before Armistice Sunday I had my 44th wedding. 44 since this year commenced. The bride came to see me about the hymns. She was with her mother. They decided to have only one hymn as they said there would not be a big 'audience'.

Trigo goes every Sunday evening to a military canteen in Hessle. It is very good of her to give up her Sunday evenings to this work. It is a four hours' job, 6.30 to 10.30. When she went off last Sunday evening I said, quite in fun. 'If you come across a chess player, send him along here.' About 7.30 there was sound of many footsteps at our front door and Katie and I looked at each other, wondering what it meant. In walked Trigo with a couple of hefty soldiers in tow. 'Here you are, daddy, here are your chess players', and she deposited two nice looking young soldiers, one of them a corporal , and she returned to her work at the canteen. I think Katie and I were rather glad of a little company. Stephen has told us recently how very good some Norwich people have been to him and we feel we should be passing on kindness like that to some of the soldiers now stationed in this district. Well. They were very moderate chess players but very good company and they stayed with us until 11 p.m. I hope they will come again. We never learned their names. One of them talked to his wife at Wembley by using our telephone and he was careful to pay me the trunk call fee of 2/4d for six minutes.

You remember my story about my tailor and my coupons. My friend has just telephoned to me to ask me to call, so perhaps after all I have not heard the end of that story. I was wondering how the coupons were getting on at the bank. Best love, Phil.

B.S.88 8th December 1942

Let me begin with geese. The geese don't seem to worry too much about aeroplanes. Ever since I came to Hessle I have heard the geese flying about overhead at night time in the late summer, November and early December. You stand out in the garden and look up and you can see nothing, but you can hear the geese, they don't seem able to fly without cackling, or whatever you call their cry. One night, some years ago, the geese settled down on the house tops of Hessle. The village was full of the geese, every house had a goose or two on its roof. Why they did it that way I do not know. As a rule they fly over Hessle and get onto to the mud banks of the River Humber where they spend their nights.

And now to end this coupon story. It seems that not only do I give up all claim to 26 coupons at Barclay's Bank but also I have to pay £9 12 6d. Great Scott. That's a big figure for a suit of clothes, leaving out the coupons altogether. Nearly £10 for a suit of clothes is a bit thick. I have now worn my new garments once or twice. I notice there are no 'turn-ups'. Well. That is something that I quite agree with. The tailor has to make his trousers straight, so to speak, because there is a war going on. That's funny. It takes a war to break down a silly and unclean custom about men's clothes. Then he hasn't given me any buttons on my coat sleeves. Here again for a very long time I have refused to have buttons on my sleeves. They used to hinder my violoncello playing. I could not play with buttons on my coat sleeve; the buttons now and then struck the wood of my instrument. So I have removed them whenever the tailor put them on the coat. So that is another foolish idea the war has brought to an end. The tailor says I must have a hip pocket in the trousers. I don't want it but I have got to have it, there is a war on. I am not allowed to have a breast pocket etc. I can't have it, there is a war on. I am not allowed the little watch pocket in my coat to which I am accustomed, there is a war on. I have to carry my watch in my trouser side pocket. It isn't safe there so I leave it at home. I cannot have my watch because there is a war on. Goodbye, Phil.

B.S.89 22nd December 1942

The other night my friend Mrs. Harvey telephoned to ask me to make up a four at bridge. She knew that Katie would be going to help at the military canteen and that I should probably be alone. She told me that Professor Milne would be spending the evening at her house and she wanted to entertain him. I accepted the invitation gladly. Arthur Milne was a Hessle boy. I remember him as a boy. He began his education at the local church schools which are under the East Riding Education Board. The same school that my boys went to later on. Arthur Milne won a scholarship to Hymers College, Hull, and from that college he won a scholarship that took him to Clare College, Cambridge. I believe he had a brilliant career there and became a Fellow, whatever that may mean. At the present time he holds some high office at Oxford University. I am not well up in these affairs or I would have told you more exactly. Anyhow Arthur Milne is a well-known Professor at Oxford. I asked Katie, 'What is he a professor of?' 'Astronomy', Katie replied. So I said to myself, I must not talk about astronomy.

It was pleasant and nice to talk to him. I gathered that he had been out to Texas with a party sent there to observe a total eclipse of the sun. So Katie, as usual, was right. Professor Milne lost one penny at bridge. I won it. Good Biz. He and I left the house together and, as we walked down Davenport Avenue and faced due east, we could not help noticing the brilliance of the planet Jupiter. It was just below Castor and Pollux, the Gemini twin stars. The three, one planet and two stars, made a brilliant picture in the clear heaven above. Notwithstanding my resolution to refrain from astronomical subjects, I could not resist speaking about the conjunction of Jupiter with the Gemini twins. The professor astonished me when he said he thought the bright one was Sirius, the Dog Star. I could hardly believe my ears. As it so happened, Sirius was also visible at the time, low down in the south, a little bit south-east, just above the horizon looking above the broad Humber. 'There is Sirius' I said. In Australia you see him at the top of Orion. Now as we see him here, he is below Orion.' I remember how queer it seemed to me to see Sirius the wrong way up. That was during my 1911 tour. When I got home I said to Katie, 'Did you say that Arthur Milne is a professor of astronomy?' 'Yes', Katie replied and Katie is never wrong, always right. That is the end of the story. It is like one of those told by the Western Brothers.

You know all my children had lessons on my typewriter, that is to say they just 'had a go' whenever the chance arose. Stephen now seems almost sorry that he can use a typewriter, for it seems he has been drafted into an office where his fingers are kept going pretty busily every day. The other day an official brought him a notice which he was told to type out. Here it is :-
ENYONE FOUND TAKING WASH BASIN OUT OF WASH HOUSE AND ENYONE FOUND WASHING IN BILLITTS WILL BE DELTH WITH. Good. Now you know. You will be delth with.

I suppose you never heard of Mr. Smith. He was a very old boy, 92 to be correct. He lived in Barrow Lane, Hessle. He had a shop on Anlaby Road, Hull, to which a post office was attached. Even at 92 the old boy went off to business every morning. A year or so ago his shop was completely blitzed, but he soon got going again, post office and all, elsewhere and near the old place. Only a few weeks ago he was at Buckingham Palace where he received an O.B.E. from the hands of the King. I heard much about this visit to His Majesty. It was the talk of Hessle but it all came to an end when the old boy was knocked down on the Anlaby Road by a motor vehicle, and killed. The coroner, in giving his verdict of accidental death, said he thought Mr. Smith had gone on a bit too long. A man should retire before he gets to 90. So say I. But I knew Mr. Smith and am sorry he has gone. Goodbye, Phil.

1943

B.S.90 5th January 1943

Thank you for César Franck. In my B.S. 81 I said that if anyone came across a second-hand copy of César Franck's *Sonata for Violin and Piano* I should be very glad to have that copy. I don't think French published music is obtainable in this country. On New Year's Day a brand new copy of this work arrived from Victoria B.C. It was a Christmas present from Kittie. A jolly good present, too. Trigo and I were rather keen to have a preliminary run through this Franck sonata but, alas, when she opened her violin case, the tail piece had collapsed and the instrument was in a sad condition. We have not got it going again just yet and I have to be content with the piano part alone. Trigo has now a pretty big library of violin and piano sonatas. We have just been through Mozart's 19 sonatas, one of which, the *Fugue in No. 13*, floored me. We are now studying Beethoven's *No. 4 in E flat*, a real beauty. Fancy an old man and a professional musician , nearly 71 years of age, learning Beethoven, Mozart and Brahms, and now César Franck. You can see this violin business has done me a world of good. I practise these sonatas almost every evening. With the kid, if she's available, if not, then without her. A new musical vista has opened out to me in my old age.

Yesterday one of my bowling club friends came up to the organ. Mr. Brindley Evans. I have known him for several years. 'Well, I had no idea you played the organ,' he said. A remark that caused me deep reflection. Nearly 42 years I've been at that job!! And one of my many bowling friends. Well. Well. Well. Best love and a Happy New Year to you all, Phil.

B.S.91 19th January 1943

What do you think of this next story and choir discipline: Last Sunday at the end of the Creed the one and only tenor, Len Emerson, turned to the one and only alto, Mrs. Katie Chignell, and he said, 'T'owd tin pot's done.' You can't guess this one. — The old tin pot referred to is the silver teapot won in 1883 by Private W.H. Chignell of the Artists' Volunteers, which came into my possession so many years ago that I forget how it came to me. T'owd tin pot has been under repair. When Len Emerson has a watch or anything else to repair you don't go into his shop to ask if the job is finished. Some day you will meet him in the street or in the church and he will then, from his trouser pocket, produce the repaired watch, name a price and leave you to call when you like with the money to pay him for his work. But I wonder what Charlie (our vicar) would have thought if Len Emerson, at the end of the Creed, had produced t'owd tin pot and with a flourish had handed it over the choir seats to my beloved wife. I wonder what the choirboys would have thought about it. Best love, Phil.

B.S.92 2nd February 1943

So far this winter, the fourth winter of the war, we have had no ice or snow and the weather has been very open and pleasant. Snowdrops are now showing and there are many signs of a coming spring. There is still time for a nasty spell but so far we have had a very easy winter. I, for one, am thankful because I hate frosty weather. I hate it more and more as I grow older. Well. There has not been much to grumble about this time.

In the past few days I have lost two very good bowling friends, the vicar of Sutton (Charles Paley) and the treasurer of our Hessle Bowling Club, J.W.Sharpe. Parson Paley was a keen and good player and it was always nice to see him, with his Sutton men, trundling the merry woods and taking a lively interest in the scores and the match, and in fact enjoying himself as much as any of us. Jack Sharpe succeeded me as treasurer of the Hessle Club about nine years ago. He was a schoolmaster by profession and he was certainly one of the leading lights in our club until a year or two ago when it was said he was suffering from heart trouble and was forbidden to play bowls because of the stooping. Jack Sharpe is the only player who has won the championship twice. In the summer of 1939 I was fortunate enough to beat Jack in the final or he would have had his name engraved on that cup for the third time. Jack was only 61 years of age when he died yesterday morning. Four years ago he retired from his school work and spent most of his mornings in his garden. I got into the habit of paying him a visit every Friday morning about 11.30. We used to have long talks about our boys and about bowls and buzzers and bombs and blitzes.

Philip's sister, Isabel ('Jezebel').

Last Thursday, January 28th, my services were called upon for a memorial service at Hessle church — Mr. J.W. Powell — a gentleman I knew quite well. He was managing director of Hammonds Ltd. (Hull's Selfridges). You probably remember the huge building close to Hull Paragon Station. This very big and up-to-date establishment was completely knocked out in the blitz of May 1941. The ruins have all been cleared away now and the site stands ready for the new buildings that are bound to rise up as soon as someone gives the 'go ahead' order. Business now goes on in various buildings nearby the old site. Every department was closed last Thursday and the staff came over to Hessle to attend the memorial service. In addition, there were a great many Hull business men and Hull Masons present. The queer part about this service was the absence of any coffin or hearse. The body had gone off to the crematorium. I just gave ten minutes' music, including the *andante* from a string quartet of Schubert. A short lesson, a psalm, two or three prayers and then Beethoven's *Funeral March,* all standing. All over in a few minutes. Funny, but why this fuss? Mr J.W. Powell never came inside our church, so why hold a memorial service for him there? Why not on Hammonds' ruined site? Perhaps I shall charge two guineas on this occasion. It was my show anyhow. The other chap didn't turn up. I must think it over. Best love, Phil.

B.S.93 16th February 1943

Another yarn of a domestic nature — the price of electricity. I have just paid my electricity bill for the three months, October, November and December, 1942. I find that for the past quarter the electricity cost me a trifle less then 5d. a day. You cannot grumble at that. During the winter months we had house lighting every day from 6.30 to about 9.15 a.m. and then again from somewhere round about 5 to 11.30 p.m. often three or four lights going. Electric kettle whenever tea or coffee or shaving water is wanted. Two electric hot plates for pans, sometimes used when the kettle goes wrong. An electric oven and a grill — but there I don't really know all the cooking devices there are out at the back. I know I can get a cup of tea in the early morning in two minutes. Once or twice lately in the dead of night I have had an attack of cramp. Beastly business. Remedy — come downstairs and make a cup of tea. Cramp all gone. Creep back to bed and forget all about it. Well. Then there is the wireless business. Our wireless is run by electricity. We don't give the motive power a thought. If we want the wireless we turn a switch and it is on, if we don't want it we turn the switch off and there you are. No trouble at all and all included in the 5d a day. Then we have an electric fire that can be used in half a dozen places in the house. I find it very useful in my little attic study. It warms the place up in no time and it can be run at half cock if desired. The same fire is very nice on a really cold night in the bedroom, but we don't often use it in that way. It is nice to have it as a standby. Perhaps Trigo wants to do a bit of fiddle practice in a room where there is no fire, the electric heater meets the case in five minutes. The piano tuner may call or a stray visitor may turn up, the electric fire comes in splendidly. This electric fire is our property but the stove and the kettle and the electric boiler and an electric iron, which so far I have forgotten to mention, belong to Hull Corporation who charge us rents for these commodities and keep the same in good going order. The 5d. per day covers all these rents. It is not a bad bargain and we should all be very sorry to return to gas. We do not use gas anywhere in the house now but we were one of the last houses in The Weir to make the change over.

Stephen is at home this week for a few days. He came to us from somewhere up in Perthshire. We are still puzzling why his homeward route took him to Norwich for a few hours, but it did. On his return ticket from Norwich to his depot, or whatever you call it, he managed to drop off at Hessle station and there was nothing to pay. I don't know how he managed it. This slickness reminds me of 'Gumgum' who had a lot of tricks up his sleeve in the railway travelling line. John wants me to send him a typewriter to Gibraltar. No matter the cost. I have that little matter on hand just now. We get letter-cards from Stalag VIII B fairly regularly but we can do nothing but answer them in a guarded manner. Oh. When will it all end? Best love, Phil.

B.S.94 2nd March 1943

It is evening. The blackout curtains and blinds have been drawn up (7 p.m.) and I have shut myself in for the night. I hope I have a nice and quiet evening, in the good company of my Corona typewriter, my Marshall and Rose piano, my Mullard wireless to hear what the Brains' Trust has to say, and the two books I am reading just at present viz. *Country Doctor* (Balzac) and *Precious Bane* (Mary Webb). My pocket set of chessman is close at hand but just at present it does not appeal to me very much. I have locked the front door and bolted the yard gate. Nobody can get at me. I will not answer the door to anyone. Katie and Trigo are both out for the evening and I am alone and I want to be alone, too. This brings me round to a difficulty we have had here just lately. How much hospitality is due from residents in Hessle to the troops stationed here just now? It is a big question. Hessle has not much in the way of entertainment to offer these young men, men of all classes and thought. There is the Plaza cinema but two visits there a week is about the limit, I should say. Katie is at the local canteen at the present time, but it is not a very cheerful place from what I hear. Not well heated, refreshments on the light side, not much room for games, cards or billiards, nothing very attractive about it. It is true Hull is only five miles away and there are a good many cinemas running there, although one or two have been blitzed out altogether. There are one or two theatres and music halls in Hull but the last 'bus home to Hessle leaves at 9 p.m. and that is too early for anybody.

No. These good soldiers find Hessle a dull place and I am sorry for them. Last night one of them called here at about 6.30 and asked to see me. He said he was a violinist in a well-known dance band and he wanted to borrow a violin. The whole question was settled in five minutes. I could do nothing for him, I was not going to suggest that Trigo should lend her instrument and I did not feel called upon to go surety for a violin to any of my Hessle friends, seeing I had never seen the man before, Anyhow my new friend settled down in an armchair and made himself comfortable. He stayed and had a bit of supper and eventually cleared off at 10.30. Four hours we had of him, just talking, and I had mapped out my evening just as I have mapped out this evening. No wonder I have locked my doors tonight and will not reply to any bells or knockers.

John, Henry and Stephen have told of many friends they have made in various places they have been stationed. We feel that we must make some effort to pass on the hospitality that has been shown to our boys. But tonight. Well. I have locked myself in. I want to be alone.

A parcel came from Stephen yesterday morning, a few things he did not want to take away with him. He has gone off goodness knows where. It may be weeks before we get any news of him, and yet my telephone bell may ring and I may get talking to him as I have talked to all three of them many, many times on long distance calls. A bob or so and you can talk for three minutes. For this alone our telephone has been worth having. I am afraid we shall get no more distance calls for the present. Phil.

B.S.95 16th March 1943

We have had lately some very extraordinary weather. Quite unusual for this time of year. Day after day it is just the same. No rain or moisture. Hard, dry and frosty in the early part of the morning. Warming up as the sun gets going. Afternoons of glorious sunshine and warmth. This is the sort of weather that suits aeroplaning, I suppose. Our evenings have been rather disturbed lately. An alarm last night brought our total up to 771. All the same, that only makes our figure for 1943 to 20, which is not very alarming. 20 in 74 days. Best love, Phil.

B.S.96 30th March 1943

This is a good day for a B.S. letter, is it not? The Old Man's birthday. One hundred and two years ago today. I wonder how many of the children born in this country today will be talked of with affection in the year 2045. My typewriter almost refuses to type out those figures, the time seems so remote.

I played three games of chess last night with Ted Starkey, a member of the Hull Chess Club. I had almost forgotten all about him, the club being now closed and inactive. He telephoned to me about tea time and asked if he might come over for a game some time or other. I fixed up with him to come over at once. I had rather a shock when he turned up. How he managed to ride a bicycle I could not imagine. His left arm was all wrong. Smashed up. Poor fellow. He looked half a corpse. He had been in the wars and was lucky to be alive, even in the poor condition that I saw him. He had been bombed at sea, thrown into the water half dead, rescued, taken into hospital somewhere over there. Not particularly well treated. Patched up so far as possible and, after a month or two, bundled off on to another ship for home and country. Bombed again and once more rescued from the sea, and once more treated in hospital. This time, a home hospital and doctors and nurses of his own nationality. He will never be fit for work again but he can play chess all right. All his bombs and half drowning don't seem to have spoiled his chess. He won two games out of three against me. All the same I promise you he won't do that again, not the next time he comes over to Hessle on his bicycle. Next time I shall think of chess only and not of bombs and shipwrecks.

One day last week, March 18th, to be correct, I went off on a little charitable excursion. I was asked to visit the grave of a young Australian airman who had met his death, by accident, in this country and is now buried in a little churchyard about twelve miles from here, at Leconfield. A bus ride of 50 minutes and a walk of three miles and I was in the little churchyard where Kenneth S. Cadd now lies buried in company with about twenty other young airmen. For March it was a perfectly brilliant day. Spring flowers and especially the daffodils were all in flower. That March day was borrowed from June. It seemed quite wrong to think about these two dozen young airmen, dead, sleeping the eternal sleep here in this little countryside churchyard. I called at the vicarage and the door was opened by his reverence — Douglas Birt — very pleasant and kind. What can he find to do in such a little place? He was pleased to know that I intended to write to Cottesloe to say something about Kenneth S. Cadd's grave. But what can I say? I can't send Kenneth home again. There are no flowers on his grave. It is too fresh. One day, perhaps, I will visit it again. Perhaps there will be a rose or a violet or even a daffodil growing close to the grave. One day, perhaps, I will send an English flower from that little country churchyard over to sunny Australia. All the same, even Australia could not beat the beautiful March sunshine as I saw and felt it in the little churchyard up country there, where Kenneth S. Cadd and his friends are buried. Alack. Such is war. We have no idea where Stephen has got to. P.

B.S. 97 13th April 1943

I celebrated my birthday yesterday by having a game of bowls in the afternoon followed by an egg for my tea when I got home. Some festivity, that. It is not often our bowling season opens so early in April as this. The weather all through this year, so far, has been of a mild nature and we have escaped any really cold wintry weather. Everything, including bowls, is in advance of its usual time.

We had a very extraordinary day last Wednesday, April 7th. A violent gale sprung up and worried us all day long. About dinner time the weather-cock on the top of the church spire took a sudden leap downwards and brought with it some of the stonework from the spire. This fell right through the roof of the church close to the font and did a great deal of damage. The church spire now looks like a man with a bald head. I keep on looking up to see which way the wind is blowing but the iron bird has now retired from work and lies in the corner of the church. Hundreds of people have been to see it and to talk about it for this bird has a story and the story is this: About 60 years ago Freddie Coulthard, who lived in a house almost next door to the church, fired three shots at this harmless and inanimate but useful bird. With his third shot Freddie hit it, so the story goes, but nobody ever knew why he wasted his powder and shot in this way. True enough, there is a bullet hole in the tail of the cockerel, and all these visitors want to see this hole and talk about it. The poor old cockerel lies there, the centre of the talk and the interest, with its 60-year-old bullet wound and a queer little vacant look in its one little eye, the eye a mere hole in the metal but with a certain amount of expression, even in this mere hole. At choir practice every choirboy had to have his share in this excitement before I could begin any kind of work with my little gang.

On one side of his tail there is an ornamental inscription — H. NEWMARCH B.A. Vicar. JOHN CLARK, G.S.HAYES, Churchwardens 1853. On the other side of his tail — H.NEWMARCH B.A. Vicar, J.W.PEASE, A.BANNISTER, Churchwardens 1877. There is no mention of the organists of those days. I suppose he was not so important a person as he is in more modern times. One man told me that on Wednesday he looked up to the top of the church spire to see which way the wind was blowing. A minute afterwards he looked up again and the cockerel had vanished. He could not believe his eyes and wondered if he had overstayed his time at the Marquis of Granby. Best love, Phil.

B.S.98 27th April 1943

Our fine old church spire has scaffolding right up to the top of it. Scaffolding that has taken a whole week to erect without doing any kind of repair. This little jump of the church weather-cock during the gale of April 7th is going to cost the church a pretty penny. It will be weeks before the little cockerel is re-erected and then there is the gaping hole in the roof, just over the font at the west end of the church, which will have to be repaired.

It is rather depressing to think of all the pounds and pounds spent by Hessle church upon insurances — insure this and insure that. If I sprained my ankle in playing the *Hallelujah Chorus* on the organ on Easter Sunday, some company would have to shell out, but if the weathercock up aloft does a jump and goes through the church roof, well — that's that — It's a big joke and nothing to do with any insurance company. I have no doubt that the expense will be met all right but there seems to be something wrong somewhere. You know we had a big church hall erected in 1938 on a site next to the churchyard and due south. As a going concern it had just started on its career when the war came along. It was commandeered as a hospital for air raid casualties and the church is being paid £250 a year for the use of the hall. So perhaps the cockerel's little escapade will be paid for out of the church hall's rents. Perhaps.

The sooner they get the little cockerel back on his pedestal up aloft the better for me and my choir practices. The little beggar at present is spending his days and nights in the church vestry where we hold our choir practices. The choirboys don't seem able to give me any attention with the little cockerel looking on with his vacant hole of an eye; he seems to be looking all over the vestry at the same time, regarding myself and every one of the choirboys. He seems to have cast a spell over us. The boys can't sing a bit and I can't teach them. I am sure he laughed, or at least his one vacant eye twinkled the other night, when Georgie Scott, reading his verse from psalm 130, read: 'Before the morning WITCH, I say, before the morning WITCH.'

Letter from Stephen today. He is somewhere in North Africa. I wonder where. Best love, Phil.

B.S.99 10th May 1943

Do you remember the weekly newspaper that came to 10 Regina Road every weekend — *Sunday At Home?* I wonder if you remember it. Mother was keen on that journal, also *Chamber's Journal*. The *Sunday At Home* is my text for B.S. 99.

I have had two Sundays free from organ playing, hymns and psalms and choirboys, since April 1939. Over four years and only two Sundays away from Hessle Church organ. I suppose it is my own concern but nobody ever suggests that my turn has come for a little holiday. The two Sundays I have had in four years were both spent in Owston Ferry on the Trent. I was half inclined to go there again for a weekend but I really thought I would go right away somewhere or other for about a week.

I looked up timetables for all sorts of places, including Worthing and Leominster. That little game gave me some amusement for Bradshaw always interests me. London and the Royal Academy passed through my mind. But I became timid when I heard my men friends at the bowling club talking about their experiences travelling — standing all the way to Leeds — standing all the way to Kings Cross — queuing up an hour before the train was timed to leave Hull. I asked at the Hessle booking office what the present fare to Kings Cross might be. A girl told me it was 36/2d. If that is the single fare, and that was what I asked for, a return ticket to Kings Cross would be £3 12 4d. It used to be about 25/- return. It is perfectly clear that the railway people do not want stray passengers on their trains, which always seem full of soldiers. An old man with no particular object in view is best at home. That is where the *Sunday At Home* came in. I just stayed at home all day yesterday. The sweetest hours were those of church time. It was lovely to sit down and think of all that hymn singing going on in Hessle Church, just over the road, and somebody else playing the organ and looking after the choirboys and putting the hymn numbers up on the boards. All the same I hope they missed me. I shall be back at work again next Sunday. Even so, three Sundays off in four years leaves me still something in hand. Goodbye, Phil.

B.S.100 25th May 1943

I have two little stories to tell you today:
What Lionel said to me.
What Oswald said to me.
Which shall I begin with? I will toss a coin. Oswald has it.

Many years ago Oswald Hillerns took me to see a new building erected in Nile Street, Hull. He opened the locked door with a master key and he took me all over the building. Oswald was proud of that building for it was the first time he had ever had one of his designs accepted. Oswald was an architect by profession. He was young in those days and a very handsome and lovable man. One of the most charming young men I have ever met. He was of German parentage but was born in this country, went to an English public school and I never heard him speak a word of German. The building that he designed was a Lutheran Church intended for German people resident in Hull or for German seamen who might be in Hull with their ships. 'How do you like it, Chig?' That is what Oswald said to me, forty odd years ago. The 1914 war came along. The hooligans of Hull threw bricks and smashed all the windows of the little church. The pastor and the congregation vanished into thin air. The place was boarded up, afterwards to become a place of storage. I don't know what was stored in it but, whenever I happened to pass the place, I could see it was being used for some commercial purpose and not for any religious ceremony. Oswald was killed in the 1914 war. He was with the English army and his services were used as an interpreter. His name is on our Hessle war memorial. Poor Oswald, he never came home again.

I cycled past Oswald's little church the other day. Blasted. Smashed up.

Windows all gone. Walls tottering. Ruined houses around it. Poor Oswald. Not even of any commercial use now. German bombs have destroyed it. And Oswald himself was a German by birth. Yes. And a great friend of mine.

And now for Lionel and what he said to me somewhere about Christmas, 1923. Lionel was a parson, he was also, *rara avis*, a musician of ability. He had, in his time, been a minor canon at St. George's Chapel, Windsor, and had given up that somewhat flashy appointment on succeeding to a very good family living not so very far from Hull. Lionel succeeded his cousin Robert Hildyard who died quite unexpectedly very soon after his ordination and before he was really established at the vicarage of Rowley, about twelve miles north-west of Hull. History relates that, once upon a time, the whole population of Rowley emigrated to America and founded a town of that name there. Anyhow you can look in vain for any town or even village of Rowley now. The vicarage and church of Rowley both stand in a fine park and, except for two lodges at the gate of the park, there is no other house to be seen. An old map will show you where the site of the old Rowley village is to be found and if, on Sundays, any congregation turns up for the services the people will come from Little Weighton, a mile or so away. Somehow or other the living is a good one, somewhere in the neighbourhood of £800 a year. So I have always heard. Lionel Hildyard very quickly regretted the change from Windsor Castle and all the comings and goings of that famous place to quiet and deserted Rowley where, apparently, there was nothing whatever to do, except what any country gentleman would find to do in a large house surrounded with gardens and paddocks. But what did Lionel say to me just before Christmas 1923? We were having tea together in a Hull café and I told him that we were, in our family. expecting 'an addition'. 'My dear fellow,' Lionel said to me, 'you'll be ruined.' I thought of that remark very keenly. When I got home I told Katie what Lionel had said to me. We talked it over. I thought it was a terrible remark for a parson to make to a prospective father. It rather frightened me. In 1923 I was working at the Hull Savings Bank for a salary that brought me in just about one third of what I was spending, everything taken into consideration. I have all the figures in front of me at this moment. In 1923 the bank paid me £132 and my expenses were £396. John was seven, Henry five, Stephen getting on for two, and then this addition was coming along. Of course, the position was rather serious. How was I to know that my three boys would all win scholarships? Yes. Lionel only said what he thought but it did not cheer me up very much. I remember saying to Katie, 'Well. I hope to live to the day when I can show Lionel how wrong he was to make such a remark as that.' Yes. And I have lived to the day and that day is this day but Lionel does not now live. I cannot cast his words in his teeth. Trigo, the beloved 'addition', is now 19 years of age. The boys have all gone off to the wars, but Trigo is left to us to cheer us up. I have survived the troubles and expenses of rearing a family of four. I don't know what we should do if there had been no Trigo, if the number had remained at three and not advanced to four. Trigo is the life of this house at this time of anxiety. She helps me at the church by singing in the choir and doing the work of the called-up librarian (Stephen) and, with her fiddle, she just prevents me from going absolutely stale in the matter of music. So, Lionel, you were absolutely wrong. Wrong, wrong, wrong. I have not been ruined, I have been blessed by 'the addition'. Good old Trigo. If you ever read these words of mine and I don't know whether you are or are not interested in my B.S. letters, just remember and think about what your Daddy says in his hundredth B.S. letter. And, Lionel, it is too late to say to you, 'Give thy thoughts no tongue!'

The mitoo iris in my garden, which I look to flower about June 12th, this year produced its blooms on May 21st. That shows how early things are this year. Phil.

B.S.102 22nd June 1943

The little cockerel is back on his elevated pedestal at the top of our church spire. He looks quite well and perky up there and everybody is now observing which way the wind is blowing. The little bird has given a good deal of trouble since he came down from the top of the spire during the gale of April 7th. I understand that about eight feet of the spire fell at the same time and that the firm that are still at work with the repairs have had to make up twelve feet of the spire before placing the little cockerel back on its airy swivel. Such a ceremony, too, of names to be inscribed on the little beggar's tail. I think I told you that two sets of names could be seen engraved on the little cockerel's tail. This precedent has been followed with additions. The names of our present vicar and churchwardens have been carved on the tail, but unfortunately an error was made in the spelling — Hoyle instead of Hole — I wonder whose mistake that was. Just like Hessle Church to make a muddle of things. It does not matter. Nobody will ever go up to have a look at these names. The contractor for the job and also the architect have also had their names engraved on the much decorated weathercock. Good luck to them. Nice to know of the advertisement swinging round up there with every change of wind. Well. The old man who has played the organ at Hessle church for over 42 years, who has seen six vicars and is not likely to meet with No.7, who has seen more churchwardens than he can remember, with curates at a penny a dozen. Anyhow, that old organist, to wit, myself, has the satisfaction of knowing that his name, my name, that is, does not turn round, up aloft, with every change of the wind. Another thing — If they were going to spell anybody's name incorrectly, you can bet your last penny that it would have been mine. So all's well that ends well. The cockerel is up aloft again and looks extremely well and happy and thank you for the kind inquiry. Goodbye, Phil.

B.S.103 13th July 1943

I am having trouble at home with my wife and daughter. Last Saturday they went off to Leeds on their own. I certainly had heard some sly talk on the subject of this excursion and so I was not very greatly surprised when I came into dinner, after gardening all morning, to find my meal left out and ready for me. The only trouble I was put to was that I had to make my own cup of coffee and I am not quite sure how you do it. I am all right and good at making tea or cocoa but not so clear about coffee. However, I had a leisurely dinner and left the washing up and was off to the bowling green in time for a friendly match. Rain spoiled this sport and I came home for an early cup of tea and a good long read. Then there was a jolly good Prom concert which I thoroughly enjoyed. I lit a fire in my little drawing room and was perfectly happy and cosy until THE REBELS returned home about 10.30 p.m. They explained why it was so necessary for them to go to Leeds. Here is the yarn — In May 1941 Trigo wanted a new coat. This was purchased for her at Hammond's, in Hull. Paid for and left for some slight alteration. Never delivered. That same night was Hammond's blitzed. Even now the site is a place of desolation, right in the heart of the city. However, in that case the money paid was ultimately refunded. Two years later Trigo needs another coat. That is now, in 1943. The same story. History repeats itself. The two of them trot into Hull. This time they go to Bladon's in Albion Street. Buy a coat, leave it to be slightly altered, pay for it, of course, and then Jerry comes along with another blitz (782) and the coat and everything else has gone. This time the blitzed firm do not cash up but refer us to the Board of Trade. The story is too complicated but I believe it is to the effect that, when the war is over, somebody will pay for that second lost coat. You're telling me, as they say. Now you see the reason for the trip to Leeds. It is too risky leaving new coats lying about in Hull.

I laughed on Sunday when I heard our vicar give out the banns of marriage of a couple whose wedding I had played at a fortnight ago. That is just like Hessle. Our July magazine says that the total amount collected in the offertories during June amounted to £000. 0s. 0d. Hessle Church won't get far on that. Never mind. A big change is in the wind. All the same I fancy if they have a new vicar they will also have to have a new organist. P.

B.S.104 6th August 1943

Yesterday we had another little joke from our sirens. No. 790. Nobody took the slightest notice of the raid warning. I was just getting on my bicycle for a visit to the Humber side. I just went and thought no more about the warning. I was sitting down on the Humber beach worshipping the flow of the tide under the grey clouds of a dull but breezy morning, when the relief siren sounded. The siren I heard most distinctly came from over the water, from Barton in Lincolnshire. The following notes are taken from my pocket book record of siren air raid alarms:

No. 200 — 6th November 1940.
No. 300 — 23rd December 1940.
No. 400 — 25th March 1941.
No. 500 — 13th August 1941.
No. 600 — 24th November 1941.
No. 700 — 29th June 1942.
No. 790 — 5th August 1943.

So you see the business of air raid alarms has slowed down very considerably of late. Good job too.

I wonder what is going to happen at Hessle Church in the immediate future. Our present vicar, Canon Lenton, has four more Sundays to serve. Then he leaves us. What next? No one has yet been appointed to carry on the work. When there is a vacancy like this nobody seems to be in the slightest hurry to fill it up. It is a funny sort of business. When a new vicar arrives he generally begins pretty well. One of the first things he has to do is to gather in the income that has accumulated since the date of death or resignation of the previous vicar. The newcomer gathers in the accumulation as soon as he arrives. I wonder if newly appointed organists ever find three months' salary waiting for them to handle before they play one note on their new organ. I have experienced it the other way round — you play the organ for three months before you draw a penny. That was my very trying experience at Kirkley Church in the early days of 1893. I started work there with an empty pocket and had to keep going as best I could until the first pay day. There is no doubt we are badly in need of a new broom. — All the same I am quite conscious the new broom will probably sweep me into the dust pan in the course of the general and much needed clean up. You see what I mean. I know that our present vicar has had fears lest I should die off or retire before his time was up. He has told me so much himself, and I quite understand his feelings. It is obvious that I cannot go on with my organ playing very much longer.We have two peculiar churchwardens, both good friends of mine. Neither of them will discuss this subject with me. They seem to look upon me as a fixture at Hessle Church. Well. I can only say that they may have to consider this business even before the new vicar arrives. And then I cannot make out where any new and competent organist is to be found in these war days. All the young men, all the young organists, are out there thinking of other things. Nobody bothers about organ playing when there are guns to be fired and aeroplanes to be flown. Best love, Phil.

B.S. 105 24th August 1943

I begin with two stories about choirboys, both incidents that occurred last night. Just now I have four boys in the choir who come from the Seamen's

Orphanage at Hesslewood. This large house is more than a mile from Hessle Church and the four boys come down to the practice by 'bus. The bus passes the gates of the orphanage and drops them at Hessle Cemetery corner, just in time for the practice. After the practice they walk home, up Ferriby Hill and through that beautiful avenue of big trees that perhaps you remember. It is a charming walk home for the boys but we pay their 'bus fares one way.

Last night in calling over the names and commencing the practice, three of the orphanage boys, Peter Collie, Albert Norman and Fred Hall, clamoured round me, all telling me the same story at the same time — No. 4 of their little group, Walter Fisher, had run hard to catch the bus, but had just failed. The conductor would not wait for him. I suppose it is not worth the penny that the boy would pay for his ride, so he was left behind. I had just gathered in this information, sifting the three stories told simultaneously, and the clock was just warning us all of the time for the practice when in came Walter Fisher, very red in the face and anxious to know if he had saved his time and his place. He had run all the way from the orphanage to the church and had almost, but not quite, paced the bus. Walter, by the way, is a first cornet player in the orphanage band. No wonder his wind is good for a quick mile run.

Story No. 2 now follows:
At the end of practice I told my monitor, Keith Bailey, that I was going to practise the organ and he could do as he liked about staying. I got out my music case containing Rheinberger's twenty organ sonatas and I picked out *No. 11 in D minor* and began at the beginning. I took each of the four movements in turn, practising difficult bits here and there. It is very nice to be at the organ in a lovely old church at the hour of twilight with a delightfully obedient electric blower. I don't know — there is something lovely in this — my thoughts get completely absorbed and I become lost to everything except the essence of the music. I went on and on, every now and then going back a page or two to practise a difficult passage or to enjoy one that seemed particularly attractive and beautiful. It was getting on towards 'nine o'clock news time' and supper time, when a small voice rather startled me. 'I think I'll go home now. I promised Daddy I would help him to make a rabbit hutch.' 'Good night, Keith,' I said. Fancy forgetting that lad, and he was there all that time. Very strange. I must go round and have a look at that rabbit hutch.

I have still another yarn in connection with my church work:
Sunday, August 15th, Katie came home from early communion (8.0.) and told me that there were bats flying about in the church. I said then, 'No. I'll bet they were swallows.' I went to the 9.45 service, sung eucharist, and there the birds were, a couple of swallows flying round and round the church, all over the place. You can figure out sixteen choirboys during a sermon with two swallows flying round and round and sixteen heads all turning together,

right, left, up, round and round and all over again, whichever way the birds went. The last hymn at that service, English Hymnal 469 — *Happy birds that sing and fly, Round Thy altars, O most high.* Ruth does not believe that yarn of mine so I will send her one of our printed choirpapers for August and, if she has an *English Hymnal*, she can look it up. Best love, Phil.

B.S.106 7th September 1943

Canon C.H. Lenton, my sixth vicar, has retired. He had a run of 15 years, the longest of them all — Arnold Savory, who appointed me in 1901, five years (the last of which he was an absentee for the whole year). Bishop [Richard Frederick Lefevre] Blunt, five years. The old boy became vicar of Hessle at the age of 72, Canon Lenton has resigned at 70 because of his age. Bishop Kempthorne, afterwards Bishop of Lichfield, three years. He was vicar of Hessle at the time I went on the world tour. Bishop [Francis] Gurdon another five years and Canon [Arthur Creyke] England, now Archdeacon of York and Canon of York Minster, about ten years, and lastly Canon Lenton, fifteen years. So I have said 'Goodbye' to Canon Lenton. He has gone out of my life for ever. In fifteen years I have never quarrelled with him. He went his own way and I went mine. My way was to do what I was asked to do and to pocket my salary. I am given to understand that in the day of resurrection everybody will be playing golden harps and there will be no call for organists. Well. They can have their golden harps, I don't want to have anything to do with a harp. I intend to go in for a bass trombone. I shall be able to play it straight away and I shall immediately put in a request for Schubert's *Symphony in C.* What a joy that would be. I can see myself, clothed in white, of course, and playing that bass trombone and 'jiggers' to your golden harp. I prefer brass, it gives out a stronger tone than anything made of gold.

We had a letter from Stephen the other day and he told us of a North African newspaper that had asked its soldier readers to send in a list of the six things they most missed since they left England. Stephen's list of six things interested me. Here they are:

1. Catching a 'bus at the very last moment.
2. Tickling the ivory keys. (If that was his idea of joy it wasn't mine.)
3. Anthems, as sung at home by the family quartet. (I suppose that would be Trigo, Katie, Stephen and Henry. I don't think John entered into this coterie, I forget, but if he did the quartet would be Trigo, Katie, John and Stephen, or the last couple reversed. John had a very nice toned voice and I always liked to hear him singing even after his treble voice went. Both John and Stephen seemed to be uncertain whether they were tenors or basses but Henry was definitely a bass. Would to heaven we could hear them trying their quartets once more. Even I might be persuaded to join in.)
4. Springtime in England. (That is what Browning said, isn't it? Oh, to be

in England — Now that April's there, Stephen must have been reading Browning.)

5. A table tennis party at No.19. (Stephen misses that, does he, and so do I, although I never play the game. I miss the gang of young people scrambling upstairs to the table tennis in the large attic at the top of the house. A dozen at a time. Great games and tournaments, and paper and pencil charts to note the progress of the scores. Notices pinned on the walls. Superfluous bits of furniture, such as travelling trunks, old pictures, an old oil lamp, bits of carpet and even an old violoncello, all dumped into my little nearby study to make elbow room for the table tennis players. Left in the study for Daddy to put back the next morning. Yes. I, too, miss the table tennis.)

6. A cycle ride in pouring rain. (Yes. I have no doubt that Stephen would love to be on his bicycle once more, riding along the green lanes in this neighbourhood. As to the rain — I remember that, when I took long walks from Hull to London, to Leominster, I enjoyed the rain when it came. It did not worry me, I enjoyed it even if I got wet. Well. Those were the six things that Stephen, now in Africa, misses most.) Goodbye, Phil.

B.S.107 21st September 1943

Who was the poet that talked about, 'Retired leisure, that in trim gardens takes its pleasure'? I could not have answered that question until I had looked it up. Milton it was, and I never did think much about Milton ever since I had *Paradise Lost* stuffed into me, week in, week out, at St. George's School, Windsor Castle. I have a fine book of Milton's work which I gained as a school prize at Windsor in 1877 and, so far as I remember, I have never once opened that book. The binding of the book is beautiful with the St. George's Chapel coat of arms, same as the Knights of the Garter, on the outside, with a nice inscription on the fly leaf, written by Randolph Davidson, Dean of Windsor in 1887, afterwards Archbishop of Canterbury and Lord Davidson. You can't chuck a book like that to the salvage collector, but you can have your *Paradise Lost* and all the other stuff Milton wrote so far as I'm concerned, but I will return to the 'trim garden' idea. Somebody has to trim up our front garden about once a week. If I don't do it myself I have to pay someone else to do it for me. I am indeed a man of leisure and I can spare the time to do the necessary work, but the silly old poet is wrong when he talks about the pleasure to be got out of the job. Milton did not know The Weir, Hessle, on a Saturday morning, and the number of gossips, men and women, that prowl along its pavements, with their tongues itching for chatter and talk on any subject whatsoever. No matter who it may be, so long as there is some person to talk to. The poor old man who tries to tidy up his front garden on a Saturday morning, with only a low privet hedge between him and the pavement becomes the target of the gossiping tongues that waggle up and down The Weir all the long sunny morning. My word, but don't these gossips bore me? Not 'alf, as they say, an expression I cannot explain. Just let me dot down a few items of gossip gathered together last Saturday. Mr. F. says my lawn cutter doesn't do its work properly. It wants adjusting. I say, 'Well, put it right for me.' But he goes on to tell me all about his musician son who played at a Middlesborough cinema and was called up, and goodness knows where he has got to now, and I don't remember what else, but a long yarn about the son anyhow. Miss B. comes along and wants to know what books I have been reading lately and can I keep her a good book for when she calls at the Hessle library next Tuesday (the day I help to run the library.) I tell her about *The Pied Piper:* if I can I will hold that book for her as I have just finished it myself. Mrs. B., Hessle gossip No. 3., comes along, I see her coming from afar and I turn away, she passes, and I breathe a breath of relief. She changes her mind and comes back to have her little bit of chat, mostly about bottled fruit, a subject outside my line of thought, and eventually, finding me dull on the subject, she walks into our house, dog and all, to tell it all over again to Mrs. Chig. H.W. comes along and asks me if I have been after mushrooms lately. Yes, I have, and got ever so many, such a lot that at least half had to be given away. This gossip tried to fix up a mushroom appointment with me for early one morning. Perhaps I knew where to find the mushrooms and he didn't, but I would not make any date with him. Another Mrs. B. comes along. She wants to sell me a whole stock of old music. Good lord, my dear woman, just lately I have been putting tons of old music into the salvage box — Go and do thou likewise — There is no demand for second-hand music now, none whatever. Then J.C. comes along smoking, as always, the small end of a cigarette. He stops and talks bowls stories, how he slithered in off an outside wood and ran right up to the jack. So on and so on. It was nice of him not to refer to the quid he borrowed from me some time ago and has since forgotten to repay. Best thing he can do and I am glad he did not refer to it, but he hindered my trimming. D.E., my next visitor, is a comely young woman but deaf and dumb. For some reason never explained she used to call at our house, when she was a child, whenever she wanted a penny stamp. She used to hold out the penny and try to say something, and I used to give her the stamp and take her penny and she would go off quite satisfied. I never understood this game but I played my part in it until she suddenly gave up calling. D.E. has always been one of my friends. She cannot gossip, only just smile at me and make a queer sound that might be meant for, 'Good morning.' Then E.N. comes along and he has a good long innings. I am related to him in four ways: he belongs to our bowls club, he has been in the church choir for ever so many years, at one time he was our next-door neighbour and he, on behalf of my landlord, attends to any little repairs needed at No.19. He talks to me about my very nice hydrangeas, now in excellent bloom, how to take cuttings and so on. All the same I am there to trim my garden and not to bother about hydrangeas. T.T. on his bicycle in passing calls out to me, 'Don't overdo it.' Capt. G. comes along and he is one of the very worst. He smokes a long pipe and talks about my three sons, he wants to know all about them, where they are, when they last wrote, and so on and so on. Then he goes on to tell me all about his son, his only son, who was killed in the last war, somewhere near Jerusalem. He would have given his own life to have saved his son's life, and I believe he spoke truly. Capt. G. runs the Hessle library but he was my hindrance on Saturday. Somebody wants to sell me a flag. What for, I don't know, but I have to run indoors to find a copper or two. Then old Mrs. X. passes, I forget her name. She was the good soul who helped to bring Trigo into this wicked world. She came to my rescue, or should I say Katie's rescue, in the dead of night, when there was no regular nurse available. She came quickly, too, and was pleasant and nice and business-like. I have not forgotten her. Perhaps she has more jobs on just now for she passes with a 'Good morning' and a smile. No gossiping here, no time for it.

Many soldiers pass along during the morning and many of them just look over the privet hedge and say, 'Good morning, daddy.' Yes. And I like that, although their cheerful remark gives me a bit of heartburn and causes me to wipe the corner of my eye with a dirty handkerchief. Perhaps you can guess why. Then Leslie, our young church verger, comes on a legitimate call with an order for the organ at a wedding on October 2nd — Hymns 346 and 348, English Hymnal, and he has to stop to tell me about a pending divorce case, a couple who were married only last January. A copy of the marriage certificate is required by somebody or other. I suppose Leslie gets a shilling for that. I don't know. I want to get on with my trimming. Then, worst bore of all, old W., who tells me I am not cutting my privet hedge in the right way and tells me a better way of doing it. Then he wants to borrow my shears, to take them to a certain Hull cemetery to trim the shrubs or flowers on his wife's grave, and a long story about the bus rides and the bus changes and the fares in order to get that job done. Old W. talks on and on and on until at last I leave him standing at the gate and I go into the house on a pretended errand and I watch from a window until the old boy gives me up for lost and walks off with my shears. I return to my trimming with a spare pair of shears that I fortunately possess. And, last of all, a 'holy woman' passes by. A good soul from the Hessle retreat house. She can speak to me in a low voice when she is in church and perhaps wants to borrow some little bit of music for use up there, but in the street on the pavement no glance of recognition must be made to any man. Well. Let it be so. I will get on with the trimming. Now it's finished until next time. The Lord be praised. — 'Retired leisure, That in trim gardens takes his pleasure.' Silly old fool. Best love, Phil.

B.S.108 12th October 1943

And this is Hull Fair week — You would not have known anything about it had I not told you. Hull Fair, always beginning on October 11th and going on for a week and a day. What times they were. Excursions from all over Yorkshire and Lincolnshire. Trains and trains running into Hull right up to late afternoon and all filled with country people. Buses and trams and charabancs all off to the fair and so labelled. Everybody moving along the roads in the same direction, all towards the fair. The fair was held on what is called the Corporation Field. If ever any grass grew on that field, the annual fair, with its thousands and thousands of feet wandering about all over the place, made quite sure that no grass would grow again there for a twelvemonth. It was a desolate sort of field all through the year, a fine playground for the youths of eighteen or so, who could play their rough games without worrying anybody. No grass ever grew on that field. During fair week the place became the centre of noise and tumult. Mechanical organs by the score all played away at the same time just to help the roundabouts to which they belonged. These roundabouts were full all day long. The young people, and many of the old ones too, from the city and the country never tired of the old-fashioned roundabouts. Little roundabouts for children, perhaps horse drawn, were also well patronised. There was a special kind of parkin sold at the fair and everybody bought this sweet cake, just as one buys hot cross buns on a Good Friday. If you did not go to the fair you had to eat this parkin at home for your tea. At night time the heavens were all aglow with the lights from the fair. Aglow until midnight at the very least. Weeks before the fair commenced the traffic passing through Hessle and other places nearby Hull would advertise the approach of October 11th, Hull Fair Day. I remember once cycling out to Welton one Sunday afternoon just about this time of the year. I was going along a pretty country road, you may not know it but the country roads round about Welton are delightful, when I met a couple of quite big elephants sauntering along slowly, reasonably and sedately. Perfect gentlemen in their way. I am not sure they did not nod me a, 'Good day.' Certainly their one and only keeper touched his cap to me. Elephants — Hull Fair — roundabouts — mechanical organs — fish and chip stalls — Try your strength hammers, and indicators to show how far you hit and the measure of your strength. Shooting galleries, coconut alleys. Yes, surely there would be a Bostock's Menagerie. You could hear the lions roaring but you couldn't see them unless you paid your penny. There would be a brass band of a dozen musicians blasting away in opposition to the mechanical organs. Well, I was always thankful that was not my branch of the profession. You couldn't hear what they were playing, the confusion all round was so great. On the whole I think Hull people liked Hull Fair. It always came along at a marked period of the year. People would say, 'a fortnight before Hull Fair' or, 'a few days after Hull Fair', just as you might say, 'the week after Christmas'. All over now. All quiet. I wonder where the lions and the elephants are now and if they miss Hull Fair. One thing I notice is that our local school children, and their teachers are now enjoying their Hull Fair holidays. A fortnight at least. Not a bad idea from the teachers' point of view. I suppose this means shorter holidays at other times of the year. I know what it means to my choir practices. It is Hull Fair holiday time, Mr.C. You don't suppose we are coming to choir practices during Hull Fair holidays? So I go down to our old church to hold the usual choir practice. Three boys turn up and, after a quarter of an hour, another four manage to roll up. Potato picking they say has caused the delay. It is a funny world but there is no Hull Fair just now and I wonder if there ever will be another.

The Mozart Sonatas afford Trigo and me much pleasure at the moment. Schumann is a bit in favour of the piano and neglects the violin. Schubert is too easy all round. Grieg is exciting and wild, Handel solid and stately. Bach. No, not Bach thank you. Goodbye, Phil.

B.S.109 26th October 1943

I look in *Hymns Ancient and Modern* for an inspiration for my No.109. Yes. And I find one too. *A&M* No.109. If I am allowed to change a word or two:
> 'Sweet the moments rich in blessing,
> Which upon the green I spend,
> Life and health and peace possessing,
> There have I made many a friend.'

The last job I did before I sat down to my Corona typewriter a minute or two ago was to clean up my woods, give them a rub over with a light oil and pack them away into a cupboard for their winter sleep. We kept the game of bowls going up to last week. We should have had a final turn out on Saturday last (Oct. 23rd) but the weather prevented play on that day. Now we have packed up altogether. Our season has lasted just a few days over six months. I don't know what I should do without the game of bowls, the only outdoor game I can now play. I am lucky to have an old woman at home who pretends to listen to all my yarns on bowls. I am not really deceived. I know quite well I am an old bore with my bowls stories. Trigo is candid enough to tell me so. All the same I like to tell somebody about the funny things that happen on the bowling green, and consequently the poor wife has to suffer. So there. It is all over for another season and I must look forward to my 72nd birthday as a day on which perhaps I shall have my next game.

We have now been nearly two months without a vicar and no new appointment has yet been announced. The parish and church are in the hands of our curate, Wilkes. He is doing this job very well indeed and has infused a lot of life into our church services. He likes to make things GO and he has many things in his favour, a very good singing voice and he is at times an excellent preacher. Many people, including the churchwardens, wish that he could remain on here as vicar. In choosing his hymns Wilkes goes in for shouting and noisy hymns and does not seem to care for anything of a quiet nature. In choosing hymns one should study variety, variety both in words and music. Last Sunday for instance, we had *Onward Christian Soldiers* to Sullivan's well-known tune, followed by *Now thank we all our God* to the tune *Nun Danket*. Never before have I noticed the similarity between these two tunes. The same key of F. Absolutely the same notes, but not the same rhythm in the first line. I just avoided the monotony slightly by transposing *Onward Christian Soldiers* into another key. He is entirely an *Ancient and Modern* nan and he has no liking for the hymn book now in use in Hessle Church, the *English Hymnal*. I suppose it does not matter very much. My cheque will come along next quarter day, *Ancient and Modern* or *English Hymnal*. All the same, it is a pity that, when we adopted the *English Hymnal*, twelve years ago, we did not stick to that book and all it gave us, even if we lost sight of a few popular tunes. None of the choirboys have any knowledge of the old hymn book and all the old books were scrapped long ago. I caught Wilkes out when he talked about the good old tune for *Onward Christian Soldiers*. That tune is in our *English Hymnal* but not in *Ancient and Modern*. Yes. We are having fine fun in Hessle Church just now.

One more story before I get to the end of the page — Trigo brought home a Jaffa orange the other day. The very look of it made my mouth water. I don't know where it came from. For two days it lay on a plate in our pantry. My mouth went all wet and funny whenever I looked at this orange. Then one day I suggested that something should be done about it. The orange was cut up in three rather unequal pieces. It is not an easy job to share out one orange between three people. I would not confess it publicly but I watched to see who got the big piece. Goodbye, Phil.

B.S.110 9th November 1943

It is now nearly two and a half years since Henry was taken prisoner by the Germans. For about two years we have had pretty regular letters from him. He writes about once a week but his letters come along three or four at a time. Just at this time it is about six weeks since we last had a letter from him. In all his letters he has hardly ever made any complaint or given us to understand that he was unhappy or miserable. Beyond the fact that his movements were very much restricted, he seems to be leading a fairly happy life. In fact he seemed so cheerful that we sometimes doubted if his letters, which we knew were censored before they ever left Stalag VIII B, could be relied upon to give us any truthful statements. Sometimes I felt that Henry was forced to write only such things as would please his German captors and censors. Well. Now we have been eased in this respect by Lance Corporal Charles Baldwin, until lately a resident at Stalag VIII B, but now back again at his own home in Salisbury Street, Hessle. Charlie called to see us last Thursday afternoon just as we had finished our dinner and he stayed for about an hour and he just talked to us all the time. Of course, Charlie would not have been repatriated had he not been badly wounded. He was knocked out in France just before the Dunkirk trouble. He was left behind in an emergency hospital when the Germans came along and he, with all the other inmates of that hospital, were taken prisoner and sent to various prison camps in Germany. Charlie lost his left leg but he rose to the situation by making a wooden leg for himself. He was a carpenter's assistant in civilian life and so he knew how to set about the business. I thought it was Captain Cuttle coming to see me on Thursday when I heard the footsteps coming along the passage into our kitchen where I was having a few minutes' snooze after my dinner. Charlie had seen Henry about three weeks ago and so he was able to give us a pretty good idea of the life that young man is leading just now. What he told us was very reassuring. Henry is perfectly fit and well. He is not altogether wasting the days and the weeks and even years that he is spending in the German prison camp. Some of the prisoners are still supposed to be *chained* but that business has become more of a joke than a reprisal. I suppose I must not spin the yarn any further or this B.S. will not get over to Canada or anywhere else if a censor gets hold of it. Charlie was full of enthusiasm for the Swedish Red Cross and the Swedish trains. I can imagine what the change was like in travelling home — several days as a prisoner of war in trucks, so many men or so many horses per truck, and I don't suppose the meals would be very exciting. Five nights spent in the train. Then to become an honoured passenger in a Swedish train with Swedish Red Cross nurses giving of their best. No wonder Charlie cannot say enough in praise of the Swedes. Best love, Phil.

B.S.111 25th December 1943

I did not know until this Christmas morning that there was ever going to be another B.S. letter — I am at home this morning and I am absent from Hessle Church and the organ for the first Christmas since I came to Hessle in 1901. That is to say I have played at the Christmas services here for forty-two years. That record is broken. Today I am at home by doctor's orders and my deputy is doing the work. Thinking of the past and the many Christmas days that I remember, from the time I was ten years of age until I was fifteen (1882-1887) my Christmas days were spent at Windsor. The choristers of St. George's Chapel were not allowed to go home at Christmas time. My memory tells me that this rule was not a very great hardship on the boys. We were inundated with Christmas presents and tips and we had a really good time of it. I think we liked that arrangement — the parcels and hampers that came from our homes — I suppose every chorister had his little packet of good things. Whatever our father was or was not, he was certainly a generous man and I remember that my Christmas parcel or hamper was always one of the best. A bottle of whisky for the schoolmaster, Old B, as we called him, and a bottle of port for the matron, Mother Wright, as we called her.

Of all the Christmas Day services at Hessle Church the best were in the days of Bishop Blunt, the ultra-low churchman, who never went to an early communion, but held evening communions, which the old people of Hessle attended and liked. Christmas morning service was held at 10.30. Full church, full choir, all the old favourite hymns and perhaps a carol or two. A good sermon from the Old Man, the Bishop, I mean, and everybody home to their Christmas dinner in a cheerful mood. Those were the best Christmas Day services during my long period as organist. The record, unfortunately, has now been broken by my recent illness and inability to leave this house.

I must tell you about Peter Geraghty, Trigo's best boy, so far as I know, her only boy. Just now he is stationed perhaps fifty miles away from here. Yesterday morning he got permission to go home for his Christmas dinner but he had to put in an hour or so in the air before he left. He took off from his aerodrome and made for Hessle, circled round his home and Hessle Church and then returned to his base. He told me that he found the train that brought him to Hessle for his second visit most annoyingly slow. The journey meant two or three changes of trains with long waits. At one place he managed to get hold of a telephone to ring us up and to invite Trigo to meet him at Hessle station in the early evening. What funny times we live in. Courting was not like that in our days. Phil.

1944

B.S.112 27th January 1944

They say three women and a goose make a market. I went marketing today.
January 27th as ever was. For months and months and months, another
quotation by the way, I have used but two ties, one of them a blue tie to go
with any dark grey suit I may still possess, the other, a brown tie, to go with
an old brown Scotch tweed suit that I am fond of and wear as often as I can.
It is true, the elbows of this tweed suit are 'out', as you might say. The ends
of the sleeves are frayed and have to be trimmed with a pair of scissors about
once a week so that the sleeves are gradually shortening and the unturned-
up trousers are in a like condition, only worse. In fact the whole suit is
utterly unworthy of a man in my position and that fact makes me love it all
the more. Scotch tweed it is said to be and I wear it practically every day.
Had it not been for the war, this particular suit would have been replaced
long ago. Once bitten, twice shy. I had a new suit about a year or so ago.
About ten pounds was the price and it was not so much the price that I
objected to. No. It was the difficulty about the pockets. It is a good suit but
it annoys me whenever I wear it because I am so accustomed to find a pocket
book up here and my watch down there, a few keys in another place and my
two pairs of spectacles in a pocket all to themselves, one for reading and the
other for playing bowls or snooker. Every time I wear this wartime suit I am
vexed or angry with somebody or other, I don't know who. So I return to my
old Scotch brown tweeds on a Monday morning with a feeling of joy and
elation. Everybody wears old clothes just now and I am but running with the
fashions of the times. Well, I went to market today, that is to say I went into
Hull by 'bus at about 10.30 a.m. and had a very enjoyable time, although
there was only one thing that I really wanted to buy — a new tie. In the olden
days I bought all my ties at one of the multiple shops in Hull, never spending
more than one shilling on them. Times are changed now and I expected to
spend at least eighteen pence or possibly two shillings. There was the joy of
the escaped prisoner which was a second consideration. I have been ill, as
you know, and for weeks I was not allowed to put my nose outside the front
door. When I was allowed a little freedom it meant at first just a crawl round
one or two streets or a walk down to the church. Now I have spent the best

part of the day in Hull, looking about and having quite a good and enjoyable lunch at a good restaurant and ended up with a visit to the Regal Cinema — some horrible picture of a Russian city or town after the Germans had evacuated it. I never saw such dreadful things at a cinema before. Soon over, though. Will Hay came along with the silliest film on earth but the people all laughed and thought it frightfully funny. In another film that followed the Will Hay farce like a streak of lightning you saw a fight in an aeroplane and, while the fight is going on, the lady, or the heroine or whatever you call her, jumps to the control just as the aeroplane is spinning down to a crash and the machine is righted. It is not 'one of ours', but a captured enemy plane, and that is the chief point of the story. The lady and her lover are prisoners, but they get possession of the machine after a fight and then have to face bullets etc. from some of our machines until the lady opens a window and waves a flag and the chap in the other machine, the one that is peppering us, as I might say, waves back with the same sort of 'pass along' wave that some motorist gives to another on one of our roads. And so we get home, just missing the cliffs at Dover by a miracle, because one of the dead Germans has suddenly revived and opened a plug that released petrol so that we are jolly hard put to it to get over those very high cliffs. I don't remember what happened to the dead Germans who were in the plane but it all ended quite happily.

I must tell you, though, that my tie deal did not come off. Not because I had not the cash to pay for a new tie but because I was about four days too early. My coupon book had run dry of January coupons. Now that strikes me as being very funny. No man in this world knows less about coupons than do I. I am entirely in ignorance about them. I only know that I love all my old clothes and at any time I prefer them to new ones. You could not imagine anybody living on such a small trousseau, for lack of a better word, than I do. And yet I cannot have a new tie until next Tuesday. It is a queer war, anyhow. Perhaps I shall raid the tie boxes of the three warriors who have sallied forth from this house and are now, all of them, overseas. I have no doubt I can find a suitable tie to go along with my old brown Scotch tweed suit and I can forget about coupons. No. 1 is still in Gibraltar. No. 2 is still a prisoner of war. He tells us his Stalag is now No. 344 and that a recent mail to that camp brought in 105,000 letters. Some mail that, but it is a very large camp. Many of those who were in Italian camps have been transferred to this camp that Henry is now in, originally known as Stalag VIII B. No. 2 has been a lodger in that camp for $2\frac{1}{2}$ years. The only consolation is that he is making money all the time. At the present moment he possesses more than I have ever possessed at any time in my long life. No. 3 is in Italy. We do not know exactly whereabouts. He has moved over the sea from North Africa. I wonder if he will visit Rome shortly. Strange if he does. He has already been to Carthage and I have never seen the Mediterranean. My three sons have all seen it, sailed over it, bathed in it and flown over it. P.

B.S.114 7th March 1944

On Sunday morning (March 5th) about 9.30 a young soldier called at our house and asked to see me. He said there was to be a parade of his little lot that morning, they were going to the church and he would like to play the organ for them, he said he always played at church parades. I think he rather overlooked the fact that the service would be for Hessle people, just matins. The soldiers would be very welcome to the service and perhaps the padre would be preaching the sermon, but the service was certainly not a military parade service. Anyhow, I gave him a very decided refusal but I told him he could play the voluntaries if he liked. I asked him his name — 'Vaughan Williams,' he replied. That is a name I have heard of many times lately. 'He is my uncle,' the young man replied when I remarked that I knew Vaughan Williams, the composer, personally. Vaughan Williams — a man exactly my own age — an old Carthusian, I think — he once paid me a very great compliment at a Hull Musical Festival which I have not forgotten — But about this young Vaughan Williams. He came to the service and played the voluntaries. It was Elgar's *Salut d'Amour* at the beginning. Not very correctly played but I noted that he was without any music. He did not 'dry up' very artistically when the parson was ready to begin the service. It was the second Sunday in Lent and his last voluntary was not exactly appropriate — *The Hallelujah Chorus*, using the full organ nearly all the time. Again he played entirely without any music, a thing I could not do. I wonder if I shall see this young man again, where he comes from and what work he is doing in the army just now. Phil.

B.S.115 12th April 1944

'Insatiate archer. Could not one suffice? Thy shaft flew thrice.' And you will see what I mean later on. This day seems a suitable one on which to continue my B.S. series. When listening to the early news on my wireless this morning the announcer reminded me that I am seventy-two years old today. Let it pass. It does not worry me very much. All the same today is my birthday. At breakfast time I had two nice presents from wife and daughter and three letters from brother and sisters. Good. Let it pass. The day is sunny and sweet and the daffodils are all out and golden and it is nice to be alive.

It has been a strange Easter with us at Hessle Church. Wilkes, the acting vicar, who has a very delightful voice but no knowledge of music, took the sung eucharist at 9.30 in the most perfect manner. No cathedral with a paid musical priest could have done it better. Such a change from last year when our vicar, who insisted on officiating at the sung eucharist on Easter Day, broke down completely and just mumbled through the proper preface for Christmas Day, instead of the right one. Wilkes made one funny slip, all the same. After we had sung the Easter Anthem (instead of the *Venite*) he forgot all about the psalms for the day, and went to the lectern to read the lesson. The congregation remained standing and there was an awkward pause. At the organ I waited for the psalms for Easter Day to be given out before playing the chant. Wilkes failed to notice that he had forgotten the psalms and just said, 'Please be seated.' So our matins was considerably shortened in consequence.

At the end of evensong I reverted to an old habit. I played *The Hallelujah Chorus* as the concluding voluntary. The late vicar prohibited me from doing this after his first Easter at Hessle. He considered that *The Hallelujah Chorus* was something very divine and holy and should not be treated as an ordinary voluntary. How he formed that conclusion I never could make out. Now he has gone away from us I went back to my old custom. A goodly number of the congregation stood up all through my voluntary, following a queer concert custom that you probably know about. Wilkes came to the organ when I had finished and thanked me for my choice of voluntary. So, between vicar and curate, where are you? One of my choirboys sprang a surprise on me. Alan Brown tells me that his father says he must leave the choir so that he can *get on with his music*. Well. That's a cough drop.

And now for my text. Last Wednesday (5th April) I played at the funeral of the Hessle poetess, Mrs. Honeychurch. A funny name and a funny little woman. She loved composing verses of sweet doggerel, which she caused to be printed and circulated to her friends. I am afraid my copies did not live long. A special request for the funeral was the *Nunc Dimittis*. Wilkes asked those present to do the best they could with the singing. My friend, Mr. Holstein, a German-born man, did his best to oblige. The effort was too much for him. They got him home and he died that night. His funeral was on Saturday and my orders were — everything the same as at Mrs. Honeychurch's funeral. So so. It was not quite the same. Nobody sang the *Nunc Dimittis*, at least I heard no effort. Even Wilkes, the curate, gave up the effort after the first verse. That is the end of No. 2. Now for No. 3, as per my text. I was cleaning up my front garden on Easter Monday, the first time it has received any attention since sister Ruth polished it up last November. I chose Monday instead of Saturday because I thought there would be fewer gossips about and I should be able to get on with my work without much delay. Just about 12.30 Billy Coulson came along. He stood at my gate and he chatted to me and with me until 1 o'clock when I had to send him away and go to my dinner. Billy was my solo tenor when I first came to Hessle. For well over twenty years he was one of our churchwardens. He was the clerk to our Urban District Council until he retired a year or two ago. I wrote a song about him which John, when he was a boy, sang at a parochial concert, which was very well received and is talked about to this day. Billy's garden juts out into the road at Tower Hill, it wants straightening out, and I told Billy it was time this was done. 'Not in my time,' he said. 'No,' I said, 'but the day after your death they will get to work on that job. etc. etc.' We talked a lot. I was playing bridge that same evening. The local undertaker rang me up. 'Another job for you. Mr. Coulson — and please have choirboys and hymn so and so.' Thursday at 1.45. The one shall be taken and the other left. Phil.

B.S.116 15th May 1944

'But winter, lingering, chills the lap of May.'

Well, he has never done that little job more effectually than he has done it today. I have never known such a cold day in May as this has been. I have felt cold and miserable all day long and I have used up all my available handkerchiefs. I have stoked up my fire in defiance of the strong north wind that I can hear surging and moaning past this house.

I have a choirboy story to tell you. Little Georgie Scott, a tiny choirboy, never came to a choir practice one week. Not like him at all. He is very keen on the job. 'Scottie, where were you on Wednesday night?' 'Please, sir, my shoes were wet.' I remembered that Wednesday was rather a rainy evening. 'What about Friday evening. Why did you not come then?' 'Please, sir, I went to see a solicitor.' 'What? Bigamy or breach of promise?' 'No, sir,' and all very calm and serious: 'A woman was knocked down.' 'And you saw the accident, eh?' 'Yes, sir.' 'Well. Next time tell your solicitor that you are booked for Wednesday and Friday nights.' 'Yes, sir.' And all very serious and businesslike. But you want to know Georgie Scott to appreciate this story.

Georgie is one of those strange boys that always wants to be there. If you understand my remark. He is for ever hanging round our church. Always early at practices, wanting to be putting out the chairs or the books. He seems to spend all day Sunday in the church. Hovering round the bell ringers and just itching for the chance of pulling a rope. He is too small for that game as yet. The hymn boards interest him. He will be getting the numbers all ready and, if you give him half the chance, he will somehow or other get the boards up on their high pegs, although he is miles too small for that task. After any service he will get rid of cassock and surplice in quick time and then set about collecting prayer books and hymn books. After that he will descend to the stoke hole and give a hand in that department. He is an odd boy. Goodbye, Phil.

B.S.117 30th May 1944

This morning I turned out some old papers and I came across a little note book which I used when I worked in the savings bank. (1914-1937) Here are some little snippets of conversation entered in my little note book at odd times:

'I didn't know you was a cat burglar.'

'He'ar the notes. Don't loss 'em.'

'Give us two tens!'
'Ah didn't know while ah koom darn.'
'Ah 'avn't 'ad any 'elp up to now but ah manage like!'
'Are you waiting of anybody?'
'We had to work in them days.'
'Them ain't mine.'
'Ten shilling notes like.'
'Yas — Hisself.'

The use of the word 'like' at the end of any sentence is a peculiar habit very common in these parts. One of the dear girls who worked with me at that period added this word on to almost every sentence of her conversation. — 'I am now off to dinner, like!' 'Have you balanced, like?' 'Can I have a pound in silver, like?' and so on. A very curious and common habit.

And now, what are we to do with our dress suits? Just before the war Katie made our two elder boys a present of a dress suit each. Perhaps they wore them once, perhaps twice. Will they ever wear them again? A friend of ours recently home from Gibraltar tells us that John is putting on flesh. Except for the dress suit, I am glad to hear this news. But what am I to do about my dress suit? Always have I loathed evening dress. Sometimes I would have to dress for dinner, when staying at a class hotel in holiday time. Such an idea now seems perfectly ridiculous. A summer holiday nowadays seems to imply perfect ease and freedom with as little luggage as possible. Fancy having to play the violoncello with a stiff shirt, hard cuffs and a stuck up collar. When I practised the violoncello at home I should take off my coat and roll up my shirt sleeves but when I played in the orchestra at a concert I was obliged to be trussed up and uncomfortable with all the stiff things that go with a dress suit. When I went with the Sheffield Choir round the world in 1911 I had to dress for 135 concerts and I used the same collar, a rubber one, at every concert and I had a dozen dickies which I got starched and stiffened up whenever the opportunity arose. Fancy travelling round the world with a dozen dickies. P.

B.S.118 12th June 1944

HENRY COWARD — Born 26th November 1849, died 11th June 1944.

I have a few recollections of Sir Henry Coward. At Dusseldorf I saw him conducting a very fine German orchestra at a rehearsal. A very funny affair. H.C. talking away in his West Riding style to this company of fine German musicians who took him very seriously. No joking. No smiles. Just the job in hand. Somehow or other H.C. made himself understood. At the following concert a very big wreath of laurels was presented to H.C. It did not fit him, it was much too big, for he was quite a small man. Never mind. It was all very serious and nobody laughed. Afterwards the wreath was a confounded nuisance, nobody knew what to do with it and it could not be left behind. I forget what did happen to it but it travelled about in special trains until the border was crossed on the way home. Then I suppose it was left to its fate. Then, in the following year, very many recollections. Travelling all one day in the company of Sir Edward Elgar and H.C. and joining in with the conversation. I can remember many of the things we talked about on that railway journey which included a jolly good C.P.R. lunch. Those were the days.

H.C. was a fine man with a choir, especially a choir from the West Riding. He was not much of a hand with an orchestra. I have often played the 'cello under his beat. As a rule he left the band unguided and gave all his attention to his singers. On one occasion my department of the orchestra were carefully counting twelve bars rest. Half way through this task H.C. shouted out, 'Cellos, you are too loud.' It was, of course, a rehearsal. The rebuked 'cellos only smiled. All too fond of H.C. to be vexed with him. But I must stop. I have so many recollections of H.C. I could go on for a dozen more pages and then not finish. Nice old boy. Katie and I have to thank him for everything. P.

B.S.119 2nd October 1944

My previous B.S. letter, No. 118, was written on what we now call D Day. June 6th. What a lot of history has been made since then. Stephen has been to see the Pope and seems to visit the cinemas of Naples fairly regularly. Henry is still interned at Stalag 344 in Germany, he has been there nearly three and a half years. John is at Gibraltar and well into the third year of his time there. After three years without once entering a train, early in July I managed a short holiday at Leominster which I enjoyed ever so much, although I missed Herbert, and No. 65 seemed strange without him. On August 7th (our wedding day) I sent in my resignation to the vicar of Hessle Church. Three months' notice and I still have four Sundays to go. I have not heard who is to succeed me. It will not be an easy business in these days. Phil.

B.S.120 27th October 1944

The death was announced last night of Princess Beatrice, Queen Victoria's youngest daughter and last surviving child. This announcement causes me once again to talk about those days of long ago when I was a chorister at St. George's Chapel, Windsor. One of the many royal ceremonies I attended during the years 1882-1887 was the wedding of Princess Beatrice to Prince Henry of Battenberg. On this table as I type my B.S. I have the copy of the *Form of Solemnization of Matrimony* that I used at Whippingham Church on July 23rd 1885. This copy is a beautifully bound book, octavo size, white cloth, gold lettering. I suppose the members of the choir were permitted to retain the copies provided for them in the choir seats because I kept my copy and I suppose I sent it home for my parents to see. I also suppose it was my father's idea to have my name, 'P.H. CHIGNELL', added in letters of gold just under the date on the front of the cover.

Now we will turn over: Marriage of Her Royal Highness The Princess Beatrice (you notice the lady's name comes first) with His Serene Highness The Prince Henry Maurice of Battenberg at Whippingham Church on July 23rd 1885 — Programme of the Music — The Procession of the Royal Family and Royal Guests — *March from the Occasional Overture* — Handel. The Bridegroom's Procession — *March* — W. Parratt (Parratt was the organist on this occasion. He used to say he could not compose music and never would compose any but I can imagine Queen Victoria ordering him to write something for the occasion and, after all, any organist can manage a march for the organ, nothing more easy than that, so I have no doubt Walter Parratt obliged on this occasion. I have never heard that his bridegroom's processional march, *Here Comes the Bridegroom*, has ever been performed again. — The Bride's Procession — *Bridal March* — Wagner. (Nowadays commonly known as *Here comes the Bride*. I have seen hundreds of smiling and smirking brides come up the centre aisle of Hessle Church as I have played this well known extract from *Lohengrin.*) — *Chant for Psalm 128* — Sir F. Ouseley. — Anthem:

O give thanks to the Lord: Praise him all ye people,
And ever praise His Holy Name.
Sing ye the Lord, and ever praise His Holy Name.
All that hath life and breath, sing to the Lord. (Mendelssohn).

(I remember that the final chorus from *The Hymn of Praise* was chosen after an audition in St. George's Chapel when several suitable anthems were sung by the chapel choir to the Queen, Princess Beatrice and other members of the Royal Family. Mendelssohn was a great favourite with Queen Victoria in the early days of her reign and his music was very much in request at all royal concerts and ceremonies. I remember, also, that the final choice rested between this *Hymn of Praise Finale* and the chorus *Hearts feel that love thee* (from Mendelssohn's *Athalie*) — The United Procession — *Wedding March* — Mendelssohn. All this, so far, on the first printed page of this beautifully bound book. Then come ten pages of *The Form of Solemnization of Matrimony*. Word for word as in the Prayer Book. All the headings are printed in red, the prayers, psalms etc. in black. The pages are tipped with gold and on the back of the book a crown of gold and V.R. scroll, also in gold. And what a day it was. I remember it quite well. A special saloon train for the choir and servants from Windsor Castle, from the Windsor South Western Station, straight through to Portsmouth. The Royal Yacht *Alberta* to take the party over the Solent to Cowes. What a party for a short sea trip. Everybody in uniform or fine dresses. Medals and sunshine and sparkling water. The yacht's crew in smart white uniforms. Supposing it had been a rainy day? But it wasn't. Queen Victoria was always lucky with the weather. Everybody said so. Do you remember the Jubilee Day, two years later? A glorious day. Then when we got to Cowes we, that is the choir, were driven to the Medina Hotel where light refreshments were waiting for us. A special watch was kept on the choirboys all through the morning, in the train, on the boat and at the hotel. No playing about, no shouting, no tucking in, no ginger beer or other inflating drinks. Just a quiet do and 'keep your eyes open' if you like. A drive off to Whippingham Church. No motor cars in those days. Smart horses from the royal stables and coachmen and footmen to match. After the ceremony the watch over the choirboys was relaxed and a jolly good dinner at the hotel mentioned put us all into good fettle. Not so many passengers on the *Alberta* on the return trip. The choir lined up and sang some part songs. There had been a recent choir concert at Windsor so the choir had a few items in memory that came in useful on this occasion. Then on the return railway journey the choirboys had a saloon carriage all to themselves and they had a jovial time, with no restraint. One or two of the young layclerks, especially one named Walter Clinch, preferred to join the boys rather than the men. Oh yes. It was a happy day. And I have no doubt. And all this memorizing brought back to me by our *Hull Mail* of yesterday's date. Best love, Phil.

On reading B.S. No.120 to Katie, she reminds me that there is a sequel to my matrimonial story as there is a sequel to most stories of weddings. Katie says I should most certainly write on for another page.

Some months later, one Sunday morning, I was one of a choir of seven at the Private Chapel in Windsor Castle. Sitting in the little organ gallery we were exactly opposite the royal box. The guests and royal servants and the officiating clergy were in the well, down below. We looked straight at the Queen and the Royal Family. On this particular Sunday morning we four choirboys observed that Princess Beatrice looked very ill and that she did not stand for the psalms and hymns. We knew enough about life to know that an event was pending. Such event took place that very same evening. On the Monday morning we heard that a son had been born to the Princess, and not so long after that some of the choirboys, and I was one of the fortunate ones, were taken up into the castle and to the white drawing room to sing one or two hymns at the christening ceremony. I remember seeing Queen Victoria nursing her little grandchild, now the Marquis of Carisbrooke. I also remember looking out through the big glass windows of the drawing room, out to the beautiful gardens of the east terrace of the castle and wondering why Dean Davidson wore such tremendously baggy sleeves of white lawn. I suppose that would have been about a ten bob do for the choirboys. And one last recollection of Princess Beatrice. She was a musician and could write music. She wrote little anthems and hymn tunes. We used to sing them at the services at St. George's. They were put on just when the Princess could attend the services and then they were put away and never heard of again as far as I can remember. In this respect Princess

Beatrice followed her father, the Prince Consort, who was quite a good composer. P.

B.S.121 15th December 1944

This Christmas shopping business — What a worry it is and how thankful we all are when it is over and done with and everything ready for the great day, the day of carols and turkeys and puddings and so on. But the shopping business — what anxiety and excitement it causes. It amounts almost to a fight in these days. So many people out on the prowl and so little in the shop windows for them to buy. I went to Hull yesterday in a bus crowded with ladies all on the same errand as I — Christmas shopping. I noticed that all the ladies in the streets carried little bags and they were all half running. They all had a sort of Christmas run. It was the same everywhere. Everybody in a hurry and anxious to get through with this Christmas shopping. I looked at a fruit shop and saw grapes, mouldy, some of them, marked at 15/- per lb. and I passed on. I walked on until I got to the *White Hart* bar, a favourite resort of mine and a very historic building. It has fortunately escaped any war damage and men meet there every day to have their morning potion, perhaps to do a little business and perhaps to while away idle times. Anyhow, I like the place and, if I do have to spend 1/1 for a bottle of stout, I like the big fire, and the armchair and the friendliness of the barmaid's, 'Here's your change, dear.' or, 'It's a cold morning, daddy.' All in good part and in good cheer. I am sure to pick up a pal if I sit in one of those arm chairs in front of the big fire. This time it was a man a few years my junior. We soon got talking about the war and the state of affairs in Athens and so on, and then we both found we had sons in Stalag 344, prisoners of war in Germany. His son was taken to Dunkirk — told to guard a bridge and he guarded it until the Germans came along and took him and the bridge as well.

But to get on with this Christmas shopping — I had a walk round Woolworth's — a nice warm place compared with the street — Christmas cards — nothing under sixpence and poor at that price, not in my line, I have not sent a Christmas card to anybody for at least forty years. Katie asked me to pick up some envelopes if I could and I looked about for envelopes — a few poor little packets of about eight or ten in each packet — sixpence — Not for me. I make my own envelopes in these days or re-use those sent to me — No need to buy any, not for home use at any rate. After Woolworth's I felt like a spot of lunch — Kardomah Cafe and a hope that I may meet Mr. Chapman, a worthy chess opponent, and I do meet him — not exactly by luck as he knows my Thursday habits. Game after game we play and I forget all about time and my Christmas errand. About 3.30 when Mr. Chapman at last remembers he has some business to do before the day is over, I leave the cafe and behold all the shops are shut and all the half-running ladies and their shopping bags have vanished. I have to catch a 'bus home and my day's work is done. I am only afraid of one person in this Christmas present business — Trigo — I know she will give me a present and she will expect one in return — I can owe my good lady another Christmas or birthday present. I don't know what the score is now and one more added on will not make very much difference. So the whole thing is quite satisfactorily finished and I have only to tell you the end of this pretty story. Today at breakfast time, a meal taken before daylight in these dark times, I was reading the *Yorkshire Post* and I heard Katie and Trigo discussing some dress problem. What it was I do not know but I heard Trigo say, 'But I haven't any coupons!' Now I don't want to pose or pretend to be funny but I really know nothing about this coupon business, it does not trouble me in the least for I never see any of the coupons that I hear really belong to me. Without looking up from the *Post* I said, 'How about some tokens for a Christmas present?' 'Oh yes, daddy, that will be fine.' 'All right,' I said. 'How many do you want?' 'Three,' was the reply. I was staggered by this remark. If I had been asked for thirty or three hundred I should have agreed and gone on with my toast and marmalade. All the same, it seems like giving a three-penny bit. If anybody else wants a coupon or two for a Christmas present I shall be delighted to oblige. It will be quite easy. I believe I have a boxful of coupons somewhere or other in this house. So that is the end of my Christmas Present Prowl.

The end has come. I am no longer the official organist at Hessle Church. At the end of October I gave up the job after holding it for 43½ years. I might write a whole chapter on how it feels to be free from chants and hymns and choirboys and choirmen and surplices and cassocks and vicars and curates and to be independent of all of them. Just take this evening, for instance, a nasty, cold and foggy evening in mid-December. I can stay at home in front of my nice fire and forget all about the weather outside, I have not got to attend the choir practice, or to open up a dark and possibly a cold church. I have not to bother about window blinds or choir seats or choir books and a crowd of noisy boys. I am at home and the Lord be praised. There will be no carols for me this Christmas. Hooray. Phil.

1945

B.S.122 4th May 1945

The first B.S. of this year, 1945. I have no excuse to offer for this falling off in production. I suppose I am getting old, 73 last 12th April, and one cannot go on for ever at any job, whatever that job may be, even if it takes so little effort as typing out one's thoughts. My mind is all in a whirl today — so many things to talk about — so much history being made on these days of early May, 1945. First of all, I remember the early May of four years ago. Air raid alarms by the score. Two terrific air raid attacks on Hull and round about, Hessle included. See my B.S.46. if by any chance you have preserved your copy of that number. The night I stood at my front door and saw all Hull in flames, the light of which flames turned our night into day and floodlit the fine spire of Hessle Church. The blitz repeated the following night. The very same show. All Hull burning again, or so it appeared from our front door, but I remained in bed that night. Stayed in bed and buried my head under the bedclothes and wondered if *our* house was to come down on top of us, the same as many of those I had seen all over the place. Well. That is all over now. The official news is that we are to have no more sirens. Finished. Total number of alarms 824. The *Yorkshire Post* yesterday talking of this official intimation stated that at Leeds they had actually had 87 air raid alarms during the war. Poor old Leeds. Sorry for Leeds, but more sorry for Hull with its 824 alarms and goodness knows how many actual raids. Of these raids, the two in early May 1941 were by far the worst and they will be remembered for many a long day.

Mussolini dead. Hitler dead. Damned good job too, if the news is true. Who will write Herr Hitler's history? All these fair German cities in ruins. Many of them have I seen and loved in days gone by: Aachen, Cologne, Coblenz, Bonn, Trier, Dusseldorf, Leipzig, Dresden and even Essen. I have been an honoured guest in all of these places and many others in a fair country in happier days than these and I lament the past history of the last few years and of the last few days. The fate of those who lived in these fair cities was the fate those very same people had prescribed for us, we who live in Hull or Hessle or London or Liverpool and many other places. It was a game of chess. Only one winner and one loser. 'Mate' it is now. The game

Peter Geraghty (middle figure) when serving with 102 Squadron, Pocklington, 1944.

is won. He who planned the gambit opening and the quick humiliation and defeat is himself trapped and his king cornered to the final 'mate'. It is hard to realize this ending of a great warfare. It is hard to realize what the ending might have been had the gambit opening succeeded.

John came home from Gibraltar a few days ago. Not quite unexpected, as he had given us notice that he was due for leave. He was on the Rock for nearly three years. Now he is at home on a leave of 28 days. What has happened since he arrived home on April 19th may prevent his return to Gibraltar. At present his instructions are that he must return there about the middle of this month but he anticipates other orders shortly.

Trigo has become 'engaged'. The young man called the other night to obtain Papa's permission. I look upon that obtaining permission as rather a silly idea. For a long time it has been obvious that Peter Geraghty and Ruth

Chignell had paired off. You know the way these young couples carry on. It is always the same story. Everything gives way when Love rules. Now Katie and I are really fond of Peter Geraghty. I am as fond of him as I am of one or other of my own sons. I have often said to Trigo, 'Peter is a splendid chap. Keep him if you can.' Of course, he is a splendid young man. I don't know how many times he has been out bombing the Germans and their cities. A rotten job, of course, but a dangerous job. The man who does that job requires courage and fortitude. I think Peter has well over thirty runs to his credit and he has returned safely from all of them. The Lord be praised. Many a time has Trigo sat at home and listened to these bombers going over our heads and over the sea to their death-dealing missions. Listened to them, knowing that her Peter was in one or other of them. Would he return safely? I marvelled at so little emotion shown by this young woman in this case. I cannot tell Trigo's thoughts. I know my own and at times I feared. Now it is all over. No more bombing, at any rate for the present, and Trigo can admire the pretty little diamond ring that adorns her third finger.

Of Henry we know nothing. Where he has got to or what he is doing at the present time is a complete mystery. Of course, we are anxious about him. So many different things may have happened to him. Yesterday I saw pictures of concentration camp horrors from Germany. Filmed pictures. Moving pictures. Horrible pictures. Only produced at the English cinema to make English people understand what has taken place in that God-forsaken country. The pictures were received by a completely full house in deadly silence. I think I have never sat in an audience so completely silent as was that at the Regal Cinema, Hull, yesterday afternoon. I, for one, shall never forget what I saw then. Of course, I don't think Henry has come in for any treatment like that. Certain, sure, we shall be very thankful to have him back at home or at least to have some news of him. He was at Stalag 344, overrun by the Russians in January last. No news since early January, the date of his last letter.

News of Stephen has also dried up. He has been in Italy for well over a year. Business there seems over and settled but it will take some time to calm down and to get home again. The mails seem interrupted. Perhaps we shall have news from Stephen pretty soon. What a whirl life has become, even for the poor old man who takes no part in anything but just tunes in and gets his news by wireless. Never knowing what is coming next. P.

B.S.123 15th May 1945

My last B.S. is but ten days old and yet it is now ancient history. We have passed through ten historic days from a domestic point of view as well as from an historic or an international one.

Henry is at home again. That is the first thought that comes to me on this bright May morning. At home once more after an absence of five and a half years and after four years spent in a prison camp in Germany. At home again. If you should have kept my B.S.52 (22nd July 1941) it would be worth reading it over once more in view of the happiness that has now come to us by the return of Staff Sergt. Henry Chignell 21821. The figures mean nothing now. They are worthless. I just write them from habit. The habit of addressing prisoner of war cards to Henry at Stalag 344. 21821 was his camp number there. There is some poetry in those figures. Say them over quickly several times. My typewriter runs them off automatically.

A week ago today was the day we celebrated the coming of Peace. With the anxiety I felt about Henry I did not feel very celebratory. The day was an extraordinary one. Somehow or other it became a sort of Gossip Day. Friends came in to talk to me, to talk to Katie, to talk to John, to talk to Trigo. After an interval, or at least a little talkee varying in length according to the talkativeness of the visitor, one friend departed and another friend arrived. The telephone kept us busy in addition to our visitors. It was all talk and very little else. I am not grousing. The flags were all out and the children running about shouting and playing and nobody quite knew what to do with themselves. Talking on such a day is not such a bad occupation. There was a very nice service at the church at 7.30. A very large congregation and I found much comfort and consolation thereat. All the same I wished I could have been at the organ. Of course, I could have done the job so much better etc. etc. So I thought, anyhow. The war over. Hitler dead. Mussolini dead. The German army overthrown and defeated and scattered. No more air raids or even alarms. No blackout rules and regulations. Henry still missing. Where has he got to? So much for my thoughts on V.E. Day.

The following day, 'V.E. Day Plus One' as they called it, was about the quietest day I have ever known in Hessle. Nobody in the streets, no aeroplanes up above, no cars on the streets, the shops mostly closed. It was quieter than any Sunday. A Bank Holiday, but why so quiet? Bowls in the afternoon and a game of bridge in the evening with Katie, Trigo and John. And so to bed. A peculiar day.

'V.E. Day Plus Two' a Thursday and another very strange day. I spent most of it in Hull. Crowded out everywhere. And such crowds. Hull is still a ruined city more or less, although here and there some streets and shops remain untouched. On Thursday the crowds surged everywhere, not only on the streets but all over the ruined and cleared sites. Nowadays one can take short cuts where once big and fashionable shops stood. Instead of nicely dressed women, and presentable men and perhaps well ordered children, as in the pre-war days, now to be seen are crowds of badly dressed women, painted to the eyebrows, with perambulators and a bevy of ill-clad and ill-behaved children, adorned with flags and ribbons to celebrate Peace Day. The pubs, or those that remain in Hull, were crammed to suffocation. No getting near them and, if you could get inside, you could not catch the eye of the barmaid. No chance that way. The cafés were full. Long queues of men, mostly in uniform, with their girls, waiting for a chance of a cup of tea etc. More long queues waiting for ice creams. The staffs of the ice cream stalls working overtime and the day was not too warm either. The streets blocked here and there by crowds, mostly young women, of the painted lip variety, rushing about to see a procession with a band and a noisy drummer at its head. In Carr Lane I got into a public eddy and I was tossed about, not knowing where I was going to. I missed the bus I hoped to catch for home. Oh, but I am tired of talking about this noisy day in Hull.

Friday, the next day in this eventful week, brought us a telegram in the afternoon from Norman Emery. The first intimation we had of Henry's homecoming. It told us that Henry was on the way home and would be here in a day or two. No address was given and I have never met the gentleman but I am exceedingly grateful to him for the message. It gave us instant relief from anxiety. Two hours after the telegram Henry telephoned to us. He had arrived in England and hoped to be with us on Monday, or possibly Sunday. That was really good news and we were greatly cheered by it. Henry turned up by the last train on Sunday which arrived at Hessle just before midnight. John and Trigo were at the station, on chance, to meet him. Katie sat up and waited but I went to bed at the usual time. I heard the fuss of his arrival and I was on the point of getting up again and going down to welcome the long lost visitor but Henry ran up to my room and we met there, for the first time for over five years.

Henry looked very smart in a new Staff Sergt's uniform. He has filled out a lot but on the following day (Monday) I noticed that he has a strange expression in his eyes as though he has gone through much trouble. He is cheerful enough and he is full of the most interesting yarns. It seems that he remained at Stalag 344 until the end and was moved away from there by the Germans just before the Russians overran the camp. He was moved by train to various places and eventually his party were dumped at a camp at Moosburg, 25 miles north east from Munich. This Stalag was captured by the Americans on April 29th and it was gradually cleared of its prisoners. They all came home by air. Henry flew from Moosburg to Brussels. Changed planes there and was brought to this country on Friday (May 11th), the day he telephoned to us. After the customary routine, fixing up with clothes, coupons, ration cards and so on, he was sent to London from Horsham by train and thence home by the 5 p.m. train from Kings Cross. He has 42 days' leave. After that ? Best love, Phil.

1946

Like a symphony there will be three movements to this B.S. letter.

First movement. Stephen has returned home from Italy in which country he has spent the last two years or so of his life. Now we are as we were in the summer of 1939. Six of us living in this house, 'No. 19' as I usually call it. But what a difference there is, to be sure. In 1939 Ruth was still at school and the three boys were just getting into business habits in various Hull concerns. The war came upon us. Two of the boys were whisked away from No. 19 in next to no time and of them we were to see very little for five years or so. Stephen was too young just then, but before very long he too went off 'to the war' and for about three years all the boys were away. They had various experiences and each one of them had close touches once or twice, but they all came through the ordeal without any serious mishap. Henry with his three and a half years at Stalag 344 came off the worst of the three. On the other hand, he had the experience of a fairly long visit to Palestine and Egypt. He had seen Jerusalem and many other towns in the Holy Land. He spent some months at Athens and was 'picked up' in Crete.

John was at first on Home Defence at Spurn, Hunstanton, etc. Then he got out to Gibraltar where he was stationed for two years. Then it was North Africa and finally Italy. He travelled all over Italy, south to north, ending up with some time at Trieste, from which place he returned home when the time came for his release. Stephen followed John to North Africa and then into Italy. He seems to have visited every important city in Italy, both south and north. Now they are all at home again and Katie has to cater for a family of six, which is no light job in these days of coupons and rations. No domestic help is to be had and we have to do all our own work. Well. We have something to work for and nobody wants to be idle in these days. So that's the end of the first movement.

(2) I have oiled my woods and put them away. I shall never use them again. Nonsense, you say. But in the few games I have had this season I found out that I have lost the stength that one requires to bowl a bonny wood. I have dropped out of my position in the club just because I cannot bowl a bonny wood now. I don't grumble. I have had a good innings but,

Henry's 60th birthday, September 1978: (left to right) Henry, Ruth, John, Stephen.

obviously, the time has come for me to pack up and be off. There will be an interval of seven months now before there is any more bowling on our Hessle Bowling Green. After that seven months I don't expect to resume playing. I have loved the game of bowls and I have done pretty well at it and I have made ever so many friends on the bowling green. Is it all over? Yes. I am sorry to say it is. Goodbye.

(3) The Nazis. To be hanged in four days time. What of them? I cannot sleep sometimes for thinking about them. I am not sorry for them. I like some of their faces. Good, intelligent faces. It is hardly to be believed that they could work such devilry in the world. As a boy I learned to think that war was a matter of past history, that it had vanished for ever from the world. There was no need to pray for peace. Peace was just like daylight. There was no need to pray for daylight. No need to pray for peace.

Well. They are going to hang the 11 Nazi leaders next Tuesday morning. Four days from now. Am I sorry for them? Why, no. I would not raise a finger to spare them. Only I remember that the best friend I ever had in all my long life was a German. Carl Hillerns. The friend I could not do without in the first fifteen years of this century. Carl, Uncle Carl, as I used to call him, died in 1918, but his friendship and happy disposition still lives in my memory. The best friend I ever had. And what about Beethoven, Brahms, Schumann, Schubert, Mozart, Haydn and many others? And these 11 Nazis are to be hung next Tuesday. Not permitted to be shot. I don't see much difference between shooting and hanging, but I suppose there is a difference. It would be all the same to me which way they did it. Oh, for goodness sake get it over and let us get on with the next chapter. What will the next chapter be like. I wonder. What a pity we cannot get out of Germany and leave them to settle their own affairs. I suppose if we did leave them alone they would be up and at us again before another 20 years had passed. we might not get off next time. So get along and hang those beggars. They have troubled the world enough. P.

[Philip Chignell's letter writing was now interrupted by a serious illness].

B.S. 128 18th December 1946

I have had an unfortunate day. Things have been against me from the very start. That start was soon after 4.30 a.m. I was wide awake then. No chance of any more sleep. My rule of life is to get out of bed at 6.0 a.m. and not before. So I had well over an hour to think things over. Blessed old hymn tunes run through my mind at such times. Quite a habit with me now. Not that I care for hymn tunes in my old age. I am tired of most of them, but they come into my mind without any invitation. All the harmonies and everything. I know them all by heart. Treble, Alto, Tenor and Bass. I don't invite them to come into my mind. I don't choose which tunes are acceptable and which are not. They just come without invitation. So there you are, we will call it 5.0 a.m., and a whole hour to pass before I may get up and turn on the teapot and light the kitchen fire. One whole hour of hymn tunes. Up at 6.0 and it is, at this time of the year, uncomfortably dark and cold. However, a cup of tea revives me and I soon get a nice fire going and all hymn tunes have cleared away from my mind. My next trouble is about trousers. I have only one pair of trousers warm enough to wear at this time of the year. That leaves no margin. I must have a duplicate pair of trousers for winter wear. I don't want a new winter suit at fifteen guineas. I can carry on with what I have with the addition of a thick pair of trousers. Yesterday I consulted my usual Hessle tailor on this point. I was politely told, 'Nothing doing', and so on. Plenty of explanation but no satisfaction. This morning Katie took my measurements — Waist 34, Length 29 — and with these figures written on a slip of paper I walked into Marks and Spencer's, Whitefriargate, Hull, at about noon this morning. Plenty of nice thick trousers there. I would certainly have a pair even if I wore them just for knocking about in the house. After all, about ten bob for a pair of trousers and you don't risk very much. Another thing, the nicely clothed man or woman in these days is a *rara avis* but every one must have clothes of some kind or other. Of all the trousers displayed at Marks and Spencer's none tallied with the size I required. The girl tried to sell me a pair of 34 by 31 but I did not care to take the risk and so I left that particular multiple shop without doing any business. Next I went and prowled round Woolworth's hoping to find a Biscuit 'Kew' running. But today biscuits were sold out. However, I got a pound's worth of silver from the cashier's office (I find Woolworth's a useful place for change) and went on to the White Hart Inn where I had one with Bill Brown, a chance friend I met there. I usually have my dinner at the White Hart on a Thursday. As a rule, quite a good and inexpensive dinner served in a delightful old wainscotted room. Today I was refused entry — crowded out — no chance, not even if I waited half an hour. So off I went to the Kardomah, the café where chess players congregate. All too busy and too crowded today to think about chess. I should say the lunch I had there consisted of potatoes, bread and butter and coffee. You take a tray and walk up to a counter and help yourself, there are no waitresses to the tables. You pass along to a cashier's desk, she looks at your tray and says, 'One and nine', and you pay on the nail and then search round for a vacancy. When you have found your seat you sit down and eat your potatoes etc. All the time one or two girls are trotting round and whisking away any empty trays or plates. Almost before you have finished, your last plate or cup has returned to the kitchen and you get an uncomfortable feeling that you have out-stayed your time and must be off. However, I found a vacant seat near the door and rather far away from the feeding counter, also near a nice fire. There I sat me down and had a quiet doze and nobody disturbed me. After an hour or so at the Hull Library I came home to tea. Now, at 8 p.m. I am alone in the house. Four of the family have gone off to *The Messiah* concert in Hull and the other one, John, has gone to the annual Christmas party given by his firm, Smith and Nephew. So I am alone. I rather enjoy an evening at home and all alone. But there is a snag this time. Our wireless conked out last night. Tonight it is silent and dead. It is strange how one misses the wireless if it is out of order. It is, all the same, a boon companion to a lonely man. Once upon a time just before Christmas I used to play in the orchestra for *Messiah* performances twice and even three times in one week. A tedious job. I suppose you have heard of the 'cellist who dreamed he was playing in *The Messiah* and he woke up to find that he really was playing the 'cello in that work. As an old cellist I can appreciate that yarn. We have been *Messiah*-mad in this house for the past week or two. Everybody, except Daddy, singing and humming bits of *The Messiah*. Getting together and singing some of the choruses. Stephen singing *Comfort Ye* and *Every Valley* and doing it very well too at one of the Sunday evening services at Hessle Church. Ruth with *There were shepherds* sang it at church last Sunday, or is it to be next Sunday? I forget which. But she will do it well. Had there been an opportunity both John and Henry could have managed some of the *Messiah* solos but other members of the Church choir had to be considered. I shall be glad when this *Messiah* craze has passed. Also glad when Christmas has passed and the dark dull days of mid-winter have given place to another coming spring. End of the page. I hope I have not bored you. Best love to all. Phil.

[Philip Chignell died on 3 January 1947, only just over two weeks after the last letter was written. Mercifully he did not have to endure the unusually cold and long winter which started in earnest on the day of the funeral.]